W9-BTG-665

Daughters of Anowa

Daughters of Anowa

African Women and Patriarchy

Mercy Amba Oduyoye

ORBIS BOOKS
Maryknoll, New York 10545

Queries regarding rights and permissions should be addressed to: Orbis Books, P. O. Box 308, Maryknoll, New York 10545-0308.

Published by Orbis Books, Maryknoll, NY 10545-0308
Manufactured in the United States of America

Cataloging-in-Publication Data available from the Library of Congress, Washington, DC

ISBN 0-88344-999-4

To my mother,
Oseneniibaa Yaa Dakwaa,
and her sons,
Ewudzi, Addo, and
Kaakyire Bamfo, the tenth child

WOMAN WITH BEADS

I am Woman
I am African
My beads mark my presence
Beads of wisdom, beads of sweat
I am Woman
I am Bota
The precious black bead
Skillfully crafted from black stone
I do not speak much
but I am not without a voice
The authentic black bead does not rattle noisily
I am an African woman, wearing beads ground
by Anowa and from the womb of Anowa
Other beads I have which do not belong to her
They have come from over the seas
They are glass and easily shattered
Created by humans they can be ground
back to powder and remodelled.

I am Woman
I am African
Here I sit—not idle
But busy stringing my beads
I wear them in my hair
I wear them in my ears
They go round my neck, my arms
My wrist, my calves and my ankles
Around my waist will go the
Most precious of them all
And from this hidden strength
Will burst forth the New Me—for
I am in the process of giving birth
To myself—recreating Me
Of being, the Me that God sees.
I am Woman
I am African
My beads mark my presence
And when I am gone
My beads
will remain.

—Mercy Amba Oduyoye, 1995

Contents

Introduction

The Fire of the Smoke

For the vast majority of African women there is no food without fire. I mean *firewood* fire, producing smoke that stings your eyes and makes you cry. One ought really to say there is no life without smoke in Africa. An Akan proverb, almost untranslatable into felicitous English but far more crisply expressive than the banal English proverb, "Where there's smoke, there's fire," goes like this: *Biribi* ankɔka *mpapa a anka mpapa anye krɛde.*[1]

Two "world" wars emanating from Europe and engulfing her colonies caused dramatic changes in the first half of this century. This experience, far more traumatic than previous colonial pillage, resulted in a global awareness of many different historical realities and began to unmask the historiography that had registered only the stories of the powerful. Emerging from the kitchens were women who cooked in other people's kitchens so that the hostess might be complimented while the men who worked tirelessly for other men began to drop their tools, saying they were not women. Every kind of liberation movement surfaced, as the boiling lava beneath the patriarchal calm began to erupt and a multi-vocal theme song rumbled forth like the beginnings of a tropical rainstorm.

In Africa, the eruption took the form of struggles for political inde-

---

[1]J. G. Christaller, *Twi mmebusem mpensa-ahansia mmoano* (Basel: Basel German Evangelical Missionary Society, 1879). Christaller explains that when one hears *krɛdɛ*, you can be sure something touched *mpapa*. *Mpapa*, the dried outer cover of a palm branch, when freshly stripped, is used as rope and in basket making. When dry, however, it is very brittle. *Krɛdɛ* is an onomatopoeic word that represents the snapping sound *mpapa* makes even when it does not actually break.

pendence. The smoldering embers of dying protests against colonial exploitation suddenly caught fire and began to rage like the proverbial fires of the West African harmattan, the dry, searing seasonal wind from the Sahara. By the 1960s, young people in educational institutions had crystallized the issue as that of authority, and they demanded to know why they should not be involved in the processes that determined their lives and shaped the world. During the same period the machinery of white racism was entrenched in Africa and the struggle against it took dramatic turns as the human species became more and more polarized into races.

Other poles began to emerge—North versus South, rich against poor—and the pecking orders that developed in between have become our normal atmosphere, polluted with power and the love of death—other people's, of course. Cutting across all this is the gender question, one of the oldest power struggles of humanity. This, too, has become more visible since the 1960s. Three United Nations-sponsored meetings have given the women's movement a global voice and a dramatic visibility.[2] In 1985, the world's women met in Nairobi, the continent whose men pride themselves on having women who have no need to seek liberation as women.

While the Nairobi meeting was in session, African men were still snickering. But something new had touched the women of Africa, and they began to voice their presence. Women were standing up, abandoning the crouched positions from which their life-breath stimulated the wood fires that burned under the earthenware pots of vegetables they had grown and harvested. The pots, too, were their handiwork. Standing up straight, women of Africa stretched their hands to the global sisterhood of life-loving women. In no uncertain terms, African

---

[2]Mexico City, 1975; Copenhagen, 1980; Nairobi, 1985. Under the auspices of the World Council of Churches (WCC), women met on specialized issues in Christianity and on human rights issues in Berlin, Accra, Venice, Klingenthal (France), and Sheffield. Other meetings included regional, national, and local undertakings. The human rights issues raised from the women's desk under the directorship of Brigalia Hlope Bam, a Black South African, crystallized for the churches into the Community of Women and Men in the Church (CWMC), a study lodged in the Faith and Order sub-unit of the WCC for three years under the leadership of Constance Parvey, a white American woman from the Boston area. See Melanie May, *Women and Church: The Challenge of Ecumenical Solidarity in an Age of Alienation* (Grand Rapids, MI: Eerdman's, 1991).

women announced their position on the liberation struggle and their solidarity with other women.

Before Nairobi, there had been solidarity, but it had been crouching under global issues of North-South economic, racist, and militaristic struggles for power. Euro-American women were quick to name women's heightened consciousness as a liberating experience. They intensified their demands for recognition as human beings responsible for their own lives and for the ethos of the total community. But no sooner were women's movements born than the women's liberation movement was trivialized into "women's lib" and articulated by people who cannot distinguish "b" from "p" as "women's lip." In Africa, the move by women to seek more humane conditions for themselves was simply denied. When it was detected, it was assigned to the cracked pot of Western decadence, unbecoming to Young Africa. The deriding voices were mostly those of men.

Over time, African women had learned to know their oppressors, but had held their peace: "When your hand is in someone's mouth, you do not hit that person on the head."[3] So African women used tradi-tional coping devices: they smiled at the insensitivity of husbands and brothers and sons and bosses; with equanimity, they went about their self-assigned jobs of ensuring life. As long as the pot boiled, men re-mained blissfully innocent of whose life-breath kept the firewood burn-ing. African men preened themselves on how well-behaved and docile and content their African women were. They crowed loudly to the world: "See! We told you, our women are different. Of course there are a few bad eggs under the influence of decadent women of the West, but these deviants we can ignore." However, Nairobi was different; though its full impact is yet to be felt, it seems to me that Africa must get ready for more "deviants." Before and during the Nairobi women's meeting, African men insisted that liberation as applied to the African woman was a foreign importation. Some even called it an imperialist trap that would do Africa no good.

This work is written from a Christian perspective. Two of the key words I use require explanation. First, the word "liberation," as used

---

[3]I was fascinated to find a version of this Akan proverb taught to Rev. Dr. Katie Cannon, an African American ethicist, by her mother. "When your head is in the lion's mouth, you treat the lion gently." The African American writer Alice Walker calls this coping device unctuousness.

here, presupposes the existence of an unjustifiable situation that has to be eliminated. All limitations to the fullness of life envisaged in the Christ Event ought to be completely uprooted. Jesus came that we might have life and have it more abundantly. Jesus' reading of Isaiah could, in our contemporary experience, be stated as:

> The poor will hear good news.
> Those who are depressed will feel the comfort that
>   stimulates action;
> Those who are oppressed will be encouraged and
>   enabled to free themselves.
>
> Abilities rather than disabilities will be what counts.
> All who are blind to their own and others' oppression
>   will come to new insights.
>
> And God will pardon all at the jubilee.
> It will be a new beginning for all.
> That is liberation.

The second word is "church." I am writing in the context of Africa as a person with roots in the Christian church; however, any attempt at a theologically satisfactory description of that church would take us too far afield from my immediate concern, which is how liberation relates to African women and women relate to the church. Since it is the church I specifically want to call to task, I am broadly defining church as an organization for performing Christ-like functions in the world. I want to examine the church's attitude to the growth of women into Christ-like persons. I speak broadly, then, of Christianity and Christian churches.

AFRICAN WOMEN AND LIBERATION

In Africa, the very idea of a "free woman" conjures up negative images. We have been brought up to believe that a woman should always have a suzerain, that she should be "owned" by a man, be he father, uncle, or husband. A "free woman" spells disaster. An adult woman, if unmarried, is immediately reckoned to be available for the pleasure of all males and is treated as such. The single woman who manages her affairs successfully without a man is an affront to patriarchy and a direct challenge to the so-called masculinity of men who want to "possess" her. Some women are struggling to be free from this compulsory attachment to the male. Women want the right to be fully human, whether or not they choose to be attached to men.

Liberation for women must also happen in the church. It was a "church father" (Augustine of Hippo, a city in ancient Africa), who declared that a woman apart from a man is not made in the image of God, whereas a man apart from a woman is. Furthermore, it was a "protesting" monk, pastor, and theologian, Martin Luther, who declared that women were fit only to go to church, to work in kitchens, and to bear children. So, who defines the humanity of woman? Is it the male or is it God? If it is God, how do we get at the God-originated definition of womanness? Is family life a vocation, a demand of biology, or a convenient base for organizing human society? Patriarchal systems often forbid questions of this genre.

So, in the heightened debate surrounding the role of women, some Africans are puzzled when Christian women say that it is the will of Christ (if not of the church) that women should be free to respond to the fullness God expects of all human beings. What constitutes this fullness, and who determines its dimensions? Women want to join in the search for the truth about human life and how to live it; we want to decide for ourselves, for our day and situation, what constitutes a liberating and liberative life.[4]

Given the pluralistic nature of cultures and religions in Africa and my own conviction that personal experiences are a valid source for understanding gender issues in the organization of human society, I have deliberately chosen a personal approach to the subject. I am a Methodist. In 1835, the Wesleyan Missionary Society began work on that coastal strip around Cape Coast in Ghana where my father's roots are, in the towns of Apam and Ekwamkrom, near Winneba. By birth and upbringing in Ghana and subsequently by choice in Nigeria, I belong to the Methodist family and, hence, to the group of churches described in these pages as Western churches, a brand of Christianity that

---

[4]See Sharon Welch's discussion of liberation theology and the politics of truth in Chapter 2 of her book, *Communities of Resistance and Solidarity: A Feminist Theology of Liberation* (Maryknoll: Orbis Books, 1985).

participates in the Euro-American ethos. The churches referred to as Western churches in Africa are the primary target of my call to social awareness. I do not absolve completely the churches begun *de novo* on the initiative of Africans. These are the African Instituted or Independent Churches (AIC).

I am also circumscribed by my matrilineal Akan roots. My maternal grandfather, Ampofo, is, in fact, a Brong, a group that seems to have escaped all patriarchal influences. Coming into contact through marriage with the patriarchal Yoruba culture of Nigeria was a traumatic experience for me. The women from that Yoruba background have provided me with a control group, a point of reference and comparison. I cannot pretend to write about all of Africa, West Africa, or even Ghana. The living center of my study is the Akan of Ghana, and specifically the Asante, one of three major streams of Akan life.[5] A decade and a half of residence in Ibadan, Nigeria, and affinal relations with the Yoruba have also stimulated this study. But the sisterhood that has nourished the study spans the face of Africa. It is, therefore, my hope that this work will bear the nature of a true African child, a daughter of Anowa, the mythical woman, prophet, and priest whose life of daring, suffering, and determination is reflected in the continent of Africa. It is this that leads me to name Anowa Africa's ancestress.[6]

WHY RESPOND TO FEMINISM?

Born in Ghana of Akan parentage in a matrilineal society, I define myself politically by my mother, as do the majority of Akans. The

---

[5] The term Akan is used to cover several ethnic groups in Ghana whose languages may be defined as dialects of one language. The Akan, about two-fifths of Ghana's population, divide into two large groups: the Twi and the Fantse. Of the Twi, the Asante (Ashanti) form the majority.

[6] Anowa is a Fantse name popular in the Mankessim and Saltpond areas of Ghana. Anoa, a variant of Anowa, is the feminine form; the male version is Anoo. I have chosen the feminine variant of Anowa for my title. In *Anowa* (London: Harlow, 1970; Longman-Drumbeat, 1980), Ama Ata Aidoo recounts that Anowa was born to be a priestess but was not formally apprenticed. In *Two Thousand Seasons* (East Africa Publishing House, Nairobi 1973), a radical epic on Africa, Ayi Kwei Armah names Anoa as a mythical woman representing Africa. In this account, Anoa is a prophetess. Armah's epic describes Africans in the Sahara before their flight south

same is true of my brothers. Akan women are the center of the kinship unit and girls are brought up to feel the weight of this responsibility. Without women "a lineage is finished," the Akan say. So I grew up with a keen sense of my own importance and the necessity to play my role faultlessly.

I went through school, passing exams like any boy. I was led to choose teaching, a field I later came to realize was not very competitive, but did instill in its members a keen sense of community. All the women I knew worked: farming, trading, or processing and selling food and other daily necessities. Marriage did not change women's economic involvement. Only two of the women I knew were exclusively homemakers, although one of them had previously been my mother's teacher. Marriage, therefore, only added responsibilities to these women's lives. It seemed to me, however, that the more these women made others comfortable and dependent upon them, the more they felt alive. I absorbed all of this.

For the Akan, family meetings included both women and men. Women's concerns in the larger community were taken care of by a chain of decision-making that culminated in the *Ɔhemaa* (Queen Mother), who is in fact senior to the *Ɔhene* (King) in the ruling hierarchy. Even then, I had serious questions about how the African principles of complementarity and reciprocity operated, although I did not think in those precise terms. By and large, I could live with the system. In theory, nothing prevented me from being myself, a member of a group sharing the responsibility for its being, integrity, and wholeness. Outside the group I was a non-entity, or so I felt. As a child I had no place when members of my father's family met, but neither did my brothers.

The idea of participation shaped by my Akan background was gravely shaken when I discovered that among the patriarchal-patrilineal Yoruba of western Nigeria, a wife is a member of the work-force in

---

from patriarchal ideological encroachments seeping in from the north that brought slavery and Islam. Anoa's people were characterized more by a communal instinct than a "selfish urge for self-glorification," and more by "peace than clamor for heroic action. Like Anoa they learned to hunt for food, not for war; not for pleasure but for stopping the aged lion and the wild hog and to keep the hyena at bay." Both Aidoo and Armah portray Anowa as a woman who opposed slavery and slave trade. She was the epitome of a woman participating fully in what is life-sustaining and life-protecting, someone worthy of being named an ancestress.

"her husband's house," but not one of the decision-makers. Added to this were my experiences of what British-style patriarchy had done to women in what we have come to call the modern sector: church, university, government, and in economic development. I began to question my mother-centered world. Did I owe westernized Africa and patriarchal Nigeria the same self-abnegation, of living for the community, that I had been brought up to accept as part of my mother's lineage? Would dying to self in these alien structures result in living harmoniously with myself? Was I willing to acquiesce to the systemic sexism that I found unjust?

I felt that I was standing at a critical fork. Behind me was a world I thought I had left behind. Ahead to the right was a global patriarchy whose tentacles threatened to engulf all human institutions. Ahead to the left was a world in the making: a world of relationships yet to be realized and maybe even yet to be created, a world full of potential for affirming the humanity of all.

This book describes why I have come to see that situation as a false dilemma and how, instead, I have come to realize that by looking more critically around us, as well as deeper into our history, we can be motivated and empowered to create structures that obviate all that we have denounced in patriarchy.

The ancients tell us that as the Akan, the Children of Anowa, progressed south from northern Africa toward the savannah and the Atlantic, they became thirsty and there was no water for miles around. With them was a priestess named Eku who had a dog. They came upon a lake, but they were frightened to drink the water lest it was poisonous. Eku let her dog drink of the water. Nothing happened to the dog. Then Eku herself, as leader, tried to prove to the people that the water was drinkable. She drank and nothing happened to her. Whereupon all the people shouted "*Eku asɔ*" (Eku has tasted) and they ran forward to drink. The place where the incident happened is known to this day as Eku-Aso.[7] Most migration stories of the Akan do put women at the center, with women leading the community to freedom and prosperity.

---

[7]Eku-Aso, however, is a place name in Ghana. This myth was recalled for me by Graecia Adwoa Asokomfo Tewiah, a Ghanaian woman from Apam who is a veritable repository of Fantse myths and folktales. Although academic linguists may label this "folk etymology," the real significance for me is that it is told about a woman and not a man.

My fear is that the way of life of the African community is turning into a reverse safari through Africa's vegetation, moving from dense primeval forest back to barren land. This is a frightening vision, for we might emerge in a dry, sterile desert rather than the fertile green fields of Anowaland where oppression is eliminated and reciprocity is the way; we may not reach the land where variety and the celebration of all that is life-giving is the norm. If the direction of our contemporary journey is left solely in men's hands, we may not get to where our ancestress Anowa struggled to lead us; we may not reach the waters of Eku-Aso, where our religious leader Eku saved us from the fear of death by thirst.

As a Christian African woman, I seek to understand what the "daughters of Anowa" are experiencing today and where they are going. I seek the quality of life that frees African women to respond to the fullness for which God created them. It is my experience that Christianity as manifested in the Western churches in Africa does little to challenge sexism, whether in church or in society. I believe that the experience of women in the church in Africa contradicts the Christian claim to promote the worth (equal value) of every person. Rather, it shows how Christianity reinforces the cultural conditioning of compliance and submission and leads to the depersonalization of women. Isidore Okpehwo tells the story of an African woman's retelling of the Adam and Eve story. In her version, Eve's burdens reflect her own experience: "You will weed. The rain will beat on you there. The sun will burn you there as you think of your husband's soup. For that is what you choose."[8] Accepting the myth of the Hebrew Bible, this African woman appropriates what it means to be a woman in her own culture, and accepts it as punishment. This internalization of the church's teaching shows its negative effects on the self-image of African women.

Like African men, African women are well aware of the impact of colonization and the attempted Christianization of Africa. African women are aware of bearing more than half of the life-support burden of Africa, and Christian women feel more than anyone else the church's capitulation to Western norms, which it then propagates as Christian norms. This is the backdrop of the life of the "daughters of Anowa."

Anowa, the protagonist of Ama Ata Aidoo's drama, has never ceased

---

[8]Isidore Okpehwo, *Myth in Africa: A Study of Its Aesthetic and Cultural Relevance* (Cambridge University Press, 1983), pp. 112-13.

to fascinate me. Anowa's dreams and her would-have-been priestly vocation haunt me. Her insistence on chosen toil as self-realization and her ideal of life-in-community empower me. Yet, the most powerful vibrations from Anowa—and this is what most frightens me—is her final capitulation to the dictates of society. And I ask, why?

Ama Ata Aidoo's personification of Africa as a woman makes sense to me, for if there is anything that characterizes the continent it is love and respect for life, of people and of nature. And yet, nothing seems to work. Africa continues to produce structures and systems barren of all creativity, not because her sons who run the affairs of the continent are intellectually impotent but because they use the strength of their manhood on what does not build a living community. Raped by the patriarchal manipulation of the North, Africa now stands in danger of further battering by home-grown patriarchies.

The "livingness" of the daughters of Anowa is limited to their biology, and their sons and daughters continue to climb onto "slave ships," leaving their mothers desolate. As this goes on, Anowa, our mythical ancestress, and her daughters, the women of Africa, are expected simply to look on, to keep the peace; they are not to seek heroic actions and/or learn self-defense, for the lions and the wild hogs and the hyenas that threaten the communal life are their own brothers. The daughters of Anowa are expected to be supportive and to hide from outsiders their festering wounds. They are supposed to be custodians of all the ancient healing arts and keepers of the secrets that numb pains inflicted by internal aggressors. They are to pray and sing and carry. They are to tend the wounds from battles in which they are not allowed to fight. They are only permitted to look on from afar, "for their own good." So they stand by, shaking loosened wrists in desperation, powerlessly watching their brothers flounder.

The daughters of Anowa sit, holding their bursting heads in their hands while their men mouth political or economic platitudes, speak the language of law and order, or pay lip-service to democratization. When their brothers have unburdened themselves of their many words, the daughters of Anowa pick up the old hoes and their wooden trays and go to the farm to gather the familiar harvest and the firewood so that the familiar soup may be ready. Meanwhile, the mindless talk about fruitless five-year development plans and multi-party elections continues. With quiet desperation, the daughters of Anowa try to apply ancient remedies. But, from what I see around me, the ancient remedies can no longer cope with our modern wounds. They heal little, for the causes of the injuries are more complicated. This is the mythopoetic radix of my work. The daughters of Anowa, standing at the fork in the road, must determine which direction to take. As we stand there together, a myth is being created within me, an imaginative presentation of the reality as I see it, a film constantly being screened before my very eyes, my vision of the New Woman in the New Africa.

ISSUES FOR THE NEW WOMAN IN THE NEW AFRICA

For more than twenty years, a number of socio-economic studies have come out of Africa, authored by scholars, both African and otherwise (but mostly others). They have begun to tell a tale different from the assertions of Africans, which are often born out of nostalgia for the past. Studies of development have been most revealing, but they have struck me as incomplete. Several writers from the North have been impressed by the position of West African women in the local economy. This traditional role is rooted in traditional political systems and, therefore, has religious ramifications. Yet, these connections have not yet been made.

The role of religion in the life of the African woman gives rise to many questions. Does her modern role as church-founder give her an entry into political power? What is the effect of her exclusion from certain types of religious enclaves? What is the relationship between religion and psychology for African women? Perhaps it is my bi-national (not dual citizenship) living experience as well as the intellectual nature of my studies in religion that point me to these missing links. With a heightened consciousness of the centrality of my ego, formed in the womb of a largely matri-centered environment, I cannot be thrown into an overly patriarchal pot without seeking a way of crawling out.

Both the Akan of southern Ghana and the Yoruba of southern Nigeria maintain strong kinship ties and constitutional monarchies.[9] Both are characterized by agricultural economies, marketing skills, and the pride of peoples who know themselves to have large numbers and strong

---

[9]These anthropological categories are based on numerical majorities; neither all Yoruba nor all Akan fall neatly into the groups to which I have assigned them.

political and military organizations. Both the Akan and the Yoruba apply a primary structure of ascribed hereditary status; however, a system of meritocracy also operates, based on personal excellence, especially when a high premium on martial arts enabled people to acquire respected titles.[10] Both the Akan and the Yoruba are people who have had to contend with white culture and religion, and who, when it seemed they had succumbed, have yet managed to safeguard the things they hold most sacred: the non-material culture of religion and the ideologies on which human relations were built.

Religion in Africa, as elsewhere, has a variety of manifestations. World religions like Christianity and Islam claim many adherents and, by and large, they have become dominant religious factors in African peoples' lives. But it must never be forgotten that culture and religion are so significant within African life that neither Muslim nor Christian in Africa can be totally free of the values that emanate from the traditional African religions. There are—and this too must not be overlooked—large and critically influential sectors of African communities (among the Asante and the Yoruba, at any rate) that remain faithful adherents to the religion of their forebears. We must not forget that these persons operate entirely outside Western parameters and usually ignore the attempted standardization of national laws.

Women from the Asante and the Yoruba communities must be viewed as being under the pervasive value system of these three religions, African, Christian, and Islamic, and adherents of one or the other. Few persons in Africa, male or female, declare themselves "free thinkers," agnostics, or atheists. We are dealing, then, with the experiences of women living in communities that take religion seriously, women who admit the influences of religion on their worldview and, consequently, on their way of life.

It is often argued that traditional African religions and cultures afford adequate and requisite participation for women. This ignores the fact of women's common experience in Africa, that by the time a woman has spent her energies struggling to be heard, she has barely the energy

---

[10]Kwame Arhin, *Status Differentiation in Ashanti in the Nineteenth Century: A Preliminary Study* (University of Ghana Institute of African Studies) *Research Review*, 4:3 (July 1968), p. 44. Cf. Robert S. Rattray, *Ashanti* (1925; reprint, Westport, Ct: Greenwood/African Universities Press, 1971), p. 35; Robert Frazer, *The Novels of Ayi Kawei Armah* (London: Heinemann, 1980), p. 86.

left to say what she wanted to say. It is true that women close to royal thrones were formidable powers and may still be. But one also ought to hear the women who warn us against basking in the glory of "old shells," retained to govern social relationships when the material causes that gave rise to those structures are no more or are fast fading away.

The "our women are not oppressed" stance is an ideological statement that emanates from Africa *ad extra*. It seeks to render feminism a non-issue for Africa. The rest of the world is expected to believe this, while the women of Africa are expected to collaborate with this essentially male propaganda. The same is true of the call to African women to be African, especially when that connotes submissiveness. There can be no agreement on who is the authentic "African woman," not even among African women. That is just as well, and truly healthy and liberating, for all women are not one.

In Africa our received teaching treats both "African" and "woman" as generic. For the former, one knows that the primary sense in which Africa may be said to be one is geographical. Africa shares the intricate politico-economic traumas of the First World and, to a large extent, is affected adversely by these relationships. Moreover, for religiocultural considerations, Africa may be treated as one on the basis of the similarities one observes from nation to nation. These are the only justifications for the appearance of a "generic" Africa in these pages.

THE WOMAN'S NARRATIVE

I have organized my narrative in three cycles of interlocking circles of stories.[11] The first cycle in Chapters 1 through 3 deals with language. The second cycle, Chapters 4 through 6, deals with culture, the continuing process of action and reflection that goes on in any historical moment. I devote the third cycle, Chapters 7 through 10, to tales of us as women—who we are and what we dream to become.

The first cycle of storytelling begins with myths from Ghana and

---

[11]The number three is an important and auspicious number in Akan numerology. Its use here is based on the traditional practice of most occasions of "asking" being done thrice. This is always necessary because of the carefully structured processes of consultation. The practice finds expression in the proverb, *ɔbosom anim wɔkɔ no mprɛnsa* (One has to be ready to present oneself before a divinity thrice before receiving an answer).

Nigeria that throw some light on the humanity of women. In the second chapter I move on to the folktales that are our common African heritage, our school for moral behavior and for learning proper relationships in our communities. The third chapter concludes with proverbs, memorable sayings that are an integral part of all African languages. They are the "givens" of daily language and an unfailing court of appeal. It is interesting to note that these proverbs are often resorted to by contemporary African literary and theological writers to support one point or another.

This first cycle surveys cultural issues as they are portrayed in current African pronouncements on women and probes their roots in language and concepts arising out of and woven into myths, folktales, and proverbs. It is impossible to ignore the meaning and ideological use of this received oral wisdom of the Akan and other West African peoples. In this cycle of telling, I highlight and discuss sources of cultural norms—seemingly inscribed in stone—that shape "acceptable" social roles and practices.

In Africa in general and more specifically among the Akan, gender- and age-based roles are strictly adhered to, especially during customary religious and social rites. So, the second cycle, Chapters 4 through 6, moves from the area of language to action, examining how African women live up to the imagery of the "folktalk."[12] African women are described in terms of culture (Chapter 4), religion (Chapter 5), and marriage and patriarchy (Chapter 6). The cycle examines how these institutions affect women's roles and participation in Africa through their involvement in politics, the economy, social structures and arrangements, and in the manifestations of religion. In all this I have tried to portray the present—what we do as Africans—and what, if any, modifications have come about as a result of contact with Euro-American cultures. The dynamism and resilience of African culture are noted, with a view to discovering its impact on women. In this second cycle I attempt to discern what changes women have brought about and what impacts of the North women have struggled to fend off. The narration at this point draws on research of social scientists, historians, and those studying the phenomenology of religion in Africa.

---

[12]I have chosen "folktalk" as an appropriate shorthand for myths, folktales, and proverbs, the source of the popular ideology that governs the people's lives.

The stories are aimed at demonstrating that, by and large, the Akan woman is not so much an active participant in her own suppression as a passive victim of the culture whose life-giving aspects she seeks to protect. Cultural factors lead the Akan woman to avoid confrontation in order to avoid ridicule, intimidation, or even pity, which she deplores, thus paying a price for the stability of her status.

At the core of the culture is an ideology that has absolute priority: the corporate personality of the family, clan, or nation is always chosen over the personhood of the individual, especially when that individual is a woman. Self-affirmation is seen as selfishness. Egocentrism is denounced as the antithesis of this communal personhood. These assigned roles, I argue, stifle human development. Talents are undeveloped and unused when innate abilities are circumscribed by societal canons. I maintain that the communal ideology becomes counterproductive and, in the end, detrimental to the very welfare of the community it seeks to engender.

When we gather for the third cycle of story-telling, I dedicate Chapters 7 through 10 to what women have begun to be and what women want to be. In this cycle I turn to women's dreams, our bringing into being new arrangements of reality. We dream of what we want to be and we identify who is going to create the environment in which we may be ourselves. We dream about the future relationships of men and women in Africa. We begin to design the future home of humanity and to weave new myths from our real lives. Homes become living structures, with movable walls, not places where we women are placed but a space in which to be human.

Our dreams come into being in the Christian ambiance of life in Africa, holding believers in the *ecclesia* of Christ to account. Doing right by women, of course, places responsibility on all religions to be a voice that calls for promoting more humane social structures and for safeguarding or reviving life-affirming traditional structures. To display and teach life-affirming principles, we women must bind onto ourselves the duty to set our own homes in order.

Doing right by women calls for enlightened legal codes that people will understand. It also calls academia to account and asks for reviews of priorities in what we study; specifically, it seeks women's studies in the humanities as well as the integration of gender factors into all studies.

In Chapter 9 of this last cycle, we look to our own homes and ask questions of societies that seek to continue our domestication. This is a call to initiate new meanings of "life-in-community." As women we affirm our being and we begin to weave a new pattern of womanhood from the threads in which we feel comfortable. Through the telling of our stories, I attempt to demonstrate the political nature of gender hierarchy and its effects on man-woman relations. This is the life-giving center of my story-telling venture, my belief that human nature, though complex, is one. Our dreams become a new cloth with an African pattern that fits into the global women's *asaasaa*.[13] All must be open and flexible, a style of being that is the antithesis of death-dealing patriarchy.

At the close of Chapter 10, "Beads and Strands," a new cycle of story-telling links the experiences of previous cycles together to become the empowering myths of today. I do not share a view of history that places human beings on a railroad track running straight from beast to deity. Rather, I see a constant striving to be what we already are, but do not manifest fully—human beings in the image of God, truly human among humans.

---

[13]The *asaasaa* shows up in American culture as quilt-making. In Ghana this patchwork cloth represents the creativity born out of poverty. The poor clothed themselves by piecing together the surpluses from the rich, who invariably bought more fabric than was needed for their garments. The feminist *asaasaa* will be a new creation from a world torn to shreds by patriarchy.

The First Cycle

Language

Sankofa
Go back and fetch it

The Adinkra symbol for learning and wisdom
from the past.

1

Mythical Images

FOLKTALK AND ITS FUNCTION

The area of a religio-cultural corpus covered by the term myth varies from people to people, and the word itself has acquired several shades of meaning. In ancient Greek, *mythos*, as opposed to *logos* and *historia*, represented a fable, a tale, talk, or speech. It was located, therefore, lower down on the scale of human narratives. I have used "religio-cultural corpus" to include the vast sources of traditional influences on life, and, more specifically, the language and imagery of proverbs, folktales, and myths. The latter two I call "folktalk" to show that they are the heritage of all people rather than just the learned or the elderly. Unlike proverbs, the very drama of folktales and myths being passed from one generation to another makes them memorable.

A second reason I have grouped them together is because the line between what is myth and what is folktale is not clear. Clarifying this is not my primary interest here. Rather, my interest lies in their impact on life. When folktalk is about the origins of the earth, of people, of animals and other aspects of nature, and of social institutions, what some call myth could be called folktales or even legend by others. Folktalk, as such, has general currency in Africa. Myths and folktales shaped and continue to shape social relations, even under modern political systems. African literary writers depend very heavily on this corpus of folktalk; as they create their images on paper, they reproduce the many images preserved in oral transmission as if they were terra cotta.

I have put proverbs in a separate category. Weighty and couched in formalized language as they are, they very easily acquire the status of potent speech; once spoken, they become authoritative statements with a life of their own. Second, not all people can interpret proverbs or use them in appropriate ways or know how and when to insert them, even when they are apposite. Moreover, each proverb has more than one level of meaning; when they are used in the right context, people sit up and listen, regarding them as a legal precedent. The Ifa divination poems of the Yoruba, most of which begin with a proverb, show how proverbs, myths, and folktales are interwoven.[1]

This body of folktalk, dynamic and malleable, interplays with the changing conditions of life to direct individual self-perceptions and to shape the entire community. My primary interest is to see how this corpus of folktalk reflects or is actually used to shape women's lives and to answer the question, What is woman?

A complete study of the literary quality of folktalk lies beyond my competence. But as a person whose early life was lived in African compounds, with an extended family of not only grandparents, but also granduncles and aunts, their children, their children's children, and a host of other relatives and "apprentices" and with access to many other compounds equally regarded as home, my lived experience of folktalk is my guide. Growing up in a traditional four-generation home enabled me to "hear" a period of over one hundred years and to attempt to capture and retain our family's history and ethic. This religio-cultural corpus that I call folktalk, then, is the social history of our people as the collective memory wishes to have it remembered. A mirror on life, it also functions as an authoritative source for decision-making, even in the present. Among the Akan, as a person moves from child to adult, as elders pass away and new ones are chosen, and as family property passes into new hands, the practical applications of Akan tradition and customs are obvious. Culture, as manifested in folktalk, serves a regulatory and preservatory function for what is dear to people.

Folktales may be ingeniously constructed and entertaining; when effectively told, however, they do become an authoritative source for describing how life is and prescribing what it ought to be. The listener

---

[1]Wande Abimbola, *Sixteen Great Poems of Ifa* (Paris: UNESCO, 1975) and *Ifa: An Exposition of Ifa Literary Corpus* (Ibadan: Oxford University Press, 1976). Abimbola, the author of these two works on the Yoruba oracle Ifa (composed of 256 poems), was himself a student of the oracle. I have also drawn on the study of Ifa by Judith Gleason with Awotunde Aworinde and John Olaniyi Ogundipe, *A Recitation of Ifa, Oracle of Yoruba* (New York: Grossman Publishers, 1973).

is led to identify with the characters, and to draw certain didactic and moralizing conclusions. Good storytellers weave contemporary experience into tradition's rich imagery and linguistic expressions, creating something that is not easily forgotten. Often persons who hear these folktales cannot wait to repeat them. Thus, folktalk (tales and myths) functions for Africa as a history of thought, a philosophy of life, and, in my particular study, an attempt to find an answer to the question, "What makes a woman?"[2]

MYTHS OF ORIGINS AND RELIGIONS[3]

Myths inform social activities, shape men's and women's lives and attitudes, and give expression to people's fears. Creation myths, for example, are replete with imagery that echoes of how society functions, of the nature of social relations relating to families, the economy, the running of the community. The myths help us see, at times, the society's attempt to think through the paradoxes of life. An awareness of this function helps liberate us to some degree from the negative effects of myths. Myths then cease to function as "canon law" and become a source in the search for meaningful community.

Living among the Yoruba of southern Nigeria and reading about the Ezon and Ibibio of the Niger Delta, I have come across rich myths of origins that the Akan cannot boast of, and I have come to understand more clearly my own background as an Akan. I have also developed more appreciation of the extent of the influence of myths on our self-perceptions.

The Myth of Olodumare and Obatala

The first myth of origins I will explore belongs to the Yoruba of southern Nigeria.

In the beginning Olodumare, the Supreme God, sent the male divinity Obatala to the watery regions beneath the sky. Olodumare

---

[2]Nikki Giovanni, *Gemini* (New York: Penguin Books, 1971), p. 145.

[3]Akan myths of origins are very skimpy indeed, especially on creation; however, many of the motifs in this genre of narrative are found in Akan folktales.

gave Obatala a snail shell full of earth and some iron. Accompanied on his descent by a hen and a chameleon, his mission was to
make dry land. Arriving in the watery regions, Obatala constructed the foundations of the earth with the iron. He emptied the
earth on the waters and the hen spread it around with her feet.
They rested and waited for the earth to dry. It was the chameleon
walking carefully and gingerly on the newly created earth who
proclaimed it firm enough for habitation. That done, Obatala
proceeded to mold human beings. Male and female he molded,
and Olodumare, the Supreme God, breathed into them so they
became living beings. Sex differentiation was there from the
beginning and God's agent, Obatala, was a male divinity.

To supervise the human community and to direct affairs on
earth, Olodumare sent seventeen divinities, one female (Osun)
and sixteen male. The sixteen male presidents of the community
went about their political tasks, totally oblivious of the presence
of the female divinity Osun. Things kept going wrong until,
exasperated, they finally consulted Olodumare, who told them of
the missing factor—the female Osun. They could no longer
ignore her. When the sixteen male divinities tried to involve her,
however, she sent her son as an extension of herself and did not
attend in person.

In this myth of origins all the main actors are depicted as male,
while the only female, Osun, declined involvement. There is, however,
a variant that names the molder of humanity as Oduduwa, whom the
Yoruba regard as a goddess and the wife of Obatala.[4] The symbolic
representation of Oduduwa in Yoruba art is the hen. In this version,
Oduduwa and Obatala are co-creators.[5] What interests me in this myth,

---

[4]E. B. Idowu, *Olodumare: God in Yoruba Belief* (London: Longmans, 1962;
New York: Praeger, 1963), pp. 71 and 199. In art, Oduduwa, the female counterpart
of Obatala, and Obatala are sometimes depicted as two parts of a calabash container,
the upper half being Obatala (sky) and the lower half Oduduwa (earth). The essential
point is that two entities were needed to beget life.

[5]In the New World, and more specifically Brazil, Obatala is transformed into a
Roman Catholic saint, male when he appears as Christ and female when she appears
as "Our Lady." G. S. Afolabi Ojo, *Yoruba Cultures: A Geographic Analysis* (Ife:
University of Ife Press; London: University of London Press, 1966), pp. 162-89. See
also Ulli Beier, ed., *The Origin of Life and Death: African Creation Myths* (Ibadan:

though, is that all human beings, male and female, are of divine origin
and live because the breath of God has been breathed into them.

Woyengi or Tamarau, the Great Mother

A second creation myth also comes from southern Nigeria but belongs to the Ezon (variously written as Ijo, Ijaw). The one who creates
is a woman called either Woyengi or Tamarau, the Great Mother.

> In the beginning Woyengi seated herself on a stool and with her
> feet firmly planted on the Creation Stone and a table before her,
> she began to mold human beings out of earth. As each person was
> completed, each was embraced by her and each became a living
> being as the Great Mother breathed into each.
>
> Then Woyengi posed the question, "Which do you want to be,
> male or female?" So, what each person chose is what he or she
> became. Each was given a destiny. Where you desired to be born
> is where you were sent, and how you desired to die is how you
> died. Only by very special religious ritual could any of this be
> changed.

In this myth the creator is a woman. Sexual differentiation and one's
destiny are premundane choices that are unalterable. Again, we can
conclude that the quality of human beings, male and female, is embedded in the divine ordering of life. When differentiation appears among
human beings, traditional African religion explains this with the notion of the premundane choice. What, then, is the origin of gender-
based roles? Two myths from southern Nigeria throw some light on
this.

Ogboinba's Destiny

> Ogboinba, the strong-hearted, had chosen not to be a mother, but
> to have mystic powers. At the time of her creation there was
> another who had chosen to be a woman and to be the mother of
> rich and famous children. Since both had chosen to be born in the

Heinemann, 1966), pp. 22-41, 47-50, where the fowl that accompanied Obatala is
described as a cock.

same village, Woyengi sent both of them to the same village and they became good friends. Ogboinba used her powers to help her friend to raise her children, who became rich and famous. Then Ogboinba regretted her choice. "Why can't I be both mother and a woman with mystic powers?" She decided on a hazardous journey back to Woyengi, the creator, to change her destiny.

Ogboinba set out to go back to Woyengi to ask for a change of destiny. It was a hazardous quest, but her mystic powers overcame obstacles placed on her path by mystic beings. Some of the mystic beings were trying to turn her back to earth for her own good. The further she progressed on her return journey to her origins, the more powerful she grew, for the powers of the mystic beings she defeated accrued to her.

Inexplicably, Ogboinba decided to challenge Woyengi, the source of her powers, to a trial of strength. Disgusted by this affront, Woyengi stripped her of all that she had, returning the powers she had acquired en route to their original owners, those who had been defeated or destroyed by Ogboinba. Only her presence of mind—in her quick move to hide in the eyes of a pregnant woman—saved her from being eliminated by Woyengi (for Woyengi had herself decreed that a pregnant woman should never be killed).[6]

The story ends with, "That is why when you look into a person's eyes, you find a face staring at you." The face you see is the hidden Ogboinba. The story may be saying that by identifying with the pregnant woman (the woman whose children she helped to raise), Ogboinba did not have to become pregnant herself to gain society's acceptance. It also says that her daring act of acquiring more and more mystic powers was unacceptable, especially because her motive was self-centered. She wanted children *and* mystic powers and was ruthless in her quest to get them, to the extent of challenging the Great Mother who was her creator.

Hearing and understanding the story of Ogboinba, what woman would dare challenge her destiny? It is also clear that the myth clearly upholds the validity of Ogboinba's original choice of role. Woyengi,

---

[6]Beier, pp. 23-24; Isidore Okpewho, *Myth in Africa: A Study of Its Aesthetic and Cultural Relevance* (Cambridge: Cambridge University Press, 1983), pp. 137-38.

the Creator, gave her a companion who would be a mother and through whom Ogboinba could experience mothering by assisting her in nurturing her children.

Now we turn to a second myth, the Ozidi saga that shows society's approval of the daring acts of a man.

The Saga of Ozidi

This Ezon saga takes seven nights to narrate and to perform; I will, therefore, briefly describe the three main characters and give an outline of the plot. The hero is Ozidi, a boy born after his father's death, who grows up to avenge his father, who had been assassinated by his companions. Ozidi's mother, Orea, is a plain woman who is the source of the newborns needed for religious rituals. Her most glorious moment comes when she accidentally stumbles on a cure for Ozidi, who had been struck by smallpox. The most formidable character in the saga is Oreame, Ozidi's maternal grandmother and his protector. Oreame is a witch, a keeper of the tricks, secrets, and stratagems of Ozidi, who goads him on in his career of vengeance. She decreed that Ozidi must not get married.

Ozidi grew up under the influence and tutelage of his grandmother to come to an understanding of how his father, a general, had been murdered by his comrades during a hunting expedition. Moreover, to spite Ozidi's family, the traitors made his idiot uncle, Temugedege, king in place of Ozidi's father. Fired by this knowledge and by the belief that his father's spirit would never rest unless the murderers were punished, Ozidi sets out to avenge his father and to retrieve his family's past glory. Aided by his grandmother and having the favor of Tamarau, the Supreme God and Great Mother, Ozidi traps and murders all those who betrayed his father and their associates. He shed so much blood that the gods began to feel he had overstepped the bounds of revenge with his irresponsible carnage.

To punish him, Tamarau sent Sopona, the god of smallpox, to visit Ozidi with the disease. The powers of Ozidi's grandmother were useless against Sopona. In panic, his mother remembered that Ozidi had not had childhood yaws and proceeded to treat the smallpox with the medicine for yaws. The smallpox god (Sopona) was disgusted for being mistaken for common yaws and so left Ozidi, and the disease disappeared.

In the end, Ozidi is strong and enjoys the admiration of all, after having killed men, children, and women, including Oreame, his grandmother. (The latter he killed by accident.) Ozidi is left victorious, is given a bride, and then is closeted in a shrine.[7]

The saga is rich, and when it is performed over the course of seven nights, the people jubilate. The entire saga raises several issues that concern women. When read in company with the myth of Ogboinba, we see a clear contrast between Ogboinba, a *woman* of power and courage, and Ozidi, a *man* of power and courage. The two myths illustrate that a woman's powers may be used to destroy other powers that are malevolent to the whole society. Female power must never be used egotistically and it must never undertake life-denying pursuits. All of the women in the saga illustrate these roles, but Oreame's support of Ozidi is particularly to the point. (And we do note that in the saga, Tamarau, the Great God, is addressed as "Oh, God, the woman who bore us all," reflecting the creation myth of the Ezon.)

Women and the Primacy of Life

Furthermore, the primacy of life for the African woman is emphasized by the "right" use of power, which Ogboinba undertook at the outset by helping the entire community and by enabling her friend's children to survive. She offered protection and companionship for her "procreating sister." This role, too, is expected of childless women, as it is of all women in the African communities of these myths. Nurturing the next generation is a communal duty and all the women of the community become one's mother.

Nobel prize winner Wole Soyinka gives us a vivid description of one such community mother in *Ake*, an autobiographical novel.

The bookseller's wife was one of our many mothers; if we had taken a vote on the question, she would be in the forefront of all the others, including our real one . . . Of all the women on whose

---

[7]John Pepper Clark, *The Ozidi Saga* (Ibadan: Ibadan University Press and Oxford University Press, 1977).

backs I was carried, none was as secure and comfortable as Mrs. B.'s . . . We slept often at the bookseller's. Mrs. B. would send a maid to inform our house that we would eat and sleep at their own house for the night, and that was that. When we got into trouble we ran behind her and she shielded us: "No, no, I take the beating on myself."[8]

In the Ogboinba myth, it appears it was Woyengi herself, the Great Mother, who led Ogboinba into partnership with the procreating woman, an indication that that was an appropriate role for the childless woman. Ogboinba is censored for being too daring and too strong-headed. The story, which tells of the defeat of egotism in one woman, could also be a warning against the personal ambition that lurks in all of us and the wrong use we might make of our capabilities. After she had been stripped of all her powers, the only way for Ogboinba to survive was to be protected by a life-bearing woman. The sacredness of the bearer of life mediated for the aggressive Ogboinba and represents the "taming" or transformation of feminine power through pregnancy and the restoration of life. Having lost her mystic powers, Ogboinba allied herself once more with the role of the child-bearing woman to survive.

By listening to this dramatic presentation of what happened to one woman (albeit mythical), we can see the image of woman as the community sees it. The Ogboinba myth tells the story of life-creating females: first of God, the Great Mother, and then of several females whose interventions caused Ogboinba to spare the lives of spouses. In other parts of the myth, she defeated and killed other men after they had given her hospitality—a behavior that is taboo in Africa. The Ogboinba

---

[8]Wole Soyinka, *Ake: The Years of Childhood, An Autobiographical Novel* (London: Rex Collings, 1981). It is impossible to overemphasize the centrality of child-bearing in the African woman's life. Many of the 256 poems of Ifa have to do with women seeking to bear children. Similarly, among the Akan, the power of procreation is one of seven blessings. For an Akan man or woman to be *obonini* (childless) is considered a great misfortune, if not an outright curse. The bookseller's wife in *Ake* would be called *osebo* (tiger), meaning one who has only one child. This, too, is considered abnormal. One other religious belief to note: the bookseller's wife was unfortunate in that she was the victim of an *abiku* (Yoruba) or *kwasamma* (Akan), a quirk of destiny or the work of a witch. It is believed that infant mortality results from the same child crossing the boundary between life and death several times. Such a child comes only to taunt and tease couples striving to fulfill their religious duty of procreation.

myth emphasizes the inappropriateness of the "crude" use of power[9] and its incompatibility with being a woman in African society.[10] This latter factor is striking when we realize that Oreame, Ozidi's grandmother, was not censored when she used her powers to protect and enable a man to fulfill an ambition.

Even more glaring is the admiration heaped on Ozidi in his career of blood-letting. Every "victim" of his is considered a "sacrifice" for the peaceful repose of his father's soul and he is cheered on; only one person lived. The childless Ogboinba's story ends in "defeat," as "powerless and in fear and shame, Ogboinba flees."[11] Ozidi is left straining and strutting, looking for more deeds of greatness to take on; he then is rewarded with the acquisition of a wife to ensure his own immortality. Ozidi, the male protagonist, is rewarded with even more visibility, while Ogboinba, the female protagonist, disappears.

Oreame restrains Ozidi from killing his treacherous idiot uncle, Temugedege, on religious grounds. "That's your father. Once you kill him, whatever battle you undertake afterwards, you shall lose. Leave him alone. When God herself [Tamarau] brings about his death, then you can take him away to bury."[12] Oreame's influence on Ozidi remains untarnished. Her aiding and abetting—indeed, her active participation in his career of carnage—has the ultimate aim of supporting life, and life is defined by the earthly honor and survival of the family, as well as its spiritual well-being. Ozidi eliminates his uncle Temugedege in an act of self-preservation. However, for Oreame, such murder is irreligious, even though it might be dictated by common sense. In the end, Ozidi "accidentally" kills his grandmother Oreame, the one strong power directing him and the only power to restrain him. There was no one left to pass judgment on Ozidi.

As we construct an image of women from this saga, the following aspects are significant. When Ozidi set out to avenge his father, he massacred those who stood in his way and was hailed as a hero. On the other hand, when Ogboinba set out to change her destiny, she conquered and destroyed others; in so doing, she incurred the anger of the

---

[9]Okpewho, p. 141.

[10]Ibid., p. 149.

[11]Ibid., p. 138.

[12]Clark, p. 373. It is interesting to note that Tamarau, a female name, is also used for God in the Christian literature of the language variously called Ijaw, Ezon, or Ijo. Temerau is a version of this name.

creator and had to seek refuge in pregnancy, the only state that protected a woman from execution.

Ozidi's grandmother was hailed when she used her mystic powers to overcome Ozidi's enemies. Similarly, the creator was pleased with Ogboinba when she used her powers to help her friend's children. It seems that women may have and use power, but only when it serves the good of others. Both creation myths affirm the biological role of women as carriers of life.

The wrongness of a woman choosing *not* to procreate is demonstrated by how much Ogboinba was prepared to undergo in order to change her destiny and to produce her own children. Presumably, although the spirit world saw nothing wrong with a childless woman full of power for doing good, the world in which Ogboinba arrived so scaled preferences that she became dissatisfied with being only an enabler to a mother. To this day, no African, man or woman, wants to be called *obonini*, a childless one.

Women and Power

The collage of scenes from the two narratives, "Ogboinba's Destiny" and "The Saga of Ozidi," forms a portrait that says: a woman does not wield power, at least not in life-denying ways. The Ogboinba myth is sometimes read as an attempt to explore the contradiction between power and femininity.[13] This alleged contradiction has been and is used to manipulate women. I would not deny that "Ogboinba's Destiny" is clearly a tale of the contradiction between femininity and the egotistical use of power for life-denying pursuits. However, my interpretation is that while there is a contradiction between being a woman and destroying life, there is *no* contradiction between being woman and being powerful. We should also keep in mind that Ogboinba destroyed so-called "benevolent" powers that were attempting to restrain her *for her own good*; in the tale of Ozidi, on the other hand, Oreame's powers were used against evil persons and evil powers. A question to be asked at this point is: Who determines what is "good" for Ogboinba?

It would be good if audience reactions to both "The Saga of Ozidi" and "Ogboinba's Destiny" allowed us to conclude that *all* power—both female and male—is a gift to be tempered with grace and used for

---

[13]Okpewho, p. 150.

the benefit of the whole society. In an African community, child-bearing is a duty, not a choice; in the same way, children are obliged to ensure proper burial of their parents, which gave impetus to Ozidi's exploits. It is the fulfillment of these duties that maintains the eternal cycle of life. This single factor of the ability to procreate wields tremendous power for women and men in love with life, both in this world and in the realm of the spirits.

Women as Sacrificed Beings

Another legend from Nigeria illustrates the complex nature of women's bondage to religion and culture. It is the story of Aiyelala, a Yoruba goddess perceived to be a guardian of social morality. She is said to have been a human being whose real name is now lost, but who is remembered and celebrated as a goddess. Aiyelala is popular in the Okitipupa division of western Nigeria. She was an innocent slave woman who worshiped the sixteen divinities. The legend tells that she was sacrificed to bring peace between the Ezon and the Ilaje, whose hostility had been caused by a case of adultery. Her sacrifice saved the life of an adulterous man, thus ending the hostility between the Ezon (the place of refuge) and the Ilaje (the home of the adulterous refugee).

At the time of the sacrifice of Aiyelala, it was announced that the rules of male sexual morality were being modified: instead of being put to death for adultery, men were asked only to pay a fine. Overwhelmed by this bizarre sense of justice, the slave woman was only able to say *Aiye Lala* (the world is great) when asked to say something before her execution. The world is great, indeed, when women pay for the follies of men! Aiyelala's reward was deification as a goddess of sexual morality and fair play.[14]

It seems that women in male-dominated cultures are often left with only two alternatives in their relationship with men: to defeat men by non-physical means (for example, witchcraft) or else to allow themselves to be shaped by culture and the demands of society. When women are not allowed to use physical means to challenge male oppression, men often live with the fear that women will use mystical powers to

---

[14]J. O. Awolalu, "Aiyelala, a Guardian of Social Morality: A Study of Religion and Society, with Particular Reference to the Okitipopa Division of Western Nigeria," *Orita: Journal of Religious Studies* 11:2 (1968), pp. 79-89.

avenge themselves. Men kill, beat, rape, and enslave women; yet, it is women's silence that troubles them most, leading them to their fear of imaginary female aggressiveness. In Africa, this imagined silent activity of women is called witchcraft. Thus, the Akan saying, "fear woman"—a slogan written even on public buses—represents a real psychological war between the sexes. When a woman resists being sacrificed or taken advantage of, she is classified as being other than normal, perhaps even a witch.

Myth and the Politico-Economic Environment

In trying to assess the power and importance of these myths for today, we need to understand something of the context in which they are told or performed as ritual or religious drama. The Ezon and Ibibio both live in the delta regions of southeastern Nigeria. They are oriented to water and the sea, with little solid land to work on. They seek employment along the western coast of Africa, often turning west toward Ghana, where even today Ezon communities are not uncommon. This migration of men makes the remaining Ezon and Ibibio families in Nigeria mother-centered. In these water communities on the Niger, Ezon women farm and fish, and they worship a female god.

In this area, women hold the families together and feature prominently as counsellors and custodians of great power, which is channeled to benefit the whole community. The language, the social economy, and the total worldview of the people witness to this mother-centeredness. This centering perhaps accounts for the fear that, left in power, women have as much capacity as men to be brutal avengers.[15] Indeed, myths such as these are read as a theory of how an originally patriarchal organization is taken over by women. Sometimes, if this happens, other myths have developed to contain the power of the women.

Women and Religion

Several West African communities have exclusive men's secret societies associated with creation and agriculture that provide the means

---

[15]In an episode in Ozidi, Oreame, Ozidi's grandmother, laments that she could not behead her victim herself. "O, what a shame," she says. "That I did not come as a man is terrible" (Clark, p. 224).

for keeping order in the society. This is true of the Ogboni and Oro of the Yoruba and the Poro societies of Sierra Leone. The annual demonstration of male power over women in these religious festivals helps to perpetuate women's inferiority in the minds of growing boys and girls and to ensure that patriarchy reigns where once there was parity or, perhaps, even female leadership.

According to the Ibibio of Nigeria, there was a time when only women knew the secrets of the divinities (the avenging spirits) and those of the Great Mother (the supreme creator). In those days, there were more women than men, and men did all the hard work. By accident the men captured the shrine of the Great Mother, which was the women's cult. The younger women voted to teach the men the secrets of the cult. When the men came into possession of this knowledge, they beheaded the priestesses and took over the shrine. This, it is said, is why the priests of the cult plait their hair and dress like women. Since all farming secrets were associated with the cult of the Great Mother, the men learned how to farm and forbade the women to plant yam, the staple and ritual tuber.

The yam festival, held to honor the earth goddess, thus became a men's festival, and the goddess became the deity of the men's secret societies. This is why today, when the statue of the goddess is in procession, women must hide. They are not to be seen nor heard.[16] The Mother Goddess, who used to be the source of power for women, has been appropriated by men and is now the reigning deity of men's secret societies that demand that women remain voiceless and out of sight. Behind the masks terrorizing women are none other than their own male relations, including sons, husbands, and fathers, who act for the ancestral male spirits.

One of the economic consequences of this overthrow of women is that while women still do farming, they can cultivate anything for themselves except the prestigious and economically high-profit yam, which has become the exclusive prerogative of men. Yet, the women have to

---

[16]I do not speak of things that used to be, for twice, once in the streets of the city of Ibadan and another time travelling in the Ijebu area between Ibadan and Lagos, I have been made to hide crouched inside a car to keep out of sight of a procession of males. See Idowu, p. 193; Gleason et al., pp. 41-42; Willie Fitzjohn, *Chief Gbondo* (Ibadan: Daystar Press, 1974), p. 71. For the creative retelling of a historical event involving the women of Abeokuta (Yoruba) and the elders of the Ogboni cult, see Soyinka, *Ake*, Chapter 14.

hoe the yam (the hard physical work) because their own crops, primarily vegetables, are planted in between the rows of yam. The meaning is clear: the yam represents actual economic power and also symbolizes religious power. Yam is the staple in the diet of several forest regions of West Africa and it is also a ritual food used in festivals for the feeding of the divinities and the ancestors, the departed human spirits.

BREAKING THE SILENCE

The mystery of men's secret societies in West Africa is now being questioned by women. Why should women close their eyes and seal their lips? To denounce injustice is a necessary prophetic work that might lead to healing for the whole community. As nurturers of the generations, women must mediate this sense of urgency to share the powers and mysteries of life without resorting to violence. If they do not do so, then women lose their vital role as the communicators of life in its pristine wholeness.

I would like to reiterate one notable theme in both the Ogboinba and Ozidi myths. No one condemns power if it is used benevolently. Violence done in the name of the survival of a community or as duty to the community, as in the saga of Ozidi, does not end in grief as does the use of violence in search of personal ambition. For example, a mother can unleash power sufficient to turn away the dreaded god of smallpox. Similarly, when the affronted Woyengi turned with vengeance on Ogboinba, Ogboinba was saved only by Woyengi's covenant to preserve the life-carrier, a pregnant woman.

There is a tendency in folktalk to use women to illustrate negative human traits, as if men never behave like Ogboinba. Women are expected to be the custodians of the positive qualities of the whole community. A person who supports the community's survival, but who does not demand applause and acknowledgment is admired by the African community because, after all, "it is one person who kills the elephant for the whole people to feast on." While this ideal is expected of men, it is *demanded* of women. So, women ask for evenhandedness in this search for community spirit.

We might say that, in the end, Ogboinba came to grief because she challenged the accepted structure and, in the process, destroyed benevolent powers, whereas Ozidi was combating a murderous bunch of principalities and powers. Human aggression ought to be turned toward the destruction of what is not life-oriented. The rule is that a good woman does not put her own needs first, for her selflessness is the *sine qua non* of a healthy community. A woman's silence is upheld, while the prophetic disruptiveness that points to the possible new ways of being (as seen in Ogboinba's behavior) is deplored. Myths are structured to make sure that all female rebels are duly contained. These myths are society's way of pleading with women to put community welfare above their personal desires. Through these myths, the society demonstrates the futility of a woman's efforts to change her destiny. The society thus preempts any outcry of rebellion on the part of women.

On the surface, the myth of Ogboinba is an aetiological tale explaining the reflection in the pupils of another's eyes. Yet, on another level, the telling of the story is used by society to warn everyone of the potential misuse of woman power. Ozidi's exploits are narrated to affirm filial duties, but the myth also reaffirms patriarchy. It shows that males can choose a place for themselves in society, but that women are placed there. The women who seek veneration as goddesses are, in the end, those who allow themselves to be sacrificed.

If we re-read and retell these myths to bring parity and justice to human relations, we should look for the *human* traits that are desirable for building up and maintaining personal (not just male or female) skills in this communal task. Our search should be focused on what it means to be human, not to be feminine or masculine. Neither patriarchy nor matriarchy alone can transform relationships between men and women. Indeed, these relationships comprise a good deal of what we mean by living fully. If we view patriarchy and matriarchy with the image of a pendulum, we see them at opposite sides, and we know that the pendulum eventually will stand still in the middle. If, instead, we look at the relations between men and women as a spiral, we see that life is movement and being, a continuum of dynamic creative and empowering relationships moving ever upwards.

The study of myths shows there are several ways in which this religio-cultural corpus relates to the lives of women today. We rejoice in the traditions and continuity of many of these tales. But when the imagery and message of traditional folktalk conflict with contemporary needs of women, we must stop the spiral movement to ask the question: What is womanly behavior? The spiral mode permits us to retrace our steps to seek other myths, folktales, or proverbs to move our quest to a qualitatively different level. We know that folktalk often serves to legitimize sexism; nevertheless, there is a continuing recognition that change and movement are a part of life, that visions of other relationships are possible.

The study of Nigerian myths enables women to challenge the traditions that exclude women from the art of divination and from politics. Women's readings of the lives of goddesses free them to participate in public life and to seek wisdom according to their ability and inclination. Myths that emphasize reciprocity and complementarity recall efforts to transform relationships between women and men. Reciprocity in hospitality challenges the assumption that men have no services to render to women. Each action, each person, each man, each woman, all remain complete wholes and the relationship is one of interaction for mutual benefit.

The women and men who people the mythic realm are very "human"; sometimes they mirror our stereotypes, but at other times they exhibit traits that challenge us and cause us to re-examine our rules and roles. The Ezon creation myth, for example, begins with a procession most uncharacteristic of Africa. A procession of women and men prepared for the arrival of the creator (the Great Mother); the women swept and the men collected the sweepings. Such a scene never happens in African society. The shock disappears, however, when it turns out that what the men collected was the medium of exchange. So, indeed, the women worked and the men were paid. A similar impression is created in the myth of Ozidi, where the grandmother, who was the obvious power behind Ozidi, is accidentally killed and Ozidi alone gets the "glory." While scholars recognize the ideological nature of these narratives, it is for African women and men to build more just relations from these myths—or to discard them as no longer relevant.

For me, African myths are ideological constructions of a by-gone age that are used to validate and reinforce societal relations. For this reason, each time I hear "in our culture" or "the elders say" I cannot help asking, for whose benefit? Some person or group or structure must be reaping ease and plenty from whatever follows. So, if that harvest seems to be at my expense, then I shall require the proceedings to stop until I am convinced that there is good reason for me to die that others might live.

2

Women in Folktales[1]

Once there was a palm wine tapper whose name was Ohia. He had
a wife called Awerehow. A good woman, she was kind, honest,
understanding, and very hard-working. She shared long periods
of adversity with Ohia as well as the hard work of tapping palm
wine. Many times, she was the one who sold the palm wine. The
two could never quite make ends meet.

One time a deer led Ohia to a strange land where he was
granted the power to understand animal language and was told not
to expose his secret on pain of death. Ohia returned home and,
using his newly acquired skill, things began to brighten. The
unquestioning Awerehow was content to enjoy their new status.
With the coming of affluence, however, Ohia acquired a second
wife. She was blind in one eye, sensitive and suspicious, jealous
and selfish. Whenever those near her laughed, she would accuse
them of mocking her for being blind in one eye.

One day Ohia overheard a hen and her chicks discussing how

---

[1]My early years were spent in Asamankɛse (Akyem Abuakwa), Akyinakrom,
Effiduase, Kumasi (Asante), Sunyani and, Wenchi (Brong Ahafo) in the 1940s
when most of these places had no electricity. We could still appreciate the moon,
still sit around the fire and hear these stories told and re-told. Most of these tales are
common currency among the Akan. Here, I am using documented versions collected
and edited by W. H. Barker and C. Sinclair and by Robert S. Rattray, for the benefit
of readers who wish to do further analysis. The editors, mostly Europeans, often
collected these folktales as one does curios or shells from the beach. Now, of course,
there is an entire science of oral literature in academies around the world that pursues
analytical studies of these stories that I was brought up on.

to steal his second wife's corn, and he could not help laughing. Unable to make him say why he laughed, the second wife complained to the king. Ohia was summoned before the elders and forced to tell his story. As soon as he told the truth about his understanding of animal language and why he had laughed, he fell down and died. This is how death came into the world.[2]

Akan folktales are generally "why so" and "how come" stories, but very often they introduce a moral at the end with the formula: "That is why the elders say . . ." or simply "That is why." We cannot overestimate the power of folktales as vehicles for the transmission of norms. The verbal images created for us, often as children, acquire the status of holy writ. During the socialization process, children become acquainted first with Anasesem, folktales with Spider as the chief protagonist. Later on, young people gradually acquire knowledge of proverbs with their meanings and contexts. One thereby learns to use them appropriately in the process of assimilating the society's culture. Myths and the religious implications of their respective cosmologies, such as oral accounts of origins, are learned much later, as one acquires more maturity and the sophistication to appreciate their significance and importance. Family occasions such as funerals and other public rites including festivals provide important contexts for this learning process. Among the Akan, the ordinary events of daily life are sprinkled with an appropriate set of proverbs, used for decision-making, counselling, and the offering of benedictions and prayers. Like the collected wisdom of all societies, this wisdom literature plays a crucial role in traditional non-formal education.

In Africa, the norms of relationships in this form of received teaching are invariably gender-based, and they are usually directed at the stability and welfare of the whole community. It follows that gender- and age-defined roles are strictly adhered to, especially during reli-

---

[2]Tales of humans who understand animal language are very widespread. See, for example, W. H. Barker and C. Sinclair, *West African Folktales, Story XIX* (London: George G. Harrap and Co., 1917), p. 21. According to the authors, this "very West African" tale occurs also in Serbia, but has a comic ending there. In West Africa, it is a sexist tale used to explain how death came into this world. For the story of "Ohia, Awerehow and the Thieving Deer" see Barker and Sinclair, *XIX*, pp. 105-113. Robert S. Rattray, *Akan-Asante Folktales* (1930; reprint, New York: AMS Press, 1969) also has a version of this tale.

gious and social rites. All of this folktalk, including myths (as we saw in the previous chapter), proverbs, and folktales, provides a rich source of imagery about women. In this chapter, I want to examine the language about women used in folktales, seeking to discover what is authentic womanhood—"personhood" as experienced by women—in a matrilineal society. In selecting folktales for analysis, I asked only two questions: How do they image women? In what way is that imagery still extant, modified, or in need of transformation?

By example, let us return to the story of Ohia. As it stands, the story tells of two types of wives and the curse on the man who acquires the "bad" sort. Other peoples have versions of this story.[3] A Serbian variation is worth mentioning. In that version, a cock witnessed the discomfiture of the husband and told him how he—the cock—controlled his one hundred wives by pecking at the difficult ones. Whereupon the man picked up a cane, gave his wife a good beating to bring her to order, and thereby saved his own neck.[4] (How some men love to be the "cock with a hundred wives" and to follow their animal instincts into the battering of their wives! The Akan, however, frown upon wife beating and so would not end their version in that manner.)

The tellers of these fireside tales always have personal comments to add, as I have done with the Serbian variation. They may obliquely interpolate local examples, add songs to enliven the recounting, or embellish the story by their own attitudes. Sometimes these side comments are incorporated into the next retelling of the story.[5]

---

[3]Barker and Sinclair selected and published a number of West African folktales to introduce readers to the thought and customs of West Africans. They reckoned that through them they could understand the black person's mind (Barker and Sinclair, p. 19). Some of these tales, like the Rubber Baby or Tar Baby and the Brer Rabbit series, are found in parts of the United States and are purported to have been carried there by Africans who were forcibly carried to that continent. Others have even more universal currency and may illustrate the global nature of sexism.

[4]The story is found in Wioslav M. Petrovitchy, *Hero-Tales and Legends of the Serbians* (New York: Frederick A. Stokes, Co., 1915). In *Akan-Asante Folktales*, pp. 242-45, Rattray presents another version of this tale.

[5]An example may be found in B. K. Walker and W. S. Walker, *Nigerian Folktales as Told by Olawode Idowu and Omotayo Ayo*, 2nd edition (Hamden, CT: The Shoe String Press/Archon Books, 1980). To my surprise, the Yoruba man ends this tale by saying, "This hunter was not contented with one wife. He wanted to have another one, and in getting the other one, he lost both" (Story I, p. 11).

THE ORIGIN OF AKAN FOLKTALES

In the beginning Onyankopon (God) was the owner of all folktales so they were called *Nyankosɛm* (God's stories).[6] One day Ananse the spider went to God and said to God "Sell me your stories." Onyankopon told him that the mighty cities of Asante could not afford the price of the stories, much less an individual and a poor commoner at that. Ananse insisted he could afford to buy them. Onyankopon said to Ananse, "Bring a python, a leopard, a dwarf (the legendary 'little people' of the forest called *mmoatia*), and hornets." Ananse promised to procure all these and throw in his mother Yaa Nsia as a bonus.

Ananse went to consult his wife Aso Yaa, who taught him how to secure the python and the hornets. He followed her instructions and was successful. Then came the plan for the leopard. "Dig a hole in the tracks of the leopard," she began, but Ananse cut her short; now that he understood how to trick the animals he no longer needed her. Nor did he consult her on how to get the dwarfs, but he succeeded on his own.

With the python, hornets, leopard, and dwarf in hand, Ananse said to Yaa Nsia, his mother, "*Ma berewa*" (my old woman, an endearing term), "get up and let us go, I am taking you with the dwarf to go and give to Onyankopon in exchange for his stories." Yaa Nsia got up at the son's bidding and followed. [How women want their sons to be famous!] So before the whole heavenly council, Onyankopon handed *Nyankosɛm* (God's stories) to Ananse and they became *Anansesɛm*.[7]

Thus, in this folktale of beginnings, God abdicated centerstage, handing over control of the human story to a commoner who succeeded by his wits.

Ananse's wife, Aso, also drops out of the enterprise; Nsia, Ananse's

[6]The name of God in Akan has several versions, all of which are used in the folktales. Two used most frequently are Onyame/Nyame and Onyankopon/Nyankopon. The names beginning with "O" are more formal and both Onyame and Onyankopon are used in the Bible to translate God.

[7]Barker and Sinclair, pp. 29-32.

mother, is safely returned to her maker, and Ananse, the man, gains his autonomy! In this way, the human story as perceived by the Akan has become "Ananse-centric" (androcentric), instead of "theocentric," a myth that tells of events concerning gods, and God's way with creation. Man controls the animal world, both real and legendary. Sometimes when folktales refer to God, they substitute Ananse Kokroko (the Great Spider) for Onyankopon, the name of God. It is often said jokingly that Ananse, whose role in the stories is that of a trickster, reflects the life-style of men in the communities that tell the stories.

The relationships of the three human beings in the story are worth examining. Ananse is male, a son and a husband whose ambition was to replace God; Nsia is female, a mother-in-law; Aso Yaa is Ananse's wife. In this tale the two women do not come together at any point. It is the man shunting between the two women who is their only connection. Ananse consults his wife on how to achieve his goal, follows her counsel until he feels sufficiently confident that he can go it alone, and then shuts her up. She disappears from the story. Ananse does not consult his mother; instead of asking, he simply tells. Apparently not the questioning type, she complies. Both women are instruments of the man's success. The unspoken moral of the story for girls should be: "That is why mothers say, if you know how to achieve success, go after it yourself, and by all means refuse to be used by others." Yet, through such a folktale as this, women hear and see themselves as they are actually regarded in their culture. The stories told by the Akan in the dim light of the evening fires become operational in a veiled way in their attitudes toward women and things feminine.

OLD WOMEN AND WITCHES

Many African folktales describe old women as demons. Often, they have the power of metamorphosis to alternate between human and non-human forms. They are usually witches or possessors of extraordinary powers that they use for good or ill. Women, especially when they are old, constitute a mysterious—if not sinister—phenomenon. However, since respect for old age prevents openly ridiculing or admonishing them in real life, folktales are used to play openly with this repressed assessment. The Akan often see witchcraft as the province of women (old, beautiful, wealthy, extremely ugly, or non-conformist). Few men, according to the Akan, practice witchcraft.

In the Ifa Corpus of the Yoruba one story called "Ose-Ogbe" tells the story of a king who beat palm nuts (demanding physical work) for his wife Ameri, favoring and indulging the woman. However, the woman was a witch who refused to assist him. After reciting a poem (*odu*), a diviner told the king what to do with his favorite wife. He followed the advice. Ameri was trapped, then destroyed, and the king prospered. The *odu* may be interpreted to tell of someone who has confided in an untrustworthy person, but the imagery is clear: who can be more dangerous than one's favorite wife?[8]

Folktales with witches as characters usually portray them as old women, occasionally benevolent and wise, but more often malevolent. They often use the motif of an underground queen who demands absolute obedience for the people's own good. In a typical "how come" story, Kweku Tsin, son of Ananse, stumbles upon such an underground ruler. His strict adherence to her instructions earned him the food drum, representing prosperity. When Ananse made the same trip, but went *against* her directives, he also received a drum, but it did not bring prosperity. When he returned home to show off his gift by beating his drum, all he produced was the wild animals of the forest.[9] This story is generally told for its lesson of obedience and the avoidance of envy. The first moral reemphasizes respect for the elderly, but it is noteworthy that these rulers of underground cities are usually old women.

In this genre of folktales, the characters acting out the causes of fortune and misfortune are usually young girls. In their collection *Nigerian Folktales*, the Walkers record one such story under the title "Envy can kill." A girl who has been brought up to be industrious, kind, and obedient brings wealth to her mother; her half-sister (daughter of the mother's co-wife), imitates her, but, being haughty and disobedient, only succeeds in bringing home three gourds full of poisonous insects, wild primates, poisonous snakes, and other dangerous animals.

The theme of old women appears in several stories in *Akan-Asante Folktales*.[10] One story tells of a lazy girl's encounter with an old woman

---

[8]William Bascom, *Ifa Divination: Communication Between God and Men in West Africa* (Bloomington: Indiana University Press, 1969), pp. 457-59.

[9]Barker and Sinclair, *Story XVI*, pp. 89-94.

[10]Rattray, *Akan-Asante Folktales*. Since these stories are well-known among the Akan, I am identifying them as "Rattray" to acknowledge the collector's work as

who has the pseudonym *Tena hɔ na wo behu* (sit there and you will see). The old woman had the girl complete a number of extraordinary jobs, beginning with digging up yams that begged to be left alone, and leaving alone those that begged to be dug up. The old woman was a wicked woman who had kept her real name secret; she would not free the young girl until she had learned the old woman's real name. In this way, the old woman kept her slaving away for eight days without food, until finally a crab taught her the old woman's real name. The girl uttered the name and the old woman released her.

Another motif involving witches is found in stories in which women use their sons or daughters to entrap those hunting for husbands or wives. Rattray's *Akan-Asante Folktales* includes two examples. First, there is the tale of a woman who had eleven sons whom she wanted to be rid of because she was starving while they ate all the food she cooked.[11] She sought the cooperation of the silk cotton tree and then that of Onyankopon, both of whom failed. The latter passed the task on to Female Death, who had ten daughters. In the end, it was the eleventh and tiniest son who saved them, causing Female Death to kill her own children.[12]

In a second story, an old woman with a detachable head had eight sons. When these sons encountered eight husband-hunting girls, the girls escaped, only because their brother Gyinamoa accompanied them and outwitted the witch.[13] It is noteworthy that in these tales, however formidable the women, it is a "little man" or a younger brother who, with the aid of wit or a talisman, outwits them. The stories ridicule women and project a superior male intelligence at the same time.

---

well as that of the publishing house that reissued the 1930 edition. To get a real feel for these stories, the reader would do well to read more of them.

[11]There is a legendary woman in Akyem (an Akan sub-group) folktalk who was said to have given birth to thirty children. Feeding them was a problem, but feeding herself was well nigh impossible. In the end she died because she swallowed one snail whole in order to prevent the thirty children from devouring it. Although my mother interprets it as a legend that refers to a famine, my question has always been: Where were the fathers and uncles when these mothers seemed to be handling children single-handed? In a matrilineal society, the maternal uncle would have authority over a woman's children.

[12]Rattray, *Akan-Asante Folktales*, pp. 191-97.
[13]Ibid., p. 220.

WOMEN AND MARRIAGE

A favored theme in many folktales is that girls should not be strong-willed in matters of the choice of a spouse or marriage.[14] Sometimes the folktale gives an additional caution against leaving home to live with a husband in a place where one has no blood relations. A common motif is that the heroine, having refused all the suitors approved of by her parents, goes on her own to the forest in search of one thing or another, or to the stream to fetch water or to bathe. There she encounters a most handsome man, falls in love, and runs home to tell her people she has finally found the one who is worthy of her hand. She is married amid pomp and pageantry and she goes off with her husband, only to discover that he is not what he seemed. Instead, she has married a buffalo, a leopard, a python, or some other animal that had transformed himself into a man in order to trap her. In the python versions, the husband consumes the whole bridal entourage and, just when he is about to swallow the girl, either her brother or a poor hunter shoots it. Having learned her lesson the hard way, the girl settles for her father's choice and marries a brave hunter. A Hausa story makes the point quite succinctly: if you let girls please themselves, they will bring home a man-eating pumpkin![15]

An Akan story tells of a woman, Abena, who married a foreigner, went away, and prospered in "her husband's house" (as the Yorubas would say), and never looked back. However, this is frowned upon among the Asante, since the woman belongs, essentially, to the family of her mother's people and not her father's or her husband's. If she cannot actually reside in her mother's home, she is expected to keep close contact. Abena ignored all these customs. She ignored all messages and intimations, until she faced the unhappy situation of not being present at the funerals of both parents.[16] The Asante take it for granted, as do many other peoples, that both men and women want to get married, so the stories of spouse-hunting involve both sexes. The

---

[14]Ibid., p. 53.

[15]Robert S. Rattray, *Hausa Folklore, Vol. I* (Oxford: Oxford University Press/Clarendon, 1913), pp. 300-308.

[16]Ibid., p. 123.

predominant message is that "good" girls get good husbands, but there are also appropriate stories to educate a girl for marriage. Most often, it is the girls who get the lion's share of this counseling through folktales.

Parents are portrayed as the best judges of who would be a suitable spouse, and several stories tell of fathers testing prospective husbands. Ananse was given the task of clearing a plantation of nettles without scratching himself. He succeeded, and won a much sought-after beauty.[17] Other tales take up the theme, "Who hoes farthest marries my daughter," with men always ready to make the attempt. This theme is also combined with one of misplaced confidence, in which the men who perform these feats turn out to be unsuitable husbands. Whether a group is matrilineal or patrilineal in the matter of descent, the clear message is that parents cannot make a mistake in their choice of a spouse: even if they appear to be mistaken at the outset, the girls always find that the parents' choice was good.

One additional example should suffice. A father, seeking to make the best match for his daughter, had refused many handsome and wealthy suitors. In the end, tired of his own game, he swore an oath before a divinity that he would go to "the aristocrats' fair" in a last attempt to select a suitor for his daughter and that he would marry her off to whatever or whoever caught his eye first. The secret was leaked by his best friend in whom he had confided. That man then turned himself into a wolf and was the first man at the fair, arriving at the same time as the father. However, an oath is an oath and, sadly, the girl was married off to the wolf—who later returned to his original human form.[18]

Men do not make poor matches for their daughters! It is not surprising, then, to not find tales of girls who make their choices with good results. The single example I have found tells of Kwaku Susufo (Kwaku the thinker) and Akua Susufo (Akua the thinker), two young people who chose each other to challenge the rule that parents must always choose their children's spouses.

Akua Susufo, the daughter of a queen mother, had refused all suitors until three strangers arrived in her town; she decided she

---

[17]Rattray, *Akan-Asante Folktales*, p. 128.

[18]A Hausa equivalent is recorded by Rattray in *Hausa Folklore*, pp. 312-26. See also Judges 11:19-40, where Jephthah makes a similar rash promise that ends in the sacrifice of his daughter. In most instances, when women are sacrificed to husband

would marry one of them. To test them, she gave them the task of explaining three symbols, and she married the youngest, who proved to be the most astute and who, like her, was called Susufo (thinker). So the two thinkers were married, and by their ability to speak in proverbs and to interpret and create symbols, they were able to communicate on plots to kill Kwaku Susufo and to bring all the culprits to justice.[19]

Sexuality and Relationships

In male–female relationships, as described in folktales, men see themselves under pressure to prove themselves; they perform heroic deeds, risking life and limb to win and retain the affection of the women in their lives, usually mothers, wives, or mothers-in-law. The first story I want to highlight portrays lovers—a relationship between two young people, neither of whom is married. It is a unique story, since this type of relationship was not encouraged in traditional society, as the story itself shows.

Once there was a married woman whose babies died at birth. She tried all the medicines and all the shrines. Then, at one shrine she was made to promise that if she had a baby who lived, that child would never climb a palm tree. Not long after she gave birth to a boy who was named Kwasamma (the child who goes and comes back). He grew into a handsome young man who had a special girl friend. Playing with her one day, he accidentally broke the string of her waist beads. She had to restring them, so she asked him to go and bring raffia, which comes only from the young fronds of the swamp palm. Kwasamma had no choice, so he climbed a palm tree. No sooner had he touched the frond, then the palm tree began to split in two. There he was, caught in the cleft.

His mother came around and, seeing him, raised a song: "Palm tree, squeeze him!" And the palm tree squeezed the lad. His father came, saw him caught, and raised the song encouraging the palm tree to continue squeezing the lad. So did the chief of the village.

---

or God, the father is said to know best, the girls are brought up to comply, and it is asserted that, in the end, all is well.

[19]Rattray, *Akan-Asante Folktales*, pp. 102-5.

At last, his lover came along and implored the tree to release him. It did so. He fell into her arms and both were turned into a pool of palm oil.[20]

Despite puritanical frowning against eroticism, against displays of affection between women and men or sexual flirting (of which waist beads are a symbol), this story ends with the saying, "When you see beautiful people, it is because they got to the palm oil pool early enough to anoint themselves." Anointing with the oil (of love) enhances beauty! The story is heavy with symbolism: Kwasamma's move from touching the waist beads to touching the forbidden palm tree, its opening to trap him, the disapproval of society, and the transformation of the two persons into one entity because the female cared.

Among the Akan, a mother is the most cherished person in a man's life. Even without any demands from the mother, sons demonstrate their affection with extravagant gifts. Barker and Sinclair's collection includes a story (XXII, pp. 123-28) about three sons who were so fond of their mother that to please her, they promised to bury her in an extravagant manner. The third son, Kwesi, not to be outdone by the other two who had provided an extraordinarily elegant grave and coffin, promised to place in her coffin the tail of the elephant queen. Having survived many hair-raising events, he returned triumphantly with the prized tail. It is significant to note that these men made these promises on their own accord. No woman asked them to nor were they proving themselves to a would-be father-in-law. It goes without saying that they have internalized societal definitions of masculinity.

Most damning to the image of women in Africa are tales of relationships that portray them as demanding. Women are described as persons who stop at nothing to ensure that their husbands perform heroic deeds or even risk life and limb in order to retain their affections. They send men on dangerous errands, such as stealing the devil's kola nuts or collecting raffia from the forbidden palm. Mrs. Leopard taunts Mr. Leopard into fighting Mr. Hare, with the result that Mr. Leopard is roundly beaten. Men have to find meat for the house, and women either prod them continually about this duty or simply walk out on those husbands who are incompetent. So it is that in folktales men often get

---

[20]Ibid., pp. 48-51.

wives by a display of wealth and, in marriage, women are labelled as gold-diggers who seek only material gain.

The Profile of a Wife

> Ananse, well-known for being poor, once exchanged his rags for the gorgeous cloth of his friend Kwa (Nothing), with whom he was going wife-hunting. As a result, every mother's daughter, but one, agreed to marry Ananse, while they treated Kwa with contempt because of the rags on his back. Only one woman took pity on Kwa and gave him her daughter. All of Ananse's new wives mocked Kwa's bride.
>
> On arriving back at the town of Ananse and Kwa, the girls discovered their mistake. Kwa and his wife, being generous, took them all in. Ananse grew jealous of Kwa and, with his usual meanness, managed to cause Kwa's death. Then all the women made sure that all the children mourned him forever. This is why children always cry for nothing.[21]

The teller of this story often makes asides as to how silly and undiscerning women can be. The story says that the majority of women promote their daughters' marriages without ascertaining the background of the men. Women's overemphasis on prosperity as a goal for marriage contrasts with the rigorous schemes of fathers. Even when it first appears that the fathers have made a mistake, it always works out well for the daughter.

As mentioned above, in folktales marriage often lasts only as long as the wives can live in comfort. This is demonstrated by the following tale in which the characters, typically, are hunters and their wives.

> The hunter Gyekye, his wife Boniayɛ-Kae-Dabi, and their child lived in a hunting lodge out in the forest. They had very little food because Gyekye scarcely ever succeeded in his hunting expeditions. Fed up, Boniaye went back to her village, taking the child with her. After her departure, a Mother Eagle helped Gyekye become the chief of a whole village, which she called into being for him. Her only wish was that she and her eaglets be allowed to

---

[21]Barker and Sinclair, pp. 35-37.

live undisturbed in the *odum* (mahogany tree) around which the village grew.

As soon as Boniayɛ heard of Gyekye's prosperity, she went back, accompanied by the child when things got better. She then accused Gyekye of neglecting them. Gyekye took her back and she became the first among many wives. Boniayɛ did everything to demonstrate that she was the first wife. She lived up to her name Boniayɛ, which means ungratefulness, and decided she did not want the mahogany tree and the eagles' home at the center of the city. She nagged Gyekye until one day, to get his peace of mind, he felled the tree, and the eagle and her eaglets flew away. As soon as they left, the city disappeared, leaving behind Gyekye, Boniayɛ, and their child in their original poverty. Such are the ways of ungrateful women.[22]

Among the Akan and throughout most of Africa, marriage is conceived of in contractual terms and a husband's inability to provide for the material needs of a wife is considered sufficient grounds for divorce. On the other hand, women also have their responsibilities, including a readiness to work alongside men in this joint venture; a woman who refuses should not expect her husband to play his part.

One well-loved tale has the refrain, *Gyae o madi m'adeɛ o gyae o* (Stop complaining. I have only eaten what is mine). In this story, Aso, Ananse's wife, was not willing to help him farm. She invented all sorts of taboos in relation to women and farming, in which women kept off the farms until harvesting time. Ananse knew how to handle the situation: He "died" just at harvest time, had himself buried on the farm, and proceeded to enjoy the produce all by himself. Shocked at the rapid rate at which the food stuffs were disappearing, Aso was frustrated and angry. Who could be stealing from the farm? She lamented

---

[22]Rattray, *Akan-Asante Folktales*, pp. 16-19. In this version of the folktale, the narrator interjects his own opinion of Gyekye and all men who have to deal with women whose sexual favors they seek. He interpolates: "Just like men and their foolishness . . . he could find nothing to say" when Boniaye accuses him of neglect. He just "took her back . . . spent the night with her," and reinstated her even though she had walked out on him in his indigent days. What makes a man so shabbily treated willing to reconcile with a woman? It does not seem to come into the narrator's purview that he may have been genuinely fond of her and have missed her in spite of his many other wives.

and called on Ananse's ghost to deal with the thief. Ananse replied with the above refrain, adding several verses that describe farming. He took the opportunity to recall the custom: "Since the Creator created," said he, "I have not come across a woman who would not help her husband."

The helper role of wives—a willingness to do hard work, not asking too many questions, and bringing up daughters to do the same—is a fact of life mirrored and reinforced by folktales. Sometimes, other elements like a wicked stepmother are thrown into the mix, such as in this tale of an orphaned daughter of a co-wife. The orphan is treated in a most cruel way by her stepmother, who, meanwhile, has been spoiling her own daughter. The orphan goes on an errand and encounters a dog with a bone who orders her to do the strangest things, like making rice-cakes from a single grain of rice. The girl obeys without questioning or expressing the slightest emotion to indicate how strange she finds the whole situation. When she finishes cooking, she takes the smallest portion. As a result, she is rewarded with plenty of riches, a good husband, and an entourage of wealthy men. Her proud step-sister sets off, out of jealousy, to seek her fortune. Being haughty, inquisitive, argumentative, and self-centered, she ends up with an entourage of lame cattle, sheep, and all manner of sick people. What girl would wish for such a fate?[23]

CHILDREN AND CHILD-BEARING

For the Akan and the Yoruba—and for most of Africa as well—marriage and child-bearing are thought of together. The motif of children and child-bearing is present in many folktales.[24] It is not unusual to hear of "special" children being born to mothers after years of agony.

---

[23]Rattray, *Hausa Folklore*, I, pp. 130-60. Story-telling is part of the community education process, and stories of the dismal future of spoiled children condition children for parental discipline.

[24]In the Ifa corpus, almost every time a woman devotee goes before an oracle (and there are numerous examples), it is a question of children. In the African worldview, as exemplified by the Yoruba, the three cardinal good things of life are money, children, and long life with good health. The latter is most highly valued by the Yoruba, while the Akan will put children first. See Wande Abimbola, *Ifa Divination Poetry* (New York: NOK Publishers, 1977), pp. 34, 97; Bascom, pp. 323, 459-61.

These children are often lost through the carelessness or malice of others, although occasionally the mother is at fault. There are also several "only child" stories, but I am familiar with only one that states the cause of barrenness in biological rather than magical terms. This is unusual because usually healers and priests attach taboos to the child's life. The "biological" story, how Asɔ came to be married to Ananse, is used to explain the origin of divorce.

> Asɔ's first husband, Kwasi Ninkunfo (the Jealous One), was impotent and did not want any competition. So he took Asɔ away from their town to a private settlement that he built for the two of them. God (Nyankopɔn) was not pleased with the situation, so he decreed that any man who could manage to impregnate Asɔ could take her away from Kwasi. Ananse, with his typical cleverness, succeeded in doing just that. Kwasi lodged a complaint with Nyankopɔn and expressed his own unwillingness to continue with the marriage. So, Nyankopɔn gave Asɔ to Ananse to become his wife.[25]

The message of this folktale is that by divine injunction a marriage must result in children or it may be broken up. Hence, it is not surprising to find a preponderance of stories about childless women going in search of children. In the Akan stories I am familiar with, the child-cravers are all women; they are childless either because of infant mortality or simply their inability to conceive.

These stories also emphasize the importance of keeping taboos in order to sustain the lives of such children. Two or three examples should suffice. Akosua Dɛntaa, the daughter of the Queen Mother of heaven, was born to a common woman on earth, on the condition that the child never pound *fufu* (a staple food). One day Kra made the child pound *fufu*, and, as a result, the child died. I have already referred to the story of Kwasamma, who got stuck in a palm tree after his mother had promised that he would never climb one.

In a third story, a woman agreed to give birth to an *obosomba* (a child donated by a deity), even having been told that the child would be troublesome for a long time but that, with perseverance on the side

---

[25]Rattray, *Akan-Asante Folktales*, pp. 132-37.

of the mother, he would bring prosperity to the community. This story reflects and may be behind the indulgent way in which mothers generally treat sons.[26] A variation on this theme plays on the rivalry of women. A co-wife, who by negligence has turned the other wife's *obosomba* into a fish, then cooks the child for its mother. This latter folktale clearly emphasizes the malevolent outcome of jealousy in polygynous marriages. However, the pivotal element of all of the above folktales is the centrality of children in African women's lives. Women agree to even the most unreasonable demands of the gods in order to have children who grow and thrive.

In a traditional compound, however, a mother is not the only one in charge of her children. Occasionally, stories tell of children who have been neglected when they were left in the care of others. In the absence of mothers, some of these special children turn to oil when left in the sun or run back to the pineapple field to return to their original state as pineapples. Therefore, mothers, however burdened, strap these special babies to their backs when going out, rather than leave them in other people's care. The Yoruba culture, a patrilineal group, is so obsessed with having children that tales even tell of men becoming pregnant. However, in both systems—matrilineal and patrilineal—it is the children who bury their parents, a custom requiring everyone to have a child. Some Yoruba stories illustrate this need.

> Once, the three wives of the same man put medicine to make them pregnant into some porridge. The first two wives planned to cheat the third and youngest of motherhood, so they sent her on an errand. In her absence, the first two wives ate the porridge. When the youngest wife came back, she scraped the bottom of the pot, and ate. Only she became pregnant, as the medicine had settled to the bottom of the pot.

In a second story, a man who had prepared a fertility porridge for his wife ate of it and became pregnant. A male tortoise also ate of the porridge, forbidden to men, and he, too, became pregnant. Because child-bearing is not for men, both the man and the tortoise died.[27]

---

[26]Ibid., pp. 26-30.
[27]Walker and Walker, p. 64.

THE THREADS OF GENDER ROLES

These folktales are woven with threads that specify gender roles to appropriately prepare men and women for their roles in society. The relationships between men and women in Akan stories, as in the others referred to, closely mirror reality; at the same time, they reinforce it by serving as living parables. When a girl (or a boy, for that matter) shows signs of non-conformity, the telling of a story ensures that she or he does not become an example to be emulated.

Polygamy is treated as the norm, but many stories highlight problems encountered in the system. By and large, stories emphasize competition among co-wives for the affection of their common husband and warn men of the unsoundness of showing favoritism toward a certain wife. It is true that there are examples of beautiful friendships among co-wives—both in stories and in real life. Nevertheless, it is the importance of having children, more than anything else, that keeps both men and women from abandoning polygamy.

Folktales commonly portray a married woman as a self-seeking person who cooperates in the connubial state only when conditions are "for better" and never if they are "for worse." By and large, marriage scenes are very uncomplimentary to women. Few happy marriages appear in folktales, and we are forced to ask why, if the marriage institution is such a trial for women and men, there is such a commitment to it? Or, perhaps, instead of commitment there is only coercion. Folktales also witness to a tacit agreement that unfaithfulness in marriage applies only to women. Polygyny is prevalent and acceptable, because only male jealousy is sanctioned by society.

In the sphere of economic cooperation between spouses, the tale of Aso's artless invention of female taboos is interesting, as it is usually Ananse who goes to great lengths not to work and to profit from the labor of his wives and children. Typical is the story of how Aso and her four children complete most of the work on the farm, while Ananse pretends to have died in an attempt to have the lion's share of their joint labor. However, the tales do ensure that a man who acts in this way is also called to task. Traditional societies usually cherish a sense of justice in reaping the fruits of one's labor.

The Power of the Kitchen

Taboos are seriously regarded in this context. It is sometimes asserted jokingly that the "blood" taboos originated with women to enable them to get a few days' respite each month or after the strenuous business of childbirth. But in a polygamous society and in a society where people are organized in large family compounds, it also ensures that a man never has to care for himself. Taboos say that the kitchen is out of bounds to boys and men. The isolation of women by blood taboos, together with a lack of total trust on the part of men, may be what has led to wild speculation and, indeed, allegations of women acting as bad witches and using unwholesome products for cooking, even of using their own blood instead of palm oil. "Real life" stories are often told by men (who must have good reason to believe they deserve such treatment!) who fear that their wives have been slowly poisoning them.

On the other hand, the kitchen becomes a refuge, and food then is a strong weapon in the hands of women in a culture that disparages "eating out." Women ridicule men who invade their sacred domain and haven, the only place in the home where they can exercise autonomy and make decisions that affect the whole household without having a man cast a vote or a veto. Women hold on jealously to their kitchen power, a point to be taken into account when dealing with an African woman's sense of personhood. To live out one's role as a source of nourishment is not considered oppressive. Being a source of nourishment is a symbol of the African woman's sense of self-giving in the service of home and community. Some women, indeed, regard this and procreation as the essence of their being.

Folktales clearly express this image of woman as a being conditioned to function as the source of nourishment. Culture and custom have extended her breast-feeding of helpless infants to a life-long role of self-effacing service in the home and a nearly complete absence from the pages of national histories. As is commonly agreed, traditional non-formal education (including the telling of these tales) aims at preparing a girl for her future home so that she does not become useless in society or a liability to her future husband. A woman's life is defined as male-centered and community-oriented; she achieves nothing if she fails in this respect.

Custom demands that a girl never question a male, however unreasonable he appears to be. Of course, this means that a girl finds herself in a double bind: as a young person, she must not question adult authority and, since she is usually married to an older man, her subordinate position is doubly established. She makes no choices, except as pertain to her sphere of operation as housekeeper or homemaker. What she thinks and how she sees life are almost never ascertained in the conjugal home, usually not until she reaches the position of the oldest member of her family.

Survival in such a situation depends on how skillfully a woman can manipulate circumstances to her advantage. Her status of non-being is turned into authentic being, as helplessness and powerlessness are construed as virtues. One obvious way to survive may be seen in the devices women use to ensure that they are not totally deprived of some little comforts. This, of course, differs from woman to woman. It should not be said that women in Africa are resigned to the status of "double losers," as they, too, can learn from Ananse's love of life.

The daring "witch" in all women will not die as long as they can hear stories of their power (if only that of nuisance value!). Like the witches and queens of the tales, women can dare to act autonomously or to make demands. But until now, it seems, "we hear and hear" these tales, "but do not understand." Yet to accept a male regime without questioning male portraits of women is to agree to act out a male history rather than God's history and to continue to act out *Anansesem* (man's stories), while we ought to be rereading them to discover what in them may have been the original *Nyankonsɛm* (God's stories).

3

The Language of Proverbs

Like myths and folktales, proverbs restate themes that appear in ethical and moral teaching. Proverbs can be described as short, popular, oft-used sentences that use plain language to express some practical truth that results from experience or observation. The weight and effectiveness of proverbial language among Africans is attested to by their continuing daily use of proverbs today and also by their current interest in collecting and documenting proverbs. It is also worth noting that new proverbs are being created all the time, while others are made obsolete by the changing times. (This is seen, for example, in the appearance of proverbs about white men.)

My criterion in selecting proverbs to include here was that they must refer to women and other female creatures in a way that prescribes "what is woman." Where parallel proverbs apply exclusively to men and other male creatures, I highlight them for comparison. Essentially, I question the validity of continuing to use certain proverbs as authoritative statements to condition social, political, and domestic roles and structures when there are indications that they might no longer be appropriate. I have paid special attention to proverbs dealing with themes of marriage and of reciprocity in a domestic context. To allow others to make their own assessment of these Akan proverbs, I have drawn from the 3,679 proverbs collected by J. G. Christaller, adding only a few from other sources.[1]

---

[1] J. G. Christaller, *Twi mmɛbusem mpensa ahansia mmoano* (Basel: Basel German Evangelical Missionary Society, 1879). This collection is available on microfilm at the Ibadan University Library in Nigeria and in print copy at the

HUMAN DIGNITY

There are proverbs that do assert the dignity of all human beings and others that highlight individual worth regardless of sex and status. A good example is the Akan proverb, "All people are children of God. No one is a child of the earth" (JGC 2436), that recognizes a person's self-worth as a participant in the making of history, rather than as only a keeper of customs. Such positive proverbs could be used to counteract the sexist maxims that abound in the Akan idiom and to promote mutuality and reciprocity in community relations. But, as is indeed the case, such proverbs seem to have little import where women are concerned.

Throughout most of Africa, individual achievement is encouraged and appreciated as long as it benefits the whole community.[2] It seems, however, that any emphasis on the dignity and worth of each individual is appropriated very selectively by men as they apply traditional norms in such a way as to be the history makers. The first proverb that caught my attention was "What a man wants is what he does" (JGC 2117), observing the role of men as self-creators. I also found many sound injunctions and advice to men in proverbs, although, in my opinion, much of this advice is not taken seriously by most men.

Several proverbs on marriage speak against polygamy and the disharmony it brings, such as "If there was something to be gained from promiscuity, then the goat would be king" (JGC 2021). A typical response of African men would be that men are naturally polygamous

---

Widener Library at Harvard University. I have given the source of each proverb; thus (JGC 2436) is proverb number 2436 in the collection of J. G. Christaller. The English translations are mine. *Twi* is the generic name for a group of languages, including Asante and Akuapem/Akwapim. These proverbs or variants of them are also in the Fantse language. They can be referred to collectively as Akan proverbs.

See also Hans Nicolas Riis, *Grammatical Outline and Vocabulary of the Oji Language with Special Reference to the Akwapim Dialect Together with a Collection of Proverbs of the Natives* (Basel: Basel Bahnmauer's Buchhandlung, 1854). This book is also available at the Widener Library, Harvard University.

[2]Christaller, pp. 445-59. Of fifteen proverbs on the "individual," only two address the positive side of "going it alone." See also JGC 3254 and 3256 (against individualism), and 3258 and 3259.

and that the welfare, security, and beauty of women depend on men. However, such proverbs have not prevented wife-beating. In general, the "self-creating man" conveniently forgets proverbs that do not serve his immediate interests and regularly manages to put himself above such sayings. Thus, in a way, the status of these proverbs as binding parameters for women and men is already undermined. Why should women not feel free to dismantle those proverbs that are sexist, oppressive, or limiting to the full growth of their humanity and the just ordering of society?

The Making of Man

If you go out to watch the dance of Ohintinpraku, you meet your death; if you do not go, your wife and children will ridicule you. (JGC 1385)

When a man is in trouble, a woman takes it for a joke. (IA&FC 923)[3]

Kwasi Nkroma is not a man who will not find a wife. (JGC 3587)

It cannot be that all men are the same. There must be men who have no stomach for "savage barbarism" or violence toward women, but who force themselves "to be men" according to the expected mold of tradition. Many of the tensions between women and men in marriage arise out of these traditional expectations. Brought up to be self-creators, men are reduced to nothing if they cannot prove to themselves that they are brave and all-sufficient providers. The dilemma of Akan men and women is summed up in the first proverb above: A man brought up to present a brave front in every situation and a woman socialized to expect great feats from her husband are both in bondage to traditional norms, which they, in turn, pass on to their children. Note, also, the second proverb, one from Jamaica, which portrays the woman as unsympathetic to the man's plight.

As boys, Akan men are given examples of how to become over-

---

[3]Izett Anderson and Frank Cundall, *Jamaica Negro Proverbs and Sayings*, 2nd rev. ed. (London: West India Committee for the Institute of Jamaica, 1927). Abbreviated here as (IA&FC).

lords who dominate the women in their lives. They begin their training with their sisters and dare not deviate, else they find themselves labelled "slaves of women" or effeminate. Such men would experience great difficulty later in finding wives, the exact opposite of Kwasi Nkroma, the eligible bachelor of the third proverb. All bachelors must believe that they are like Kwasi Nkroma and act accordingly, for "It is when a man wants to be ridiculed that he goes around saying 'I have neither wife nor children' " (JGC 2658).

It is interesting to note that the Yoruba have even developed a proverb to relieve men of the burden of chauvinism: "If a man sees a snake and a woman kills it, the desirable result is that the snake has not escaped" (RA 907).[4] Such a proverb ingeniously circumvents tradition or, rather, makes creative use of it.

The Making of Woman

All women are the same. (JGC 27)

What you would not have repeated in the streets, do not tell your wife in the bed chamber. (JGC 2958)

Like fowls, the women of Akropon do not forage in one place. (JGC 1844)

Women love where wealth is. (JGC 29)

The Akan generally acknowledge that no one born is destined to be like their parents. Children do not have to exhibit the character traits and mannerisms of their parents, neither do they have to acquire the same skills. Human beings are endowed with different gifts and no one but God knows the life of any individual, for "When one took leave of God [in the unseen world] nobody else was within ear-shot" (JGC 3465). Why, then, should the Akan make use of a maxim that says all women are alike in their behavior?

A common image of a woman is a person who carries the legend "quarrelsome." For example, Samuel Crowther identifies the meaning

---

[4]Raphael Areje, *Yoruba Proverbs* (Ibadan: Daystar Press, 1985). Proverbs from this source will be identified as (RA).

of the Yoruba word *gbai* as "adverb, very vociferously, loquaciously," and illustrates its meaning with the sentence *Obiri na nso gbai* (The woman is always brawling).[5] Many examples abound in which African male writers, including theologians, illustrate negatives by using images of women.

Women, the proverbs say, cannot keep secrets and they are fickle, restless, and, thus, prone to unfaithfulness. Like hens they forage all around the village.[6] They are here today and there tomorrow, depending on how much they can find for themselves. The allusion, of course, is that women prefer to seek out wealthy men.

Woman as Mother

A hen might step on her chick, but not with the intention of killing it. (JGC 1648)

The cock does not know how to look after chicks, but only knows how to feed itself. (IA&FC 581, Jamaican)

The tortoise has no breasts and yet she feeds her young ones. (JGC 1914)

When you catch the mother hen, the chicks become easy prey. (JGC 1956)

Akan society sees women in the same way it views other female animals: fulfilling biological roles as mothers, caring for their children, feeding, training, and disciplining, but never destroying. Affection and consideration mitigate the discipline that is necessary for the young ones' survival. *Akɔkɔ*, the Akan noun used in the proverbs above, is generic but it obviously refers to the female, the hen. (Note also how the Jamaican proverb observes, "Cocks rarely stay around to feed chicks.") In Akan daily conversation, "woman" and "mother" are almost synonymous; as in nature, the obviously primary role of the fe-

---

[5]Samuel Crowther, *Vocabulary of the Yoruba Languages* (London: Seeleys, 1852), p. 114.

[6]The hen-chicken imagery is widespread, showing up among the Ibo, Haitians, and Jamaicans (Anderson and Cundall, pp. 562-63).

male is birthing and nurturing the species. The aura of life and "livingness" that surrounds the woman is the center of the home and a woman is assumed to be faithfully motherly.

It is recognized that the survival of the next generation is not limited to the availability of mother's milk. Mothers not only feed, but also protect the young. All the proverbial observations about hens and chickens also hold for the human community. The welfare of children takes precedence over everything else in a woman's life; nothing else is as important: "When one's mother or child lies dying, one does not pursue disputes" (JGC 296). A strict reciprocity is expected between mother and child, which is why mothers are so central in people's lives.

The motif of motherhood is repeated in both folktales and proverbs. It is considered a most unnatural trait—yes, even a biological aberration—for a woman not to care about children. Women as mothers are presented in a complimentary manner and are publicly commended and appreciated. A woman's value as a procreator is irreplaceable and, therefore, hedged around with religious taboos. But this sacred, indeed divine, role is not allowed to affect the gender stratification that puts men before women in almost every other sphere of human activity.

Outside this sphere of biological functioning, the character of women is painted in colors that form an image of disharmony and sinister motivations. A woman who chooses to step out of line by refusing to marry or, if married, not bearing children suffers continually on all fronts. It seems that society confines a woman to a certain place and then prescribes what she must do to keep that place. If this is so, a woman is not even equal to a mother hen; instead, she becomes a breed hen for a poultry farmer. Akan women, aware of this limitation, naturally demand that if they are to be shackled, their chains had better be of gold.

As girls are socialized with these kinds of generalizations, they become "normal" women, woman-beings with womanly skills and traits that are called feminine. Men become masculine through the same process, but with the added stipulation that a man does what pleases him. If it pleases a man to carry on clandestine activities, he invokes the ancient wisdom of *not* telling his plans to a woman. African women have yet to learn this selective use of the traditional culture.

Like folktales, proverbs serve as a source of community wisdom and socialization, creating and reinforcing the image of an undifferentiated mass of humanity called "woman" and constituting a justification for her ascribed roles. Most generalizations presented in these maxims are further elaborated in folktales, and society seems ever ready to produce new living examples of proscribed behavior for women. However that may be, we cannot overlook the fact that proverbs result in a composite picture that militates against an individual woman's personhood. Such proverbs have no more validity than the statement that "all Africans are lazy"; yet, they are as restrictive to the fullness of one's humanity as "a man does not cry," or other proverbs that demand, always, stout-heartedness from men.

Prescribing the Feminine

Like hens, women wait for cocks to crow announcing the arrival of daylight. (JGC 1664)

While the male soul is alive, the female soul does not crack nuts. (JGC 178)

When a woman makes the giant drum, it is kept in a man's room. (JGC 22)

If a tall woman carries palm nuts, birds eat them off her head. (JGC 25)

The characteristics and roles of women as experienced in society are not necessarily related to their biological nature; rather, they are the dictates of society, and women learn to live with them. Take, for instance, the fact that generally women let men dictate the pace and nature of their relationships and serve as spokespersons of the family unit. Gender differentiation governs what is acceptable for women to undertake and also prescribes what roles men should play. While men are available to do the designated male jobs—like felling trees, repairing roofs, and generally cracking the "hard nuts" of their lives together— women need not concern themselves with those jobs. Female ignorance or physical weakness plays no part in this, for the Akan know only too well that when men are unavailable, women cope fully well.

Men and women are taught what is *appropriate* for them and they are firmly enjoined to steer clear of inappropriate roles. Thus, in Akan society, a person is not free to develop any competence (however much it is needed in the community) solely out of personal inclination. All is assigned by custom and "normal" persons simply adjust to these societal dictates. If a woman insists on taking on a male role, she will only add it to her assigned female roles; there will be no recognition of her extra effort and extraordinary achievement. Doing things that go beyond what the community has ordained may give women a sense of fulfillment, but, in general, men do not seem inclined to honor this urge for wholeness. Nevertheless, some Akan women seek the path of wholeness in spite of their gendered socialization. They develop high aspirations for themselves in spite of the constant advice not to strive too hard. And then, with an incontestable finality, all ends in marriage and the glory of one's achievements in a kitchen.

Gendered socialization has operated against women in Africa, resulting in high illiteracy rates and lower educational levels and attainments. Even forms of Western education have been unable to break these "proper" pigeon holes for women and men. Proverbs of the traditional culture are deterrents enjoining women not to attempt to reach the same heights as men. If a woman becomes "as tall as a man," she will only end up in disaster. It is not uncommon to hear a precocious young woman being told that "the woodpecker will eat your palm nuts" or to see her labeled as ɔbaa kokɔnini (a female cock), meaning a woman who behaves like a man. It is a woman's prerogative to wait on the sidelines ready to act *in extremis*. Indeed, some women have turned waiting into a virtue: we wait to be born, we wait to be married, we wait nine months for new life to be born, we wait, we wait, we wait. Our waiting witnesses to our passive acceptance of whatever nature and society demand.

If, on the other hand, women are expected—without prior training and practice—to take on non-biological roles hitherto marked "Men Only," gender role stratification is rightly questionable. Although sexism generally reigns supreme everywhere, during times of crisis and war (as, for example, in Europe) women have kept society running. Widows and single women have managed without men. In Black Africa, women are expected to perform economic roles as part of their mothering assignments. Gender stratification, therefore, does not seem to be based on any inherent competence of men or inherent *in*competence of women. But gender stratification has distorted the quality of human relations, and it continues to deny the parity between women and men, or to accept female and male as equivalent expressions of being human.

In the end, the principle at the heart of socialization directs women to leave the making of history to men. It suggests that as long as men are around, women will not starve: men will provide for them. Reducing a woman's humanity to her material needs, which will be provided for by a man, has succeeded in fostering unnecessary dependency relations that leave "the thinking" to men and buttress the myth that women are ordained to perform supplementary roles, roles which are almost always subordinate or inferior.[7]

In Africa one encounters a well-rehearsed criticism that current feminist movements in the developed capitalist countries stem mainly from the dissatisfaction of the suburban housewife who lacks no material comfort. "What is it that women want?" is a question often asked by African men, who are puzzled by women's insistence on re-examining situations that, in their opinion, society *as a whole* has accepted as "natural." Although the politics of decision-making varies from group to group, I believe it is safe to assert that where there is a protest, it is not unlikely to find that someone is being hurt, that a voice is not being heard, or that someone is being muzzled, often literally or physically. Men who ask "What do women want?" must listen for an answer.

Much of what has been somewhat smugly labelled as "natural" was born in an age quite different from our own. Today, it is no longer "natural" that women walk miles to fetch water for men's baths. We deceive ourselves if we think that all women who have not spoken up are satisfied with their lot in society. Men and women often coast along, resigned to acceptance even when they feel uncomfortable with the situation. "That's life," they conclude, the head triumphing over the heartfelt wrongness of the actual experiences of life. In Africa today, research in rural areas and in the growing high-density urban areas unmasks reality. "When you go near a river, that is when you can hear a crab cough" (JGC 78). Looking more closely at these areas gives a clearer picture of the presence of women and the need for change.

---

[7]See Christaller; four proverbs referring to men deal with bravery and autonomy (pp. 47-50), while thirteen proverbs on women (pp. 18-30) prescribe gender characterization by different levels of being.

MEN AND WIVES

A wife is like a blanket that will irritate a man's skin if he covers himself with it; but if he were to take it off, he would place himself in the hands of biting cold winds. (JGC 3652)

It is preferable to have a bad wife than to sleep alone. (JGC 3654)

Running to meet a child-bride will not aid her physical growth into womanhood. (JGC 3649)

If a man has five wives, he has five tongues. (JGC 3650)

A thousand wives demand a thousand stories. (JGC 3651)

When a polygamous man is sick, he dies of hunger. (JGC 26)

Female-male relations among the Akan are conceived primarily in sexual terms, as marriage is the only "natural," or rather "legitimate," link between men and women who have no bonds of lineage. *Women are expected not to associate too closely or too frequently with men who are not related by family ties*, although the reverse does not hold true for men. When men seek close associations with unrelated women, it is assumed to be a sexual bond. The order of the words I have placed in italics is deliberate: it is the woman who is expected to prevent any association from developing. Because close friendships between boys and girls have been discouraged and because a female, traditionally, was not expected to be employed outside her home, a young woman would have no male acquaintances. A woman and a man might have commercial links, but such a relationship of "the marketplace" does not involve business meetings in "chambers." Similarly, women may be patients of a male doctor or serve as functionaries of a religious cult with men.

The only natural long-term relationship between women and men other than family ties then is marriage, which, in any culture, is fraught with ambiguities and tensions. Yet, African society operates in such a way that men and women accept that marriage is unavoidable. To be a responsible adult, one ought to be married and one ought to raise children.

For a man, marriage brings a dilemma with women cast in the role of "angelic demons." Marriage becomes a necessity, a cultivated institution upheld by society for the expedience of "orderly" procreation, the preservation of property, and to provide the male with a mothering, comforting, caring female *all his own*. Even if a wife plays the role of mother somewhat inadequately, the marriage is still upheld. Throughout Africa, proverbs underline the social pressure to get married and stay married. They emphasize the negative aspects of marriage for the man who might be caught or trapped by a wife who is an irritant or a problem—at best, a necessary evil. Reversing these proverbs to have them apply to husbands does not even enter the thought pattern.

At times, proverbs on marriage seem rather ambiguous. Marriage and women are said to be unavoidable irritants in men's lives; yet, in a counseling situation, a man may be told that a bad wife is better than a casual lover (JGC 3647) in order to encourage him either to get married or to avoid such a drastic measure as divorce. Much of the ambiguity lies in the comparison between a wife and a lover. Since both wife and lover can walk out on a man as well as smother him with attention, there must be some element other than the psychological, material, and sexual needs of a man that causes society to ensure that man-woman relations are based on the formally recognized institution of marriage. The rules of marriage are known and adhered to by everybody. Both women and men are told that they have everything to gain from these relatively permanent heterosexual relations.

Proverbs on marriage and wives seem to underline men's recognition of their deep need for female companionship and their determination to go along with the institution in spite of its inherent tensions. The "male club" agrees that wives are necessary for their comfort and well-being. Wives have become so much a part of their husbands' lives that a man will take another man's wife only in order to express hatred for him (JGC 3175)! It is interesting to note this parallel to proverb JGC 430, which points out that "It is when someone hates you that he or she will hit an animal belonging to you." A woman is to her husband as a dog is to its owner. Violation of a man's property and adultery with his wife are similar acts of hatred.

On the whole, proverbs depict men as being in favor of marriage. Indeed, some proverbs describe men as so impatient to acquire wives that they must be restrained. Yoruba men will be told, "Get a wife in haste, and you may have no wife; do not get a wife in haste, and you may have a wife" (RA 520 and 521). The Akan will try to restrain men from hasty alliances and, in particular, prevent child marriages.[8]

It is of particular interest to note the large number of proverbs that suggest that polygamy may not be advantageous or that caution against taking on the extra strains of polygamy. One proverb describes polygamy as the bedfellow of poverty (JGC 3655). This formerly prestigious institution of African marriage is beginning to lose its glamour and appeal as changes in society affect the nature and demands of marriage. It is worth noting again, however, that what proverbs tell men to do and what men actually do are not always in harmony.

Wife hunting is a serious business (as illustrated by the folktales) and many proverbs govern the behavior of wife-hunters. For instance, men seeking wives are in no position to ridicule women (JGC 1262). Men should choose carefully, looking for women from families they admire (JGC 2654); but, when time is running short for a man, he cannot be choosy and he certainly cannot afford a child-bride (JGC 3433).

These remonstrations to men to get married and to stay married demonstrate a type of socialization not much different from that of women, but men seem to come off better; otherwise, why the urgency and the acquisitiveness implied in these proverbs? A Jamaican proverb is similar, saying that as soon as a man feels materially prepared, he will look for a wife (IA&FC 222). Once married, men jealousy guard their wives. Extra-marital relations on the part of the woman are taboo among the patrilineal Yoruba, and frowned upon by the matrilineal Akan. A wife, an Akan proverb stipulates, is not meant to be parcelled and sent out to others as a gift (JGC 3653). Another version of this proverb, which says that one cannot show kindness to the extent of giving one's wife away, emphasizes the exclusive nature of conjugal relations.

The woman's role in marriage is not considered to be of equal value with that of the man's. Her position is less visible and its effects are primarily psychological.[9] The wife protects life and deals with rela-

---

[8]Among the Akan and Yoruba, sexual union in betrothals is not allowed until a girl has gone through puberty rites. After betrothal, however, a young girl may have to spend her childhood with her prospective husband's people rather than her own.

[9]In time of war, a woman's responsibility is also psychological: she remains at home to taunt the "cowards" who do not enlist.

tionships. For men, material results, technology, and brute force are valued, while relatedness and a sense of the spiritual play the handmaiden. A woman's commitment is to life and peace; hence, women allow caring love to become an effective principle in human life.

At the least, the services wives render to their husbands leave the men free to develop other aspects of their personalities and to take on the responsibilities of married life. Men are brought up with a love for bravado and are socialized into believing that as potential warriors they contribute directly to the security of the nation; as such, they deserve to be waited upon by those who contribute only indirectly by procreation, and who, in time of war, can only pray and perform religious rituals.

In marriage, the services of women are taken for granted. There is a proverb, however, that reminds a man who might share in household work or even go to the aid of a wife that he might become wife-less and have to do these things for himself. It goes without saying that this proverb has little effect on men who are able to command services from women. Nevertheless, the proverb exists, as do others which, if nurtured, could promote more reciprocity in man-woman relations. For example, a husband is advised: "When your wife returns to the house with a pot of water on her head and asks you to help set it down, you would do well to assist, for you never know when you may have to fetch your own drinking water in the future" (JGC 3648). Whatever physical chores an African man may be expected to do, housekeeping is not one of them. The taboo question "Why not?" has to be asked.

Women and Marriage

A stubborn wife does not care to be beaten. (RA 425)

Marry your daughter when you can, your son when you please. (IA&FC 945)

It is the person who has a wife who knows what she is like. (JGC 2272)

If you stumble upon a brawling couple, don't make any hasty judgments, for it is only the husband who knows what the wife has done to him. (JGC 1580)

The Akan often seem frantic to marry girls off as soon after puberty as possible, while the same does not apply to boys. The Jamaican proverb above (IA&FC 945) has the identical message. Yet, even among the matrilineal Akan, the marriage relationship is androcentric. This is a universal experience that cries for reexamination. The Akan husband (and for that matter, all male heads of families) is expected to exercise a benevolent and rational control over his wife (and the rest of the household) and not make unreasonable demands on her.[10]

Several proverbs illustrate the dominant status of the husband in the social institution of marriage. There seems to be a basic assumption that in marriage the woman must be molded to fit the needs of the man, hence, the many references to stubborn women and wife-beaters. When there is domestic rancor, it is the man who must be aggrieved, just as it is the man who understands the woman. The woman's perspective is utterly ignored. Either the man is such a paragon of perfection that he never wrongs the woman or, if, in fact, he does injure her, she is not expected to raise her voice. She stands accused, but she is not allowed to accuse, except through the elders, who have a stake one way or another in keeping the marriage intact. The man acts directly, the woman indirectly. It is only with great persistence that a woman can unmake a marriage, and she knows full well that she owes a good deal of her respectability in society to the institution.

The language of marriage proverbs indicates that a wife only reflects the state of the marriage and a man's competence as a husband. If a woman is beautiful (meaning, well turned-out), she owes it to her husband (JGC 19). The state of her well-being is attributed to good relations between her and her husband and to his good care of her. Society demands that she stay married, because a woman has no dignity outside marriage. A divorced woman's status is even more troublesome because she is then seen as a threat to other marriages (especially if she is young) and a challenge to men (if she is both young and pretty). Whatever her personal achievements, they are all canceled by divorce, says the proverb (JGC 22). Once divorced, a woman loses respect and finds herself despised if she does not quickly remarry.

Her whole education has been in preparation for marriage, so a fail-

---

[10]One appropriate proverbs says, "When the tortoise wants to pick a quarrel with his wife, he tells her to plait his hair" (JGC 1928), an impossible task on a hairless tortoise!

ure here is a total failure.[11] If a woman never marries at all, it must be due to something she has done. A Yoruba proverb says: "A woman who had lost her good character lamented that she was not destined to have a husband" (RA 405). The implication is obvious: no woman is destined to stay single. If a girl proves wayward or shows signs of being flirtatious, she is married off as quietly and quickly as possible (RA 406).

Society clearly demonstrates its fear of infidelity on the part of women by proverbs such as, "A bad woman does not allow her child to resemble her husband" (RA 528). Or, "The child who takes after neither father nor mother brings about dissension between parents" (RA 5461). The Akan is crisp: "It is the woman who knows the husband" (JGC 20). Women are the only ones who can pronounce on paternity. In a system where the birth of a child is more important than its paternity, relatives may, in case of delayed conception, even encourage extramarital affairs and, in the extreme, divorce. For, while "divorce cannot destroy a city" (JGC 3435), barrenness in a woman of matrilineal heritage is an obvious disaster.

Women and Divorce

The double standard governing the relation of the sexes in marriage is clearly demonstrable in the African societies I refer to. For the most part, "the stain" of divorce touches the woman and thus the onus is hers to make the marriage work. The tension is clear here, for the maxims are addressed to the men as the persons who have the whiphand in the game. Here, Jamaicans show more realism concerning a wife's role when they say, "Man build house but woman make home" (IA 724). Among some African groups, the control persists even after a divorce: "On dissolution of a marriage a divorced husband may swear an oath restraining his divorced wife from associating with the paramour suspected to have been instrumental in disrupting the marriage."[12] It is assumed, of course, that it is the husband who seeks the divorce and that the cause is the wife's infidelity. It is significant to note that Kofi

---

[11]When it becomes inevitable, the severance of a marriage is viewed as a form of social death, though, and Akan society has rites to deal with this.

[12]Kofi Abrefa Busia, *The Position of the Chief in Modern Political Systems of Ashanti* (London: Oxford University Press, 1951), p. 78.

Abrefa Busia, a highly westernized Akan man and a sociologist, singles out this cause for divorce. Busia does not provide an example of circumstances under which a woman can sue the elders for divorce, so I must expand on what he has written. In my tradition, if a husband is impotent, cruel, or tightfisted, his wife has an option to discontinue the association. Infidelity is only one reason for divorce.

An Asante maternal uncle or mother or even a woman's parents may take steps to bring about divorce if they have cause to believe that a husband is treating their daughter cruelly or, more especially, if the woman is childless. They assume immediately that the "fault" is the husband's and they will not allow their daughter to serve a man who cannot enable her to fulfill her role as the channel by which the ancestors in the spirit-realm return to join the clan in this realm. In fact, there is an assumption that to stay in an unfruitful marriage is to declare oneself a "fool"—one who does not mind giving without receiving, or toiling without seeking a reward. Obviously, an Akan woman is not expected to derive joy in doing the will of a man who is not a blood relation. There is no pleading "in giving we receive," as Akan marriages are not set up for the purpose of uniting couples for their enjoyment. The marriage is important to the kin group because of the prospects of children. Companionship for married women is still derived from associations with other women. Personal considerations of an individual woman (or, for that matter, man) who wants to stay in a person-to-person relationship with another are only incidental.

Women and Lineage

No matter how restricted the space is, the hen will find its way to its hatchery. (RA 89)

When the hen is caught, her chicks are easily collected. (JGC 1956)

If your mother is poor, you don't leave her to adopt another. (JGC 2059)

It is when your own mother does not go to the market that you ask her co-wife to make purchases for you. (JGC 2064)

A woman is indispensable to her clan (or among the Yoruba, to the husband's clan) solely as a mother. It is motherhood that endows a woman with status and responsibility. This high premium placed on a woman, however, is only domestic in nature. Any political roles, such as women have in matrilineal groups, are carefully shielded from the public eye, and any influence a woman might have is exercised through her brothers, her sons, and the sons of her sisters.

Among the matrilineal Akan, such as the Asante, however, the role of motherhood has political consequences because one's economic heritage and political status depend on one's mother. Many proverbs either reinforce this point or simply indicate why things are as they are. The centrality of motherhood to the Akan stands out vividly when compared with the equivalent Yoruba sayings about fathers.

"The thumb," they say, "is the prop of the fingers; the paterfamilias dies and the family disintegrates" (RA 270). For the Akan, a lineage "is finished" when one's mother dies (JGC 2068). She is the cardinal point from which all directions and other linkages are traced; it is she who validates, ensures, and sanctions the status one enjoys in the larger clan. Without a mother as their rallying point and mentor, siblings are thrown into fractious disarray, thus falling easy prey to negative forces.

The close link between a mother and her child is crisply captured by *Ɛba a ɛka oni* (JGC 1), literally, "When it comes, it touches the mother." When disaster overtakes a child, the mother cannot escape its effects. This proverb is often on the lips of men when they attempt to shirk responsibility for the bad behavior of their children. One's kinship to one's mother is so crucial that it does not matter what sort of a mother she is; any mother is better than being motherless or being adopted. There is no substitute for one's natural mother, says the proverb (JGC 2059). Another proverb captures the centrality of the mother as heart of the hearth, and the one who nourishes and cares: It is only in your mother's kitchen that you can be fussy and choosy (JGC 39); however much other women are willing to oblige, they are poor substitutes for one's birth mother.

An Akan woman is expected to be not only a helpmate to her husband, but also a source of stability for her progeny. Akan and Yoruba alike agree that "mother is as precious as gold: father as the radiant glass" (RA 1059). A mother's demise is expected to lower the expectations and aspirations of a child, as a pathetic proverb tells the orphaned child: "Oh, motherless one, ask for skin, not meat, for the substitute mother is going to give the best parts to her natural children." Or in this dialogue:

Woman to Orphan: "Are you satisfied?"

Orphan: "If you had given me as much as you gave your child I would have been satisfied." (JGC 3666)

The above sentiments are taken a step further to strengthen the relationship between children of the same woman. One's first loyalties are to those who have shared womb and milk. One is expected to protect their interests over those of others, even if such others may have the same father. The Fantes say, *Wo na ba nye wonua* (True sibling relations are with those who are one's mother's children). Hence, the proverb, "When my father's child succeeds I rejoice, but when my mother's child succeeds my joy is doubled" (JGC 1239). A similar attitude is expressed in the question, "If Ko Buobi were your mother's child, would you have recommended that he carry the big drum?" (JGC 2061).[13] The well-being of your mother's children cannot be separated from your own; their well-being is your mother's joy and, therefore, yours as well.

Frequent use of these proverbs leads toward the idolizing of women as mothers and, by extension, of their mothering roles. Among Jamaicans, the height of irresponsibility and selfishness is described in the proverb, "My mother's death does not hurt me as much as getting my feet wet with the morning dew" (IA&FC 892); or, "Dog says he will not fret if his mother dies so long as it does not rain in the afternoon" (IA&FC 339). The woman who is a mother is put on a pedestal and showered with verbal adoration and deference, which, of course, is no substitute for concrete acts of solicitude for her well-being.

Yet, such an attitude can be a first step toward marginalization. Since a woman has no direct word in the public sphere, she is often ignored as a nonentity and forgotten. Political decisions are made behind her back, because she is busy keeping the lineage alive, both biologically and domestically. This current state of affairs for Akan women ought

---

[13]It cannot be a pleasant duty to carry a heavy drum on your head in a procession while the drummer walks along behind you beating it.

to be re-examined; the role of this ideology that perpetuates the idolization of women as mothers should be exposed and exorcised. Men are always ready to talk about how they honor and respect their mothers, but honoring and respecting one's mother is not the same as honoring and respecting the humanity of a woman. The language about women used in proverbs serves to exonerate men from their role in marginalizing women from the crafting of public policy.

Several stories and myths attempt to explain why women do not openly take on political roles. Christine Obbo recounts a fable of how role assignments came into being. God, she says, was calling women from their household chores to other duties. The women were so engrossed in the work they had taken on that they repeatedly told God to wait for them to complete what they had in hand. Men, having nothing much to do, were lazing around and so offered to attend to God. From that day God decreed that women's work would never end. Jamaicans have captured this in the proverb, "Man's work lasts till set of sun; women's work is never done" (IA&FC 84).[14]

WHAT SHALL WE DO WITH THESE PROVERBS?

The ancient resting place is not necessarily the resting place of today. (JGC 3240)

We recall history and analyze culture in order to understand how we got where we are and to see where we are heading; however, where we actually go depends on what we decide to do, or else we cease to be morally responsible agents. It is the woman who sleeps by the fire of gender discrimination in the modern sectors of our economy, and it is the woman in the home who knows how hot that fire is. If women are prepared to show their pain openly and to articulate their vision for a more just and a more participatory and inclusive society, then perhaps we can begin to reshape the attitudes of society as a whole.

This is not just a question of being liberated. It is one of breaking away, for never in history has a privileged group decided of its own accord to give up power and prestige in order to bring about collegial-

---

[14]Christine Obbo, *African Women: Their Struggle for Economic Independence* (London: Zed Press, 1981), p. ix.

ity. If we stand by proverbs that imply that slaves cannot free themselves, then we might as well forget all visions of full participation. This holds true for all aspects of our struggles for the recognition of the equal value of the "other," be it in terms of the economies of North and South, the tension between white and black, or the polarization of male and female that results in the marginalization of the female.

Therefore, I heartily take issue with the implications of proverbs such as, "A person who has a speck in her eye cannot remove it herself" (JGC 2131) or its parallel, "One does not sew up a cut on one's own back" (JGC 2198). Both may seem reasonable, but they are nonapplicable to the issue of just relations between persons or between nations. In the arena of economic transactions between North and South, we in Africa operate with the maxim, "When you can get someone to feed you, you are not a debtor." But if we continue to follow this maxim, we will become content with being satellites of the Euro-American economies. Of course, few Africans indeed want this to happen. Inappropriate proverbs do not empower, they weaken.

One proverb about mothers should not be overlooked: "If you do not have a mother, you ought to avoid getting a cut on your back." If the world's structures had mothers, these wounds would be healed. There would be someone to remove the blinding speck or tend the bruised back, because mothers know that the wholeness, welfare, and shalom of one is the shalom of the whole.

Weaving a New Tapestry

These myths, folktales, and proverbs are still extant among the Akan, with their counterparts throughout the world among descendants of Africans. Some may have lost their historical roots, while others simply observe natural phenomena. Some folktalk is adhered to faithfully, while other folktalk has even lost its meaning; some is ignored altogether—especially by men—even when the meaning is clear. Such folktalk often runs counter to the image men create for themselves.

Neither movements of counter-culture nor rebellions against ancient wisdom are new to the Akan. These proverbs, collected in 1829 before colonialism had its full impact on the Akan, contain examples of culture versus counter-culture. Young people undoubtedly used the proverb, "The resting places of old have been abandoned" (JGC 3240), while their elders refuted the younger generation's attitude toward tradition and found comfort in another proverb:

> Young people say the ancient resting places are not for them! Why don't they take away one of the three legs that make up the cooking tripod and try to balance their cooking-pot on only two? (JGC 2285)

The first proverb recognizes that in situations of rapid change a generation cannot be bound to principles simply because they are "traditional"; they must also be efficacious. The tripod that supports the cooking pot will be cherished and not pulled apart. Yet, even in 1829 the younger generation can tell the elders that they keep the tripod not simply because it is there but because they find it practical and appropriate. But, we should expect that, if they find a more efficient method, they shall feel free to discard the tripod altogether.

The ancient resting places do not have to be ours. This is as true of technology as it is of gender definitions and human relations. We should not allow proverbs to stem the tide of our creativity, even though the whole community is nervous when confronted with changes in the relations between men and women and in the participation of women in the communities to which they claim to belong. I say "claim to belong," because marginal or incidental people do not belong fully. No place, whether ancient or modern, can be said to be humanity's final resting place. Change is inevitable. As the school drums used to say, "As the times are changing, so human beings change." Using proverbs to insist that certain aspects of community life should remain untouched by change seems to me unrealistic and even unreasonable.

In weaving these myths, folktales, and proverbs into a tapestry of women's lives and of Akan ideals and practice of community, I have had the Kente cloth *adwini asa* before my eyes. There can be no higher expression of creativity, of design, of thinking, of weaving patterns than the Kente cloth called the *adwini asa*. But there is a plethora of Kente designs beyond the *adwini asa* that result from the many expressions of human creativity, human thinking, and human wisdom. We may despair at changing relationships between women and men, but we must never throw up our hands saying, *Adwene asa* (We have no more brains)!

I dream of a new Kente cloth, a new tapestry to symbolize the equal value of men and women. With intricate designs of mutual dependence and reciprocity, it has a pattern in which individual strands of thread may be traced, but they cannot be pulled out without destroying the whole. Although we love *adwini asa*, we have continued to weave new patterns. Remember, no matter how restricted the space is, a hen will find its way to its hatchery (RA 89). Women have set out on a journey to call society back to its divine origin and back to the dignity of the human person. This goal will be reached. And when we waiver or doubt, we should recall Jesus's story of the persistent widow!

The Second Cycle

Culture

Pempan Hwemu Dua
Searching rod or measuring rod

The Adinkra symbol for critical examination
and excellence.

4

Culture's Bondswoman

The one constant amid the changes that are transforming the character of a continent is the role of the African woman, a person whose physical and spiritual strength is nothing short of remarkable.[1]

To sleep with someone else's wife is not considered "evil" if these two are not found out by the society which forbids it; and in other societies it is in fact an expression of friendship and hospitality to let a guest spend the night with one's wife or daughter or sister.[2]

I would not describe my life as a happy one because of this strong custom that ruled over me.[3]

In discussing the relationship between women and culture, I write primarily of the Asante woman and, by extension, of the Akan, although some generalizations are obviously possible. I maintain that the identity and autonomy of women fare not much better today under the matrilineal systems of the Akan group than under the overt patriarchies of southern Nigeria, and most particularly, the patriarchal system that operates among

---

[1]David Lamb, *The Africans* (New York: Vintage Books, 1984), p. 37.

[2]John Mbiti, *African Religions and Philosophy* (London: Heinemann, 1969), p. 213.

[3]Iris Andreski, *Old Wives' Tales: Life Stories from Ibibioland* (New York: Schocken/Pantheon Books, 1970), p. 81.

the Yoruba. I also maintain that colonial rule reinforced these patriarchal systems and compounded the woes of African women by augmenting their ordinary burdens with those of their Western sisters.

In the three chapters of this second cycle, I will look at culture, religion, and then marriage. I will examine the customs and practices of the Asante as well as those of some other cultural groups. Because our approach to life in Africa is holistic, these three chapters do overlap. We cannot look at domestic, community, political, and economic structures without encountering religion, and, similarly, culture and religion will enter into our discussion of marriage practices and the political or economic power of women.

When I describe customs and practices in this cycle and in the next, I have chosen to use—in most cases—the present verb tense to recognize that although some of these practices have died out, they can be and are commonly revived to sanction a particular form of behavior. Although our culture remains dynamic and is ever changing, it, like most other cultures, has firm foundations in tradition. In any case, these traditions continue to shape women's lives, both directly and covertly.

The woman above who could not describe her life as a "happy one" is an Ibibio from southern Nigeria. She was designated as a "home daughter," a traditional patriarchal practice that enables a man to prevent his first daughter from leaving home. Such a woman remains unmarried; however, she can have children, who are then claimed as children of her father. The daughter stays on in her father's compound until she is past child-bearing age and then she may be allowed to leave. Culture-bound to her father, her sexuality is his property. This particular woman is allowed to leave her natal compound later, but on condition that she send money regularly to her father. Then and only then does she become an autonomous person. We may label this custom, culture, or traditional right; but whatever name we put to it, this is straightforward exploitation of one human being by another, for such a woman receives no compensation, not even land, from her father.

Among the matrilineal Akan, a first-born daughter is an auspicious beginning—a blessing to her mother, a little mother to subsequent siblings, a catalyst for the continued unity of that line, and an advocate for her clan before the rest of the kin group. She is brought up diligently to fulfill these roles and to be a channel for the return to this life of the ancestors, who, the Akan believe, can return only through the daughters of the clan. She is raised to develop an overwhelming sense of responsibility of the type captured in Charles Wesley's line, "If I my trust betray, I shall forever die."

Although, in more traditional times, a peasant woman was self-supporting, a farmer first and a wife second, she is now losing her autonomy to her husband, her male relatives, or local rulers. In addition, the peasant woman is also being told by her middle-class sister Nigerians that it is "through her role as a wife and mother alone that she can contribute to the development of the nation."[4]

African society expects childbearing and homemaking of its women. This is one generalization that can safely be made. It is also more or less a truism that this has usually been accepted by African women. Nonetheless, I do not know one African society in which women are limited exclusively to such functions. Homemaking is taken for granted, like breathing in air. Like the air, if it were taken away or polluted, we would fade and die. Yet women and their work as mothers and homemakers have often been bypassed, as if women did nothing beyond producing and raising offspring. Recently, when some African women have begun to question the limitations of their biological role, men have had ready answers: African women are precious, say the African men, they know their place and keep it. Should an African woman disagree with this assessment, she becomes an imitator of Western women, a model in which Africa has no interest.

Unlike beauty, however, oppression does not lie in the eye of the beholder; it tugs at the soul of the one who feels it. I remember a chorus from my childhood used in a game played by girls. It is a dialogue with a girl in "fetters." The words are as follows:

Fatima, doesn't that hurt?

Sure! I am miserable.

Then, pull it out!

No, I may not do that.
It is the practice of father's town.
It is the practice of mother's town.

---

[4]Elizabeth Obadina, "No Condition is Permanent," *The Guardian* (Lagos), Sunday, April 10, 1983.

Many women whisper, "Alas, mother, I am dying" (*Puei eno mirewu*), but continue to wear the "fetters." If Fatima finds her burden too heavy to bear, should culture bind her to it?

We seek to discard these fetters of culture; we seek full humanity and some principles to guide our lives in community. The meaning of full humanity cannot be defined by only one sector of humanity, without listening to the voices, the hurts, and the delights of all the Fatimas. Even more important, what constitutes the fetters of oppression should be defined by those who experience it and not by those who simply observe it. A Hausa proverb says, *Kworria tagari tana ragaya* (A good woman stays home).[5] A *ragaya* is a string basket that hangs in the kitchen and holds a small calabash or *kworria*. Into this are thrown small items that may be difficult to lay hands on when needed. So a good woman should always be where she is expected to be, always at hand and always useful.

If a Hausa girl is given an opportunity to examine that proverb in a given situation, she may conclude that there is more to "usefulness" than hanging permanently in a fixed place in the kitchen. She may decide that some of her particular skills may enhance the well-being of the community or that her role need not be predetermined by gender. She may then realize that just relations can be developed only when the equal value of males and females is upheld and allowed to flourish.

The silence and anonymity of the African woman are her greatest handicaps. Burdened with so many restrictions, she has not found it productive or of enough consequence to educate her Western sisters about herself. Indeed, the oppressed rarely have time for such luxuries. The result is that occasionally Euro-American women and a few African men generate proposals and receive grants to study "the African woman" under such rubrics as marriage, family, or population, but hardly ever as a person. Only when such research is thorough and empathetic does it become valuable as an expression of solidarity with the oppressed.

---

[5]George Merrick, *Hausa Proverbs* (1905; reprint, New York: Negro University Press, 1969), p. 38 (Proverb 188). Although the Hausa ethnic group is spread throughout much of West Africa, references here are to the Hausa of Ghana or Nigeria. In the end, the precise location is of little consequence as most women in Africa will experience these same demands.

THE DANGER OF GENERALIZATIONS

Making broad all-inclusive statements about African women is not just the pastime of Westerners. Africans do this also, and it reaches outrageous heights when African men generalize from one particular form of patriarchy or from one particular form of political or economic arrangements to all of Africa. A prime example of this is found in *The World of the African Woman* by John E. Eberegbulam Njoku. Such statements are not just outrageous, they are dangerous, for they are sometimes used to form discriminating laws against women. All the women of a nation then fall under what may have been the peculiarity of one small sector of a society. For example, Njoku declares, "One thing common to the African woman . . . is her responsibility to her family and rural development."[6] He is on safe ground in speaking about a woman's responsibility for her family, but it is irresponsible to assume that throughout Africa responsibility for rural development lies with women. Even if women shoulder such responsibility alone in some areas, this does not mean it is their exclusive responsibility.

On the other hand, it is true to say that, given the chance, all African women will willingly work with rural women toward economic and technological liberation. Increasingly, organizations of African women are moving in this direction in economic development and in health education. In Nigeria, a program called "Better Life for Women" focuses on income-generating programs for rural women. Similar projects are underway in Ghana, some of which aim at improving food crops, processing staple foods, and promoting the development of crafts such as basket-making.[7] The Ghana branch of the International Federation of Women Lawyers has worked hard to get laws passed and to provide legal aid protecting women's rights in the areas of inheritance and marriage.[8] Work is also being undertaken throughout much of Africa

---

[6]John E. Eberegbulam Njoku, *The World of the African Woman* (Lagos, London, and Metuchen, NJ: Scarecrow Press, 1980), p. 3.

[7]Florence Abena Dolphyne, *The Emancipation of Women: An African Perspective* (Accra: Ghana Universities Press, 1991), pp. 57-85.

[8]One of the most significant laws passed in Ghana is the Law on Intestate Succession, "making provision for surviving spouses and all children that a man claimed to be his during his lifetime to inherit the greater portion of his self-acquired property" (ibid., pp. 28-29).

by women on behalf of women in health care issues, including prostitution and the elimination of genital mutilation.[9]

The insidious nature of generalizations such as Njoku's about "all African women" becomes apparent when we see how often they work against the autonomy of women, and the way in which they are often supported by traditional folktalk and proverbs. I could spend time challenging proverbs that allow the battering of women or I could refute the research findings of Western "scholars" who portray the illiterate African woman as being under the foot of her husband;[10] more urgent, I believe, is to ascertain what practices are genuinely traditional and to what extent they correspond to our sense of justice and fair play.[11]

Elizabeth Obadina cites an example of a law from the 1977 Igbo traditional law manual, drawn up by a group of four hundred and one men and two women, which

> actually prohibited all women in certain areas of Imo and Anambra states [in Nigeria] from owning land or landed property. It prohibited all married women from divesting themselves of any landed property without their husband's consent and it stopped married women in certain others [states] from owning land.[12]

This "customary law," Obadina points out, violates the Nigerian Constitution. Yet, how can an individual Igbo woman challenge this so-called customary law before the nation's courts?

---

[9]On prostitution, for example, see the work of the Ursuline Sisters in Zaire described by Bernadette Mbuy Beya in *The Will To Arise: Women, Tradition and the Church in Africa*, Mercy Oduyoye and Musimbi R. A. Kanyoro, eds. (Maryknoll, NY: Orbis Books, 1992), pp. 155-179. On issues of genital mutilation see Dolphyne, pp. 34-40 and "Rapport du séminaire régional sur les pratiques traditionelles ayant effet sur la santé des femmes et des enfants en Afrique," Addis Ababa, April 6-10, 1987, sponsored by UNICEF and the World Health Organization, among other organizations.

[10]See, for example, Helen Ware, ed., *Women, Education, and Modernization of the Family in West Africa* (Canberra: The University Press, 1981), p. xiv, or John C. Caldwell, "Mass Education as a Determinant of the Timing of Fertility Decline," *Population and Development Review* 6:2 (June 1980), p. 248.

[11]Dolphyne makes this same point: as long as traditional beliefs are still intact, given rites will persist, such as those that disenfranchise and abuse widows (p. 24).

[12]Elizabeth Obadina, "Women in Nigeria: Homegrown Feminism," *Guardian* (Lagos), June 14, 1985.

It is important to note that traditional law often varies widely from group to group and even within a group. Thus, as a rule, generalizations should be treated with the same ideological suspicion with which we looked at proverbs beginning "all women are." For example, in speaking of the personal rights of "the African woman," Njoku says, "she has a right to own property, farm on her husband's plot, and is allowed by her husband to buy and sell (and gossip) in the market."[13] In fact, this applies to Igbo women, rather than to all African women. (How curious that people can be given permission to gossip!) Another area of great misinterpretation is the wealth that passes from the groom's family to the bride's family upon a marriage: regional and local customs vary greatly.[14]

Prior to the United Nations Decade for Women (1976-1985), Western views of African women tended to be simplistic: either they assumed that African women experienced the obverse of all that Western women were supposed to have achieved, or they read all of their own sufferings into the African woman's life. As Ama Ata Aidoo observes, "Africa and Africans have for a long time been used as a regular catalyst with which foreigners have tried to work out their own aberrations and other psychological hang-ups."[15] Westerners often see the African woman as a beast of burden walking behind her husband, carrying his children, one inside, one on her back, and many more following in a long procession of children whom she brings forth from puberty to menopause. She is clearly an inferior creature to the Western woman, a person at the bottom of the human pecking order.

Before the Decade of Women, information about African women could be found under index headings such as marriage, family, or menstruation. Women *as a social category* were virtually absent; of course, men were also absent as a social category, but then any book about

---

[13]Njoku, p. 9.

[14]The word for gifts given to the family of the bride by the family of the groom has no English translation, nor does it have a uniform connotation throughout Africa. Names such as "bride wealth," "bride price" or "dowry" do not acknowledge the reciprocity of giving that happens in marriage in Africa. Even more serious is the fact that the giving of names to the practice is beginning to change the nature of that practice: for instance, today some people are beginning to talk of "buying wives."

[15]Ayi Kwei Armah, *The Beautyful Ones Are Not Yet Born* (New York: Collier Books, 1969), p. ix.

Africa was, almost without exception, about men and their world . . . and their women. When appearing in an account, African women were portrayed as "docile doves." Christine Obbo refutes such a portrayal. Today, she says, some Ganda men of East Africa testify that their women are "too much," "difficult to deal with," and "wild." Obbo's view of the situation is that Ganda women have not recently become "too much"; rather, they have always been so, if being true to their heritage is being "too much."

Christine Obbo reminds us that the mythic foresister of Ganda women, Ggzulu (the daughter of Heaven), was the wife of Kintu, the man who is said to have unified Ganda clans into a political state. In the myth, it was Ggzulu's stubbornness that brought death among human beings. Ganda women still claim her, nonetheless, and when Ganda women leave their husbands, they do so in the name of Queen Mother Inere, widow of the thirty-fourth *kabaka* of Buganda who shocked people by remarrying, and to a commoner, soon after the *kabaka*'s death.[16]

It is dangerous to wave the flag of innocent docility over all Africa's women. Western women, unaware of the mythic foresisters that inhabit the African woman's subconscious, have not been sensitive enough in their bid to globalize the oppression of women. In their zeal to speak for women from the Third World, they have often focused on cultural manifestations they have not sufficiently understood and they have thereby alienated the very people they set out to include.

Mary Daly's *Gyn/Ecology*[17] was fascinating reading until I came to Chapter 5 and read of "African Genital Mutilation: The Unspeakable Atrocities." This material cries out for response by African women. Another radical feminist, Audre Lorde, also African American, expressed similar misgivings about *Gyn/Ecology*. She reacts:

> Your inclusion of African genital mutilation was an important and necessary piece in any consideration of female ecology, and too little has been written about it. But to imply, however, that all

---

[16]Christine Obbo, *African Women: Their Struggle for Economic Independence* (London: Zed Press, 1981), pp. 45-49.

[17]*Gyn/Ecology: The Metaethics of Radical Feminism* (Boston: Beacon Press, 1978). See Chapter 5.

women suffer the same oppression simply because we are women, is to lose sight of the many varied tools of patriarchy.[18]

Indeed, too little has been written; however, our well-meaning sisters should consider that the African woman should be empowered to tell her own story, or else be left alone.

WESTERN FEMINISM AND AFRICAN WOMEN

Western feminism has stirred fears in Africa of a disruption in the family. Dependent as family life is at present on the good will and life-loving nature of women as wives and mothers, any move, however small, to tamper with the nature of women (or men) is too radical to ignore. And yet, whenever a child is born in an Akan community, this basic "difference" between the male and the female (the outcome of their socialization, to be sure) is enunciated.

> Oh, mother, I heard good news today. My wife has
>   given birth.
> What did she get?
> A girl.
> Welcome, source of water, she will give us water to
>   drink.
> Oh, mother, I heard good news today. My wife has
>   given birth.
> What did she get?
> A boy!
> Oh, mighty man of valor, stay on if you have come.

Abaayewa-Ma-Nsu (girl, the giver of water) and Ɔbarima-Katakyi (mighty man of valor) are both welcome. She brings us the water of life and he will put our enemies to rout. But when there are no enemies for Ɔbarima-Katakyi to fight, he turns to fight Abaayewa-Ma-Nsu. That is a predominant expression of patriarchy. A proverb tries to forestall

---

[18]Audre Lorde, "This Bridge Called My Back" in *Writings by Radical Women of Color*, ed. Cherrie Moraga and Gloria Anzaldua (Latham, NY: Kitchen Table, 1984).

this form of abuse by directing Ɔbarima-Katakyi to seek real enemies of human survival to do battle with. *Ɔbarima woye no dom ano, na wonnye no fie* (Bravery is exhibited in the battlefront, not at home) (JGC 50).

To overcome the unequal value assigned to people on the basis of gender, even before they have uttered their first cry, Western women have raised aloud their voices. They have taken it upon themselves to speak for their "inarticulate" sisters. Their action reminds me of the proverb, "The strength of a woman is in her tongue."[19] This is partly why African men reject sexism as a non-African issue: if its spokespersons are Western women, it is an issue of Western women, not of African women. African men also maintain, at home and abroad, that the African woman's oppression (if indeed she is oppressed) arises also out of racism and classism, and particularly from the sins of the North in its unrelenting use of economic advantage over the South.

For an African woman, the argument is more dialectical. Her stance vis-à-vis the external world (meaning the West) is that sexism is less important. Classism, embedded in economic exploitation, creates a situation in which the poor of Africa can never win against the rich of the West. As the proverb says, "If the stone falls on the pot, woe to the pot; if the pot falls on the stone, woe to the pot."[20] The interwoven issues of racism and classism (having taken on demonic proportions in apartheid) are unquestionably the African oppression *par excellence*; indeed, given the human misery in Africa, they make sexism look like a pet peeve. That is the position *ad extra*. *Ad intra*, on the other hand, African women who can speak out show clearly how the life of a black African woman can be described as that of a slave of slaves.

It seems, however, that instead of simply talking against sexism, African women are *acting* against it. Although usually lacking treatises or theories criticizing their received teaching on African womanhood, African women make relentless efforts to recall, practice, and enhance the dignity found in their traditions. To be adaptable is to survive, and it is survival rather than the quality of life that rules Africa's consciousness. When her Western sister concludes that eating in the

---

[19]Merrick, Proverb 190, p. 38.
[20]Abraham Cohen, *Ancient Jewish Proverbs* (London: John Murray, 1911), Proverb 250, p. 103.

kitchen and not with her husband sounds like punishment or indicates her inferiority, she simply shrugs it off.

All the same, sexism is a daily experience in an African woman's life. Feminism, for her, is not just a new line in the academic industry, but a perspective that requires analysis leading to action that will orientate people and communities toward justice. As Marjorie J. Mbilinyi says, the conventional image of the servile West African woman is oversimplified.[21]

POWER, AUTHORITY, AND AFRICAN WOMEN

Any discussion of power and authority must be based on a clear understanding of the indigenous socio-political organization of a specified group. Because these structures were rarely understood by the colonizing powers, "modern" (meaning post-colonial) political structures often ignore these autochthonous, deep-rooted systems, creating a continuing source of conflict; yet, existing traditional rulers and laws (such as those governing inheritance) continue to be regulated by them.

A typically misunderstood autochthonous system is that of the Asante people who have seven *abusua* or clans that operate under two primary rules. The first rule is that descent is matrilineal: a person belongs to his or her mother's clan and a woman's individually acquired or inherited property belongs to her and her clan; a woman's husband cannot touch it. The second rule is that these clans are exogamous, meaning that a person of one clan can under no circumstances have sexual relations with anyone who belongs to the same clan. As the various *abusua* have no geographical limits, knowing membership in one's *abusua* is of primary importance. Each *abusua* has its own symbols and taboos, as well as a history that is narrated on significant occasions.[22] Any "modern" system of government imposed on the Asante that ignores or abuses the rules of *abusua* can have no more than limited success.

---

[21]Marjorie J. Mbilinyi, "The New Woman and Traditional Norms in Tanzania," *Journal of Modern African Studies* (10:1), 1972, pp. 57-72.

[22]For more complete information on Akan clans and matrilineage, see Robert S. Rattray, *Ashanti* (1923; reprint, Westport, CT: Greenwood/Negro University Press, 1971), pp. 34-35, 77-85 and Kofi Abrefa Busia, *The Position of the Chief in Modern*

Women's Role in the Family

Since Akan women and their children remain members of their matrilineage throughout their lives, it is in that group that the women function as decision-makers. More will be said about this later. Yoruba women, on the other hand, participate in their natal family on their father's side. However, both groups of women are silent observers in their husband's lineage, although Yoruba women might be involved on the sidelines to ensure their children's interests. Married women are not decision-makers in their affinal families; this factor underlines the separateness of the marriage partners.

In the affinal compound, a wife's companions and colleagues are the other wives. In patrilineal groups, these domestic establishments can become small-scale industries and trading cooperatives as the wives organize to perform their economic and homemaking duties. As far as decision-making goes, all wives hold secondary positions to the women whose birth home they have come to share. But, as with the Akan, the older the Yoruba woman becomes, the more important her position in her paternal or maternal lineage.[23]

The right of a woman to participate in domestic policy-making is guaranteed in these traditions only *outside* of affinal relations. Neither the Akan nor the Yoruba spouse is expected to participate in decision-making in his or her partner's lineage. Although a wife is excluded from affinal decision-making, she is expected, nonetheless, to comply with any and all decisions and to assist in their implementation. It is also important to note that the practice of deferring to males in decision-making or in the taking of prestigious positions and titles is not required by tradition; based on her multiple roles, a woman does so out of expedience. It is almost impossible to cope efficiently with being a mother, to be economically autonomous, and to be dutiful to her affinal group as well as to *rule* in her natal family. So in the latter, she defers to male relations.[24]

Another factor in determining the actual weight of a woman's influ-

---

Political Systems of Ashanti (London: Oxford University Press, 1951), pp. 1, 218-19.

[23]Gloria Alberto Marshall, *Women, Trade, and the Yoruba Family* (Ann Arbor, MI: University Microfilms, 1964), p. 61.

[24]Ibid., pp. 66-67.

ence depends upon her personal success and personal qualities. While birth gives status in both the Akan and Yoruba traditions, meritocracy is not a total stranger.[25] Finally, it is important to note that because neither the Akan nor the Yoruba woman has any say in her affinal home, an Akan or Yoruba wife has no part in decisions taken by others that affect her husband, nor in those taken by him, both of which may affect her directly. Thus, in domestic policy she is ruled without being consulted, so that in effect the systems of the Akan and the Yoruba are both male-dominated. One African-American scholar was so fascinated by this preeminence of the Yoruba male that he recommended that all African-Americans should return to that pattern of relationship so they could

> break the tangle of pathology as it affects the Black family structure in America and Nigeria today. . . . There is also the need to go back to male leadership. . . . The Black woman should use her education to support and stabilize her husband in his leadership capacity in the home and in public life.[26]

By suggesting that African-American and Nigerian women put aside their rights to decision-making, he ignores the traditions of decision-making in public affairs stemming back to the Ɔhemaa (the Queen Mother) and her sister rulers. While mutual support certainly tends to stabilize family life, the African husband (and this is particularly true of the Yoruba) does not expect his wife to "stabilize" him. Perhaps he should, as a step toward promoting mutuality and reciprocity; marriage, then, would become a stabilizing factor in the lives of both partners by mutual consent.

In recent times, West African women have been described as "very powerful." They have been designated "superwomen" by the language of middle-class feminism. This image has been built on the industry of market women, who are quite visible to tourists. Their retail trade plays a significant role in raising the politico-economic barometer. It has

---

[25]Kwame Arhin, "Status Differentiation in Ashanti in the 19th Century: A Preliminary Study," in Institute of African Studies *Research Review* 4:3 (1968), pp. 34-52. See especially the critique of Rattray's assertion that birth settled the status of an Ashanti for all time.

[26]George S. Lewis, *Black Heritage Unveiled* (Los Angeles: Spencer's International Enterprise, 1987), pp. 132-34.

also contributed to the overthrow of governments and has frustrated official attempts at price control. Even more recently (and this has been emphasized in the findings of the Decade for Women), we have seen a long overdue acknowledgment of the role rural African women play as food growers, processors, and distributors. It is the city market women, however, who, being closer to the seats of governments, have constituted very sensitive constituencies for political parties.[27]

In traditional politics, women functioned as policy makers. The *Ohemaa* (Queen Mother) was actually a female ruler and the kingmaker in the traditional political system of the Asante, although an understanding of her formidable influence in the history of her people eluded the British. The designation of *Ohemaa*, a term that embodies a force to reckon with, has been extended to various leadership roles in the market place. Even today, the fixing of prices is done each day by the sellers under the leadership of an *Ohemaa*. Today, while a traditional *Ohemaa* scarcely ever makes the headlines, her modern counterparts are more visible: women who have "made it in a man's world," such as a handful of market queens, high court judges, ambassadors, university professors, specialists in the medical profession, and commissioners in civilian and military administrations, not to talk of church founders. Yet, more than 80 percent of African women still till the land with a simple hoe, struggling to earn enough money for meat and clothing for their family.

A study of market women in Accra demonstrated that accounts of their prosperity and power have been exaggerated.[28] Zulu Sofola has described the power that market women still wield to protest against government price control or the forced relocation of markets.[29] Yet, the fact that they are retailers makes them directly susceptible to the peri-

---

[27]Several reasons have been given for the February 1966 fall of Kwame Nkrumah of Ghana. A popular one is the U.S.-sponsored boycott of Ghana's cocoa that caused unemployment and adversely affected the economy, including the significant sector controlled by the market women.

[28]Claire C. Robertson, *Sharing the Same Bowl: A Socio-Economic History of Women and Class in Accra, Ghana* (Bloomington: Indiana University Press, 1984), p. 119.

[29]Zulu Sofola, "Position of the Church on Womanhood and Its Implications for African Theatre Artists," a paper delivered in Ibadan during the African Regional Consultation of the World Council of Churches on "Community of Women and Men in the Church," 1980.

odic belt-tightening that has become the way of life in Ghana and other African countries. It is also evident that as commercial trade and industry become more specialized and capitalized the profits and power of women are reduced. Similarly, the numerical insignificance of African women in most professions reflects the global situation of women's lack of equal access to education. This is why African women cannot afford to look the other way on issues of global sexism. As the proverb says, "When you call Kyeiwaa, she comes with her children." When Africa imports Western systems, whether they be economic, political, or social, these systems arrive with their sexism intact. The status of women and the nature of the family cannot remain unchanged.

It is impossible today to shield our homes and familial decisions from national politics. While in the past women were involved in traditional politics, today Asante women can draw strength only from the traditional institution of the *Ɔhemaa* and what she represents in the matrilineal tradition. Although this seemingly unassailable position of authority and influence functions as a model and no more, nonetheless, the group memory of *Ɔhemaa* as the founder of the nation still holds a spiritual power over the consciousness of the Asante people. We need study and action, rather than lamentation for the past. As women we cannot preen ourselves with a false image of dominance, while we drift further and further from the centers of authority. We must remember that the market woman's hard-won image is based on a person whose position is solid because she controls her own economic resources and claims her status as a mother.

Women themselves believe that only two of their species suffer: the sterile—that is, those incapable of producing children—and the foolish. And by the foolish they refer to the type woman who depends solely on her husband for subsistence.[30]

Asante Women and Policy-Making

We in Ashanti here have a law which decrees that it is the daughter of a Queen (*Ɔhemaa*) who alone can transmit royal blood, and that the children of a King (*Ɔhene*) cannot be heirs to that stool. This

---

[30]See Ama Ata Aidoo's Introduction in Ayi Kwei Armah, *The Beautyful Ones Are Not Yet Born.*

law has given us women a power in this land, so that we have a saying which runs: "It is the woman who bears the man."[31]

Traditionally, the Akan people did not belong to one political structure, but were constituted into *aman* (nations) very much like the city-states of medieval Europe. Each nation was composed of several matrilineages that formed the Akan matri-clans spread throughout southern Ghana. This matrilineal organization differentiated the Akan from the surrounding peoples. Within the nation, each autonomous political unit (*ɔman*) had a capital (*ahenkuro*), a male ruler (*ɔhene*) whose title indicated the subgroup (for example, the *Asantehene* was the Asante king), and a female ruler (*ɔhemaa*, or the plural, *Ahemaa*; for the Asante, the *Asantehemaa*). Each town reflected this pattern with its own *ɔhene* and *ɔhemaa* and the villages also had male and female heads.

When the Asante Union was established in 1700, the *ɔhemaa* of Kumasi, the Asante capital, represented the authority of all the *Ahemaa* and, by implication, all Asante women. The social organization of the Asante is an intricate system of relationships in which women are politically and economically powerful and which rests on the principle that it is the women who found lineages.[32] In practice, however, a symmetrical system developed, with the *ɔhemaa* controlling the female line and the *ɔhene* in charge of the whole. The *ɔhemaa* directs and represents the women while the *ɔhene* rules the whole community with the support and advise of the *ɔhemaa*. She is thus an indirect ruler, the proverbial "power behind the throne." For women, the *ɔhemaa* was more or less the de facto ruler, the one who sanctioned marriages and ensured that sexual mores were observed.

As a member of the general council, the *ɔhemaa* was involved in the maintenance of order within the body politic, taking part in legisla-

---

[31]Rattray, *Ashanti*, pp. 294-95. The "throne" of Akan traditional rulers is usually in the form of a stool. The stool of the Asantehene is said to contain the soul of the Asante nation. This quotation is from a speech of Queen Mother Amma Seewaa Akoto of Mampon when she presented a replica of her own stool to H.R.H Princess Mary as a wedding gift.

[32]A *matriarchy* is a system of governance in which women have political power and direct rule. (The Asante structure is really a delegated matriarchy in that women are the king-makers and rule indirectly.) A *matrilineage*, on the other hand, is a system in which women have rights of inheritance and ownership; a person's status is determined by one's mother's line.

tion, and settling disputes relating to the customs that regulated family, property, and inheritance.[33] She ran her own court and could protect people, even from the *Ɔhene*, until she herself had heard the dispute. As chief counsellor to the *Ɔhene*, she could make things difficult for him if he were stubborn, but generally she was his most reliable ally.[34] Researchers have noted with interest that as the Asante nation was increasingly centralized, the authority of the *Ɔhemaa* moved "behind the throne."

The significance of the *Ɔhemaa* often escaped Western observers. When Robert Rattray asked why he had not been aware of the importance of the *Ɔhemaa*, he was told:

> The white man never asked us this. As you have dealings which recognize only men, we supposed the European considered women of no account, and we know you do not recognize them as we have always done.[35]

The patriarchal systems introduced by the British succeeded because they suited the Asante men. In the end, Rattray concluded that the British non-recognition of the *Ɔhemaa* was unwarranted and detrimental—unless the British intended to destroy the Akan culture. Apparently that *was* an aim of the British. Since this suited the Akan men, no protests were made and the *Ɔhemaa*'s political role was eliminated in the modern system. Westernization served to castrate both male and female traditional rulers in a way that surprised the traditional ruling houses. When the military component of the traditional system was swept away by the British, the rulers automatically lost a large measure of their political power, as the two were knit closely together. Military titles were emptied of power in much the same way as the *Ɔhemaa*'s

---

[33]See John Mbiti, *African Religions and Philosophy*, p. 179. Mbiti refers to the Queen of the Luvedu, who is both monarch and supreme rain maker; her very moods affect the weather.

[34]The Asante also had a wartime provision that made the senior wife of the *Ɔhene* (selected always by the *Ɔhemaa*) the acting *Ɔhene* while he was away at war. In actual practice, then, the *Ɔhemaa* herself ruled because the wife of the *Ɔhene* might be quite ignorant of the intricacies of decision-making. The wife was simply a figurehead, put there to safeguard the tradition that the *Ɔhemaa* did not rule directly (Rattray, *Ashanti*, p. 83).

[35]Ibid., p. 84.

stool, which, in spite of being the senior stool, was no longer invested with political power.

No women's names appeared on the colonial chieftaincy lists. Thus, Westernization abolished the bi-focal political administration that had given women a measure of autonomy and enabled them to contribute to the general discussion of national issues. This colonial fiat affected not only the Ɔhemaa but all equivalent systems throughout British-controlled West Africa. The demise of matri-kinship as an ideology had begun. Although matrilineal heritage had long been muffled—but in a subtle way—by paternal authority, the coming of Western patriarchy completed the strangulation of matriarchal voices as far as policy making was concerned.

Women in Traditional Politics

Traditional symmetrical (parallel female and male) organization is also found in some areas of southern Nigeria, although these societies make no claim to an ancient Ɔhemaa figure like the Asante. It has been found, however, that "on the West African coast and in Cameroon and the Congo region, patrilineal groups would trace their genealogies back to an eponymous ancestress."[36]

Even among the patriarchal Yoruba, it has been noted that "Although most Yoruba political leaders are male, the women do have representation at the highest level, the king's council, through their leader, the Iyalode."[37] The Iyalode (variously translated as Mother of the Town, Mother-in-charge of External Affairs, Mother of All Women, She Whose Business Is Women's Affairs) is the head of all women in the town. Each town has an Iyalode who is elected by the women and appointed by the Oba (king) on the basis of her personal qualities of leadership, influence, and wealth. The Iyalode is their political leader and advocate in the otherwise all-male Oba's council of male representatives of all the lineages. As the only female voice heard directly in

---

[36]See G. C. Mogekwu, *African Society, Culture and Politics* (Lanham, MA: University Press of America, 1977), p. 20. See also the controversy over the identity of Oduduwa in J. O. Awolalu, *Yoruba Belief and Sacrificial Rites* (London: Longmans, 1979), pp. 25-28.

[37]Alice Schlegel, ed., *Sexual Stratification, a Cross-Cultural View* (New York: Columbia University Press, 1977), pp. 145-47; and Marshall, p. 17.

traditional Yoruba politics, the Iyalode has to be an astute politician.[38]

Roles similar to that of the Asantehemaa are also played by women among the Ondo and Ijesha Yoruba peoples of southern Nigeria. Vestiges of women's representatives are to be found in the Igbo women's title of Omu (One who looks after the welfare of women),[39] and the Iban Isong (Daughters of the Land) of the Ibibio, an organization which ensures that delinquent husbands are called to account.[40] As one looks at these parallel systems, it becomes clear that these male-dominated structures made provisions for women to be heard, and even more important, women exerted leadership in their own organizations. Women were able to form a pressure group so that a totally silenced West African woman is not a political reality today, nor was she in the past.

Women's representation, as it was structured in traditional decision-making, guarded against women's complete bondage to culture as perceived by men. Today, as the twentieth century comes to an end, we cannot let these earlier achievements of West African women perish by default, as they seem to be doing. From serving as an integral part of the circle of authority, they now only sortie out from time to time. The earlier power of women is vividly demonstrated by the example of the Iyalode of Lagos, Madam Tinubu, who protested against British domination. Lagos became a British colony only after the British sent her into exile. In her absence, the British forced King Dosumu to sign a treaty of colonization. Madam Tinubu chose to die in exile rather than return to Lagos to work with a puppet.

In more recent times, Mama Urhobo Iyaloja of Dugbe market in Ibadan was responsible for a scheme that successfully "controlled the syndicate of thieves in the city, and controlled the Olulu Masquerade," which enabled men to cause panic and loot wares from the Dugbe market. Any confrontation of women with masquerades is always significant as they symbolize the power of religion to control women. Wole Soyinka gives a noteworthy account of a powerful Yoruba woman,

---

[38]It is interesting to note that there were royal mothers and royal priestesses in the court of the Alafin of Oyo (an important Yoruba traditional ruler) who seemed to have made it their delight to prevent even the Iyalode from getting the king's ear. Women against women is also part of our female heritage.

[39]Mogekwu, pp. 48-49.

[40]Andreski, p. 60.

Mrs. Kuti, whose action caused the Alake of Abeokuta, a powerful king, to flee from his palace and to go into exile.[41]

Women's political power in the traditional administration, which continues to control cultural affairs to this day, is of utmost importance to the future of women's participation in remodeling relationships. While there is no way an Akan or Yoruba woman will be told that she is *not* to be heard in public, we are still left with the question of why we are not heard in public except as protesters. We have our examples of hereditary rulers such as the Ɔhemaa of the Akan, the market "queens" chosen as a result of personal qualities, and the Iyalode of the Yoruba.

When we have said all this, we have in effect spelled out the level of tokenism in the participation of women. Do we have any compensation for not having a parallel or symmetrical women's political organ, as did the Ɔhemaa? I have pointed to the British bias for patriarchy as the beginning of the marginalization of women in public affairs in West Africa. But to what do we owe the male domination of national politics today? When women found themselves without direct voice in the colonial period, they resorted to tax strikes. Today, when family law is being handled by nearly all-male parliaments, women's voices need to be heard not only in the streets but also in the courts of law.

Military Roles

In today's West Africa, the seat of power, maintenance of public order, legislation, family law, and all other arenas of political decisions are passing constantly into military hands as civilian governments are overthrown. It may not be out of place, therefore, for West African women to return to the military tactics they formerly used to stall the encroachment of colonial governments. I am thinking especially of the anti-tax "war" fought by the Aba women of eastern Nigeria against the British government in 1929. There is an indelible image in my mind of an African woman with a baby strapped to her back and a gun slung over her shoulders. Political independence did not come easily to Africa; Africans, including women, had to fight to attain it.

For the Asante, too, political and military roles went together. In the Asante constitution, one's political status was determined by military

---

[41]Wole Soyinka, *Ake: The Years of Childhood* (London: Rex Collings, 1981), pp. 180-225.

rank and assignment; thus, if a female acceded to a position of author-ity held by a male, she also formally assumed the corresponding mili-tary position.[42] Few women actually led men into battle, although Yaa Asantewa (1860-1921) of Edweso did so against the British along with Juaben Seewa, Ataa Birago of Kokofu, and Akyia of Asansu.[43] Some women, finding themselves in the role of generals, urged their male counterparts to the fight in order to retrieve or safeguard the national honor.[44]

Other women carried out various responsibilities crucial to the mili-tary campaigns. At one critical battle, the Battle of Dodowa, the royal women carried the *sikagua*, the "throne" of the Asantehene.[45] Parading at the rear of the battle line, they performed religious rituals, chants, and dances to bring about victory and ward off evil. The women left at home carried on similar assignments and they also taunted able-bod-ied "war dodgers" to join the battle or "get lost." One *Ohemaa* actually sold herself as a slave in exchange for gunpowder for her people to use. The passion of the *Ohemaa* and of all African women, whatever their rank and place, has always been the survival of the race.

Women and the Economy

In the past, as today, the survival of African children is dependent on food produced by subsistence farming done in large part by women. Indeed, subsistence farming feeds most of Africa. Oppressive systems have taken a heavy toll from Africa: Westerners have carried away Africa's population, they have organized the remaining Africans to grow

---

[42]Kwame Arhin, "The Political and Military Roles of Akan Women" in Christine Oppong, ed., *Female and Male in West Africa* (London: G. Allen & Unwin, 1983), pp. 91-98.

[43]Rattray, *Ashanti*, p. 81; see also David Sweetman, *Women Leaders in African History* (London: Heinemann, 1984), pp. 83-90.

[44]See Arhin, p. 96. I recall learning the story of the Yaa Asantewa from playmates when growing up in Ghana. She was a great warrior queen and we spoke of her as *Obaabasia a ogyina a apremoano* (the strong woman who stood in the shooting range of cannons). I also remember changing the names of the house teams in the Methodist Girls' School where I taught from Red, Blue, Green, and Gold (chosen by the missionaries) to the names of four queens, one of whom was Yaa Asantewa.

[45]Arhin, p. 96. Note that the stools (thrones) are not seats. To be "enstooled" a person is seated three times in rapid successions on the stool and that is the only time she/he does that. The stool is a symbol of the power, presence, and soul of a person

products for export to the West (mostly luxury food items), and they have gained control over large areas of land.

Studies on women and development arising from the United Nations' Decade of Women have unmasked the real breadwinners of Africa. Africa's rural women, unaware of development decades, national five-year plans, or budget allocations for agriculture, have simply carried on the grim business of growing food for survival. While they work on, agricultural experts and extension officers with a vision of what could be accomplished rarely include women in their plans. They usually advocate large-scale plans, often heavily dependent on technology, and often appropriate land otherwise worked by the women, Africa's small-scale subsistence farmers. When women have benefitted from modernizing trends, it's largely been indirectly, by the "gossip" of women who pass on hints to other women, or by women's organizations from village to village.

Traditionally, African women have farmed, traded, processed, prepared and sold food, made pottery, woven and dyed cloth, and made it into wearing apparel.[46] To do this, we required no male direction or education. We learned through an apprenticeship with our own mother or another skilled woman. In West Africa, women specialize in food processing (oil and flours) and soap-making. Unfortunately, the making of soap and vegetable oils has been nearly taken over by large-scale producers. Food preservation remains, but its future remains doubtful as large-scale mechanized methods—owned by men—enter the market.

Next to being child-rearers and food producers, West African women are traders. The markets of West Africa are run by women. Women, with great mobility and independence facilitated by a "system of reciprocal obligations" within kinship groups, tend to distribute goods from overseas (imported by men) or farm products that they themselves bring

---

or abode of a divinity. The Sikagua Kofi mentioned here embodies the soul of the Asante nation.

[46]The customary practices that surround these activities still operate. Yoruba women may still prepare calabash (a type of gourd) for daily use in storing and serving food and drinks, although these are now sold cheaply and are quickly being replaced by plastics). The ornamental calabash for ceremonial use (and now also for the tourist trade) is reserved for the patrilineal guilds; the same goes for pottery. While the textile industry has changed beyond recognition, most hand-woven fabric comes off men's looms.

in from rural areas. Such traders have been freed from housekeeping duties by a traditional support system, so being a wife and a mother does not prevent the West African woman from being a success in business, even if it is only small-scale trading.[47] The skills needed for marketing are also acquired on the job, and husbands are not involved in the management of the enterprise, although they may provide the initial capital either as a loan or an outright gift. Traditionally, an Akan wife spends her profits on her children and on housekeeping, occasionally on herself.

While there are significant exceptions, one only needs to see the markets and, increasingly, the supermarkets to observe the growing marginalization of women in economic activity. Future changes are not likely to benefit women unless some deliberate action is taken; otherwise, the feminization of poverty will soon be a reality in Africa. At the national, or even the regional level, the question is never raised as to why rural women continue to toil under so much neglect. If they are the breadwinners, why are their voices not heard?[48] I feel this lack of empowerment has its roots in a prevailing ideology of sexism. Yet, political rhetoric would have us concentrate on the global issue of Western exploitation rather than have us begin to clear our throats to speak about "home truths," including the systematic attempts to push women off the land.

One other form of rhetoric that I feel is equally dangerous to women is that of right-wing Christianity. Christian fundamentalism seems to be making a fresh attempt to promote the image of the Christian woman who is economically dependent on her husband and who spends long leisure hours in the service of religion, distributing tracts and doing "charitable" works.

QUESTIONS OF WOMEN'S AUTONOMY

Portraits of the African woman's world could be captioned almost invariably with, "Beware, she knows her husband is her master." Yet Christine Obbo has pointed out that the myth of male control goes

---

[47]Marshall, p. 23.

[48]As an Ibibio proverb says, "Whether a woman is rich or not, it does not concern the husband as long as he eats regularly." It is her husband's land that a wife farms,

hand in hand with the myth of female submission.[49] Similarly, the novelist Ama Ata Aidoo questions the supposed subservience of the African woman in the words of a young woman to a man from whom she had just separated:

> I could not shut up and look up meekly to you even when I knew I disagreed with you. But you see, no one taught me such meekness. . . . It seems as if much of the softness and meekness you and all the brothers expect of me and all the sisters is that which is really Western. . . . See, at home the woman knew her position and all that. . . . But wasn't her position among our people a little more complicated than that of the dolls colonizers brought along with them who fainted at the sight of their own bleeding fingers and carried smelling salts around?[50]

Akan women are brought up strong in body and in will. Both Ama Ata Aidoo and Christine Obbo agree that the deference of the African woman to a man, and specifically to her husband, must arise from something other than their economic relations. Indeed, we have seen that women can manage without men and can work to maintain men. (There are even wealthy but non-literate Kumasi market women who can afford to employ male bookkeepers.)

However, while it is the duty of a Yoruba wife to defer to her husband and kneel to greet him as a sign of respect, it is an insult to expect a husband to prostrate to his wife.[51] Nonetheless, researchers have not linked these customs with age. All younger people are expected to pay this obeisance to their elders and, generally, wives are younger than husbands.[52] The practice of kneeling does not signify inferiority or dependence, nor does it measure reciprocity. More important, it seems to me, is another aspect of conjugal relations which stipulates that a wife can use her husband's property only with his permission or that

---

for upon marriage she lost the right of inheritance of her father's property (Andreski, pp. 89-90).

[49]Obbo, p. 49.

[50]Ama Ata Aidoo, *Our Sister Killjoy or Reflections from a Black-eyed Squint* (Lagos, London, New York: NOK Publishers International, 1979), p. 117.

[51]R. Olufemi Ekundare, *Marriage and Divorce under Yoruba Customary Law* (Ile Ife: University of Ife Press, 1969), p. 28.

[52]Ibid.

she must respect the privacy of his room. These customs have more serious implications.

Among the Yoruba, a husband's authority extends to the children: "Despite the relatively high degree of independence of women . . . women do not regard themselves as having equal authority with their husbands in respect to certain family matters."[53] The children are the husband's and a wife's position in affinal affairs is one of a helper. Of course, if a wife defies her husband's authority, she must leave; if she has small children, she cannot leave without being labeled irresponsible.

I began to see how complicated this is, or rather has become, when I heard a market woman in Kumasi say that when Asante women work to look after *their* children, they do so because their husbands are irresponsible. True as the statement may be in theory, when expressed like that it conflicts with what I know of Asante customary practices. Asante women with delinquent husbands have little support to fall back on, whereas traditionally a woman's brother would have come to her aid in these matters. This is an inherent weakness in the matrilineal system, which separates spiritual oversight from politico-economic interests.

Equally complicated are issues of the financial support husbands give to wives. Among Yorubas, for example, the customary law "recognizes the fundamental obligation of the husband to maintain his wife."[54] But other sources indicate that "A woman shall carry on her own private business (in trade and industry) to provide for her own substance as well as for the nourishment of her own children especially when in infancy."[55] Ajisafe adds, "The husband might provide capital, usually a gift, but it could be a loan." In this relationship, if a husband makes use of his wife's labor in *his* enterprise, he is honor-bound to compensate her with presents.

In order to understand some of these seeming contradictions, one needs to look at the impact of British colonial rule on customary law. We need also to note that women and men in West Africa live a lot of what the West would call contradictions without mental pain.[56] Yet, the question that refuses to go away is this: With all this flurry of economic

[53]Marshall, p. 255.

[54]Ekundare, p. 5.

[55]A. K. Ajisafe, *Law and Custom of the Yoruba People* (New York: Routledge, 1924), p. 62.

[56]Ware, p. xviii; Aidoo, *Our Sister Killjoy*, pp. 116 and 122; and Mabel

activity on the part of women, why do we have to resort to street demonstrations to be heard while men seem able to translate their economic power *directly* into political power?

As far as colonial economic policy was concerned, there were no women in Africa except "beasts of burden" or those kept (maintained) as wives. The Christian missionaries attempted to turn the women they westernized into kept women (housewives) who had some hobbies to occupy their idleness and who could make themselves useful as helpmates, but not by going into the evil world of the market place. The Methodist pastor's wife, the model for a Christian spouse, was specifically forbidden to trade, except in processed food. She was to knit (and no less than woolen garments, and this in the tropics), to crochet to beautify her home, and to embroider. The sewing machine was her best friend and she could train young apprentices so they in turn might become model housewives like her. Girls who attended school had a special homemaker's curriculum. My own mother went to one such institution in Cape Coast—the Wesleyan Girls' High School and Training Home, it was called—and my mother-in-law experienced similar fare in Yorubaland. Their lives were mapped out for them. Few in that generation, now in their eighties, were admitted into the professions. Even if they trained for them, they had to abandon these careers in order to become homemakers.

However, with modernization, the generation after them produced professionals in teaching, nursing, and administration. The momentum accelerated in the 1940s and secondary school curricula made it possible for girls to choose courses other than domestic sciences. The changes introduced by Western education and the ambiguities it wrought on the economic independence and autonomy of women have not been sufficiently probed.[57] In Ghana the education explosion of the late 1950s began just as the economy began its downward plunge. Women were and still are the chief victims. Over most of Africa, the switch to a cash economy greatly increased women's work, especially on the farms, but their "economic tasks continued to be regarded as part and parcel of

Imokhuede, "Conflict," in Frances Ademola, *Reflections: Nigerian Prose and Verse* (Lagos: African Universities Press, 1962), p. 65.

[57]Aidoo and Sofola, both African women writers, have pointed out that modernization shattered the traditional imagery of women, an imagery that served women well (Aidoo, *Our Sister Killjoy*), pp. 116-17.

domestic work."[58] Education for women remained "informal" and was outside the system of government subsidies.

Even today, when the GNP of modern African economies is added up, women exist only as consumers. When educational reforms are being contemplated or undertaken, women are generally counted as unskilled and unlettered. The decade of development had focused on improving the standard of living and bridging the gap between the poor South and the rich North. In all this, women were not consulted and those women who were involved were simply co-opted to work on schemes they had not helped to formulate. When economic planners became aware of their presence, women were raced through programs to improve their participation in development. But women were never given the opportunity to define what development was, and eventually women discovered that they had been cooperating in making possible their own exploitation. Until the International Women's Year (1975), the beginning of the U.N.'s Decade of Women (1976), women's social organizations were waved aside as having neither political nor economic significance. It was not until after study programs were finally undertaken during the Decade of Women that serious questions were raised about the participation of women in development.

On the whole, the position of women in the economy has deteriorated; "modernization" has bypassed the majority of African women who are still in the age of hoes and mortars. The free, compulsory education in which women placed their hopes has only succeeded in producing tens of thousands of young women able to read and write but who have no other skills. That women have survived at all is due to the effort of a small but highly educated, influential group who hold executive positions in organizations such as the University Women's Associations or the National Councils of Women. For the majority of the women, local self-help groups sometimes keep their heads above water. Yet, most often they remain without political power and are completely alienated from local government structures.

These issues are more fundamental than the modernization of the economy. They involve the criteria for modernization and who determines what these criteria should be. Why has modernization meant a decrease in the autonomy of women? I am convinced that factors other than the detrimental influence of westernization on traditional econo-

---

[58]Obbo, pp. 146-50.

mies are at work in the deteriorating status of African women. We need to investigate our roots, our culture, our religion, and we need to acknowledge frankly the patriarchal nature of the axioms that shape traditional ideologies.

African women have always worked. As we have seen, in the traditional economy they took responsibility for their own development. Traditionally, how did they perceive their work? Did they associate work with prestige and power? What were the traditional modes of women's self-development? What lessons may be learned from this to empower African women so that we might become more effective economic and moral agents?[59]

In the traditional system rewards were palpable. Sex role differentiation was clear, and although women did not generally take on prestigious roles, there were safeguards against their dehumanization. The colonial administrations, however, excluded the representatives of women from local governments. As development activities were initiated, women became invisible to economic planners; modernization brought men many more benefits than it brought women. The Western patriarchal ideology worked in favor of men, and women were expected to be "fragile and dependent." Fela Anikulapo-Kuti, a popular West African composer and singer, has captured this alien picture internalized by some African women (and men) in his song, "I Be Lady."[60]

We have seen that as the British co-opted men to produce cash crops and "schooled" and recruited them for modern sector jobs, women continued to be active in their traditional occupations (farming, trading, food-processing, and crafts), holding tight to their economic independence. The few women in the modern sector (a minority everywhere, except in nursing) occupied lower-level jobs just like their Euro-American sisters: they became shop assistants rather than managers,

---

[59]Naomi Chazan, "Different Approaches to the Study of Women in Developing Countries in Africa." The importance of refocusing research on women to take in culture, religion, and psychology was confirmed for me in this seminar given at the Episcopal Divinity School in Cambridge, Massachusetts, in December 1985.

[60]See also Audrey Chapman Smock, "The Impact of Modernization on the Women's Position in the Family in Ghana," in Alice Schlegel, *Social Stratification, a Cross-Cultural View* (New York: Columbia University Press, 1977), pp. 193-214. Chapters 13-15 of Wole Soyinka's *Ake* contain a delightful profile of Mrs. Ransome Kuti (Fela Anikulapo-Kuti's mother from Abeokuta, Nigeria), and the beginnings of the Egba Women's Union.

and secretaries instead of bosses. Meanwhile, rural Akan women held their heads high and insisted on their rights to communal land and cocoa farming. As the cocoa industry was devastated by plant disease, more women moved into trade and began distributing manufactured goods from Europe imported by colonial merchants. Colonial merchants greatly preferred dealing with men, so the women sold whatever they could put their hands on that was not controlled by men.

As women were losing their traditional pre-eminence in trade, European men were communicating the "unsuitability of women for conducting affairs of substance."[61] Meanwhile, "educated" Ghanaian men were encouraging their wives to wear western clothes and to leave the *tam* (traditional apparel) to the *adesefo*, the unsophisticated rural women. In this way, women in western dress were automatically excluded from the market place, creating an image of the husband as a man of substance whose wife has no need to work.

The Ghanaian "Victorian woman" is a lost person. She bears a name that was approved by the missionaries and then she has her husband's family name, neither of which her ancestors can recognize. She has become an extension of her husband, who has chosen from the West—and from Africa—those customs that best suit his interests.[62] The difference in access to education and to prestigious employment cannot be divorced from the ideologies of male preeminence. The cooperative labor bond between spouses (as when men brought in fish and women cured and sold them, or when men brought down the palmnuts and the women made oil from them) has nearly disintegrated. Women's cooperatives have virtually disappeared.[63] Special efforts are being made today to revive them.

---

[61]The foundation for this had already been laid in the proverb, "If you have a matter of moment do not share it with your wife" (JGC 2520). See also Schlegel, p. 34.

[62]See my article in *Bulletin of African Theology* 3:5 (1981); see also Smock, p. 206.

[63]Christine Okali, "Kinship and Cocoa Farming in Ghana," in Oppong (1983), pp. 167-68. See also Robertson. As capitalization has become necessary for trade (e.g., in the trade of frozen fish), it has been increasingly controlled by men. As a result, cooperation among women has decreased (pp. 80-90). Robertson also describes the effects of formal education on the apprenticeship system and the reduction in women's networks (pp. 159-62), and the increasing economic burdens for women and effects of westernization on marriage (pp. 177-225).

Faced with the increasing social pressure on women to return to tradition, it is of the utmost importance that women join together to define what tradition they are being asked to return to, and whether it is advisable for women to *return* while men *move on* into the twenty-first century. We should take another look at the model of the traditional West African market woman, a woman who is self-identified and who belongs to an all-female organization (or, at least, a female-directed one) with political potential. If women are to make an impact on public policy, we must look seriously at how our solidarity at the local level can be brought to bear upon national legislation. And we must do this now, refusing to let seemingly trivial issues—such as our naming by Madam, Mrs., or Ms.—overshadow questions of real autonomy, the naming and defining of who we are.

5

Religion´s Chief Clients

A woman is in religion as a client.

"Customer, come buy from me,
Long time no see. *Se daadaa*
Awon omo nko ile nko?"
(How are you? How are the children?
How is the home?)

The solicitude of a market woman for the welfare of her customer closely resembles that of a priest of traditional African religion ministering to a devotee of his shrine. The first time I ever set foot in Ibadan's Dugbe market, I was greeted by a perfect stranger with these words. I had glanced at her tomatoes and was moving on when she said in a most pleasant voice, "Aah, customer, come buy from me." How did I become her customer? Why was she inquiring about my health, my affairs, my children, my home? Indeed, market women are like priests or, perhaps, we should say that religion can be like commerce. If the practitioners are good psychologists, they know exactly what their "clients" need to make life meaningful, liveable, even desirable and enjoyable.

THE CENTRALITY OF RELIGION IN AFRICA

Given the claim that Africans are incurably religious and the fact that few months pass without feasts and festivals that cannot be divorced from religious symbols, any person who is bonded to culture is usually a regular "customer" at religious houses and of religious ritual rites and priests or priestesses. The primal religions of Africa (known to scholars as African Traditional Religion), Christianity, and Islam all vigorously claim the allegiance of Africans, while African Traditional Religion continues to be a major source of meaning and receives formal acknowledgment as a living religion. All three form the backdrop of this chapter.

In Africa, or at least in the English-speaking parts, this close interlacing of religion and culture is visible in the educational system. Studies in religion are available at all levels and are often supported by national budgets. Religion is regarded as one aspect of culture and is most often included in the humanities, by itself or as part of philosophy. A few universities locate religion in the social sciences as a companion to sociology. It is not surprising that African scholars of religion have to employ an interdisciplinary approach: given our African holistic approach to life, God is seen as involved in all aspects of the human ordering of life, including politics, economics, or sports. Seen as present in people's lives from birth to death, God is evoked as the source of approval and sanction for human activity, and God is invoked for support and direction along the way.

If we consider the frequency of attendance at churches, mosques, and shrines as an indication of peoples' dependency on religion, we can describe women in Africa as very religious and demonstrably more religious than men. In this chapter, I want to look at the actual participation of women in religious practices to examine how and why they participate in religion as well as what is distinctive about their religious involvement. I also want to examine religious practices that impact solely on women.

GENDER-FREE GOD LANGUAGE

Throughout Africa, generally, the variant ways of talking about God do not pose fundamental problems. By and large the idea of God attracts male imagery in all three religions (Christianity, Islam, and Traditional Religion), in spite of the fact that everyone knows that God does not have a body. This maleness, however, does not seem to be a cause for concern, as the language for talking about God uses no gen-

der-specific pronouns. God's "maleness" is further masked by appel-
lations of God that suggest androgyny, like the Ga name Ataa Naa
Nyommo (Grandfather Grandmother God); the Creatrix Woyengi;
Tamarau, the name given the Creatrix by the Isoko of Bendel State in
Nigeria; or the androgynous Mawu-Lisa of the Ewe.

The divinities in the traditional religions of both the Akan and the
Yoruba are associated with specific genders. However, all of these divinities are described either as children or messengers of the Supreme
Being who is the Ultimate Source and Sustainer of life and the universe, without whom nothing endures or makes sense, and who is con-
ventionally called God in English.[1] While this Source Being is not represented in any concrete form, it must not be denied, as scholars and
other intellectuals insist on doing, that in popular folk imagery and
talk, this Being is masculine. It could be said, given the way we Africans understand gender, that in African Traditional Religion the
Godhead is androgynous.[2] Yet, although both the Akan and Yoruba
have non-gender specific pronouns, androgyny is not a fact of our human experience. As a result, what we commonly do is make God in our
own image, male or female. An Akan may call God "Father" or *Owoo
dɔm* (the One who gave birth to the multitude). God may be *Ɔdehye
baatan a ɔte n'ase de neho* (the Royal Parent, self-existing and self-
sufficient), though *baatan* is a more female-specific term. God is *Afua
Panini a ofiri tete*, the Friday Woman of ancient origins. God is *Kwasi-
Asi a daa Awisi*, the Male-Female one, born on Sunday with the praise
name Awisi. These strong but mixed images prevent an exclusively
male God from reigning in the Akan subconscious, folktalk notwith-
standing.

The disinterest of African women in the grammar of sexism is caused
not only by their own languages with inclusive pronouns but also because the maleness or femaleness of God is literally immaterial to them.
Women do allow such language to affect their relationships with men
who obviously are not God.

Although the gender of God does not *seem* to have any direct or

---

[1] E. B. Idowu, *Olodumare: God in Yoruba Belief* (London: Longmans, 1962), p.
30-37.

[2] The mixed community of divinities in the Akan pantheon includes both female
and male: Akua Tia (F), Ati Akosua (F), Obo Kyerewa (F), Ta Kwasi (M), Ta Kofi
(M), a Kojo (M).

specific impact on religious practices in African Traditional Religion, we need to be conscious of the tendency for the gender of the divinities to reflect human experiences. For example, research undertaken by Professor Bolanle Awe on the Yoruba goddess Osun has shown that some of the myths surrounding Osun "reflect the female predicament in Yoruba society." Osun is depicted as a female *Orisha* (divinity) "participating in the world of male divinities" or maintaining a relationship as the consort of a divinity and preoccupied with an inability to have children. She changes spouses and causes friction with other co-wives in a culture in which a woman has status only if she has children. As a divinity, however, Osun is "known and hailed as leader and defender"; she is adept at herbal healing, the giver of young ones, and the custodian of the safe delivery of infants.[3] Her geographic expression, the river Osun, runs through the well-populated Yoruba country and Osun is worshiped in several Yoruba towns, including the now internationally well-known Oshogbo shrine. The divinity of Osun is also known as the Lady of Candleman in Brazil and the Virgin of Cobre in Haiti.[4]

Oya, the goddess of the river Niger and a consort of the divinity Sango, appears in Latin America as St. Barbara. Oya is associated in Yoruba mythology with a former Alafin of Oyo who became the divinity Sango. The goddess Oya is worshiped mainly in northern Yorubaland but also in some areas where the Niger does not flow.[5] It is noteworthy, though, that the female divinities are always wives or mothers. Even the controversial Oduduwa is represented as a mother suckling her child.[6] Fertility is a long-standing obsession among the Yoruba, the Akan, and other West African groups. It continually surfaces as a theme in the works of creative writers of West Africa such as by Ama Ata Aidoo (*Anowa*, for example) and Flora Nwapa (*Efuru*).

While several rivers and streams of Ghana mark the presence of female divinities, others represent male deities. Ta Kora, the best known of these divinities, is enshrined in the Tano river. Divinities are also associated with other natural phenomena. Asase Yaa or Asaase Afua,

---

[3]Bolanle Awe, "The Iyalode in the Traditional Yoruba Political System", in Alice Schlegel, ed., *Sexual Stratification, a Cross-Cultural View* (New York: Columbia University Press, 1977), pp. 144-59.

[4]J. S. Afolabi Ojo, *Yoruba Culture: A Geographic Analysis* (Ife: Ife University Press; London: London University Press, 1966), pp. 189.

[5]Ibid., p. 164.

[6]Ibid., p. 228.

the Akan earth goddess, is female. Yoruba male divinities include Sopona (smallpox) and Sango (lightning or thunder).

Both women and men can worship and consult these divinities, however their functionaries (priests and priestesses that attend shrines and lead cults) may be designated by gender. Osun has two functionaries: a man called Aworo, and a woman named Iya Osun. Women followers are called *olori Osun* (the wives of Osun) and they may not marry without the deity's permission. On the other hand, Ta Kora of the river Tano is expressly hostile to women, yet has old women serving as mediums (the *akɔmfo* dancers). Ta Kora's priests attribute this hostility to the ungratefulness of women. As a result, women are not allowed to touch his shrine and he has no female priests; nonetheless, priests of other divinities may enter his shrine and women devotees still seek his help. The river Tano may not be used for cooking and no dead body is allowed to cross it. Menstruating women are strictly taboo and not allowed access to Ta Kora.[7] Other divinities, such as Ta Kese or Ta Mensah, enshrine a symmetrical principle with both priestesses and priests. In the shrine of Ta Kora there are blackened stools for both women and men who had served him.[8] The chief priest and chief priestess both have their own entourages.[9] Gender plays little and often no part in who becomes an adherent of a particular deity.

Superficial observations of these customs have given rise to the insistence that under the traditional religious umbrella both men and women have equal opportunity to lead and to be led in worship and in sacrifices. This may be too generous an assessment. One would need to travel between Accra and Ibadan via Aflao and Abeokuta to do a gender count of the *akɔmfo* (mediums, ritual dancers) and *abosomfo* (chief priests and priestesses). My observation has been that the lower-ranking functionaries, the *akɔmfo,* are mostly women while the *abosomfo* are predominantly men. This area needs more systematic investigation. When it comes to clients of the shrine, women are unquestionably the most ardent and faithful, but again some scholarly

---

[7]Robert S. Rattray, *Ashanti* (1923; reprint, Westport, CT: Greenwood/African Universities Press, 1971), pp. 188-202.

[8]Rattray, pp. 160, 167, 169. A ritual stool becomes black with the constant patination with animal blood or ocher that it gets during rituals. The blood or its substitute ocher "feeds" the spirit embodied in the stool and renews its strength and potency.

[9]Ibid., pp. 155-59.

work may help to clarify why this is so. In my opinion, a certain hermeneutic of suspicion is required whenever an African male proclaims that the African female is powerful.

Both the Ifa poems and the prayers of African Traditional Religion show that Africans acknowledge that God, the divinities, and the ancestors are fully involved in the daily life and well-being of the community.[10] They also acknowledge that procreation, health, and wealth are the indices of the good life that comes from being in harmony with the spirit powers (God, divinities, ancestors) and with the people one encounters in daily life. A very common petition in prayers of the Akan is "Let the women bear children and do not let the men become impotent." Indeed, procreation brings a woman closer to the spirit powers. This responsibility for bringing children into the world is so firmly lodged with a woman that she will be the first to run to the shrine for help if she does not become pregnant. The "tragedy" of a man proved to be impotent is so final that it is the last thing to be considered, even by his wife.[11]

The role of the mother is obvious: the children are born of the mother and her connection with their blood is direct. How then does a matrilineal society such as the Akan locate the male principle?[12] If the mother is blood, what is the father? If the mother gives political status and inheritance, what does the father confer? There was an untaught feeling that the father must play some part and that his authority must be captured in some symbol. The father's seminal fluid provided the "scientific" base for him to have a part in the child; since the seminal fluid is normally unseen but is known to be liquid its association with a river deity was not difficult to arrive at. Traditionally, the Akan located fatherhood in *ntorɔ*, the spiritual principle associated with fatherhood and, some would add, physically located in the semen, a word that has no folk etymology in Akan.[13] Whatever its origin, *ntorɔ* became the spiritual element in each person's life. When one is attuned to one's

---

[10]John S. Mbiti, *The Prayers of African Religion* (Maryknoll, NY: Orbis Books, 1976).

[11]See Ama Ata Aidoo, *Anowa* (London: Harlow, 1970), pp. 61-63.

[12]*Ɔhemaa* Amma Seewa Akoto of Mampong argued that since babies are formed in and through blood they belong only to their mothers; no man contributed blood. See Rattray, *Ashanti*, pp. 77-78, 295.

[13]See Modupe Oduyoye, "Patrilineal Spirits," in E. A. Ade Adegbola, ed., *Traditional Religion in West Africa* (Ibadan: Daystar Press, 1983), pp. 291-94.

ntorɔ (for example, being on good terms with one's father), a person's *ntorɔ* guides and protects, like a large bubble that allows only good to penetrate. To prosper in life, one must observe the same taboos and practices as one's father.[14]

The male *ntorɔ* becomes the disciplinary element in the life of all persons. Femaleness is therefore subject to the spirit of discipline and conditioned to accept male domination as the norm of societal life. A woman is under the discipline not only of her father but also of her husband. *Ntorɔ* places a double yoke on mothers, for they must enable their children to learn its discipline. It is of utmost importance for a wife to be on good terms with her husband and with her affinal group (his family) as they can enable her or prevent her from fulfilling her duties to her ancestors.

BLOOD, BODY AND COMMUNITY

In the Akan view of life, blood is not only a physiological substance; it is also a theological substance, imbued with meaning for one's being. Sustaining the body, it is the crucial substance of a human being. In pre-colonial days, human sacrifices were understood in religious terms: one life was given up in order to attain more life, either here or in the hereafter. Of course, some Asante writings of the nineteenth century also describe judicial execution, capital punishment for crimes. Generally speaking, any discussion of blood, especially human blood, as a part of the practice of African Traditional Religion is avoided, since no one wants to be associated with the crude and often racist reports of early European travelers. And yet, an understanding of the religious significance of blood is necessary to unlock many of the mysteries of Akan psychology.

Some examples may clarify the significant role of blood. In the holy place of Asantemanso[15] no menstruating woman was allowed to be present and no other form of shedding human blood was permitted;

---

[14]It is worth noting that this may be a psychological prop that permits acceptance of the language of God the Father.

[15]Eva Meyerowitz, *The Early History of the Akan States of Ghana* (London: Red Candle Press, 1974), p. 217. Asantemanso was in the forest on the Kumasi-Bekwai road. It was founded in 1600 but fifty years later was destroyed by civil war. It was

neither was anyone allowed to die there. In another village, Asubenagya, on the other side of the river, these "negative" forces were tolerated. Because no male whose blood had been shed could become an *Ɔhene* (king), circumcision is taboo among the Asante. Similarly, no one who might be described as *wadi dɛm* (mutilated) could become a priest or king; this included persons with visible injuries that could have caused bleeding or physical handicaps and those whose wholeness of body had been violated. Physical perfection and purity were required for ruling or for being a sacrificial functionary or an object for sacrifice.[16]

Some of the most significant taboos in African Traditional Religion are associated with the blood of menstruation. A woman's blood is a genuine theological symbol, representing the carrying of life, the potential reincarnation of ancestral spirits, and life offered in sacrifice. Menstruation has an unusually strong potency: it seems, therefore, a form of male envy to put menstruation in the same category as a "person suffering from a gonorrheal discharge"[17]; sexual diseases represent abnormality, impurity, and inauspiciousness, while menstruation does not.

In the practice of traditional religion, a menstruating woman becomes "untouchable"; she is like a person preparing an offering and she herself is the offering. She is surrounded by the spirits to whom she is being offered; she must be avoided by mere mortals and she herself must avoid the company of others. Women of child-bearing age are both the symbols and the source of continuity of the human community.

In the history of the Asante, women participated in wars, but they had to be past the child-bearing age. Girls who had not reached puberty or women who had reached menopause went to war as carriers and nurses. First, they did not have any menstrual "power," which could render impotent charms, talismans, and other spiritual sources. Second, if these women fell in battle, they would die as individuals and not

---

situated on the river Suben. The actual location is a well-guarded secret. See also Robert S. Rattray, *Religion and Art in Ashanti* (1927, reprint, New York: AMS Press, 1979), chap. 10.

[16]Rattray, *Ashanti*, pp. 121-32; for information on taboos, see pp. 131-32.

[17]John E. Eberegbulam Njoku, *The World of the African Woman* (Metuchen, NJ and London: Scarecrow Press, 1980), p. 15. (Sometimes I feel Njoku has written "tongue in cheek," for on the following page he calls the husband the "god of all creation.")

as potential sources of human life. It is not surprising, then, that old women often undertook courageous acts to defend with their lives the people they had brought into life.[18]

As has been pointed out, it appears that in the past when women were rulers and war broke out, "they were sent for, or when they were required for important meetings, they would say *makyima* [indicating they were menstruating] and they could not perform their duties"[19]; men, nominated by the elders, then took their place. This legend, although reported from a male perspective, does not explain *why* the women could not perform their duties while menstruating; it seems reasonable to surmise that it had to do with religious traditions and taboos. Similarly, "in the olden days" if a menstruating woman entered the "Chapel of Stools," she was killed immediately.[20]

In general, menstruating women were not allowed to participate in rituals. One of the strictest taboos applied to the carving of drums, which was forbidden to all women (even the *Ɔhemaa*). Because blood was taboo to the stately *atumpan* drums (one male, one female), women were not allowed to touch them. Although the *donno* is a drum reserved for women, it was generally thought expedient for women to stay clear of drums and drumming.[21] Similarly, most rituals required male cooks, although sometimes the most senior wife of the *Ɔhene* would be responsible. Women past the child-bearing age could participate by fetching water or the white clay often used in rituals.

It is clear that being beyond the child-bearing age eliminates only one factor of femaleness, the capacity to give birth. This does not clarify why such women should be more "acceptable" from a Christian theological point of view. Is it, using western terms, the old Freudian argument that males might be willing to accept a woman because she no longer has a capacity they don't have? These questions are important

---

[18]Rattray, *Ashanti*, p. 81.

[19]Kofi Abrefa Busia, *The Position of the Chief in Modern Political Systems of Ashanti* (London: Oxford University Press, 1951), pp. 20, 72.

[20]Every palace had a room set aside for keeping the stools (thrones function as shrines) of the rulers, both kings and queen mothers. As each ruler took office, a new stool was carved for him or her. This place became the "holy of holies" within the palace, a chapel where libations were poured. See Peter Sarpong, *The Sacred Stools of the Akan* (Tema: Ghana Publishing Co., 1971), pp. 26-56. See also Rattray, *Religion and Art in Ashanti*, pp. 74-75.

[21]One significant example is the *fontomfrom*, a giant drum.

because Akan men seem to have a deep-seated fear of menstruation and, therefore, of women. This undoubtedly affects present-day relationships between men and women.

There are occasional examples of traditional male-female relationships that might prove helpful today. For example, during an Akan festival called the *Adae*, the *Ɔhene*, the king, sat in state and could not conclude the public celebration until the *Ɔhemaa*, the queen mother, arrived to greet him. This sharing of honor and responsibility was also shown in a ritual related to the Grove of Asantemanso, which was performed jointly by the *Ɔhemaa* and the *Ɔhene*, although the *Ɔhemaa* was the chief priest and custodian of the grove. I believe we can examine such rituals in search of a new paradigm for creating relationships.

The Power of Blood That Is Shed

The Akan have a well-known belief that if a man should have sexual intercourse with a menstruating woman he is sure to end up impotent. In fact, menstruation is believed to have such potency as to annul all prayer and render all ritual ineffective.[22] This paradox and the ambiguity toward blood in general and menstruation in particular bear further examination. The Asante perform puberty rites for females only and these rites are exclusively a women's affair. It is recognized that without these rites the much desired children cannot be born and the ancestors will not be reincarnated. In fact, one of the most hideous offenses for a girl and one that is severely punished is for her to be found pregnant before puberty rites have been performed. A girl is pampered and praised with the name *Wakum Ɛsono* (she has killed an elephant, she has done a mighty deed) when her first menstruation is publicly announced. Menstruation demands her seclusion to be followed by the public celebration of the promise of new life. From then on, she becomes a woman who must observe all the taboos relating to menstruating women. For example, she must not sit in court to arbitrate any case; she may not cook for adult males, nor eat food cooked for any man. She may not swear an oath, nor may an oath be sworn on her. She may

---

[22]It is also interesting to note that while life-giving blood (menstruation) can also mean death, semen is never associated with death. See Rattray, *Ashanti*, pp. 121-32 for more on taboos.

not address men belonging to certain guilds except through a spokesperson. Because a menstruating woman may not enter a house where there are men, the traditional village has a *brafieso*, a compound maintained solely as a refuge for menstruating women.

The fear behind all these taboos and injunctions begins to be apparent when we analyze why *brafo* (a menstruating woman) must not touch any talisman, any male, or participate in any ritual. *Brafo* has power to be feared. To be in contact with *brafo* is to have all one's powers annulled. Such a woman renders a man vulnerable to evil spirits and annuls all other powers. Although I have not been able to trace the origins of these beliefs, the ambivalence toward menstruation is clear: on the one hand, it is highly esteemed as life-giving power; on the other, it is feared as a powerful negative spirit. There is a similar unexplained ambivalence toward sexual intercourse, which, while obviously necessary for procreation, is still viewed as a source of impurity.

Again we see the willingness of the African to live with paradox and contradiction: blood is sacred and blood is taboo. The theological idea that blood is both sacred and taboo (meaning, to be avoided) is found in other sacrificial religions. The ethical implications, too, may be similar and related to an idea that, while we hold life to be sacred (related to the divine), people may voluntarily give themselves up so that more life may be created, assured, or lived at better levels.[23] Yet, no one has the right to shed another person's blood or to sacrifice an unwilling person. The blood from such a sacrifice spells death, not life.

On the other hand, free-flowing menstrual blood is seen as nature's sign of hospitality, and a preparation for the arrival of the ancestral spirits. Yet when this blood touches people who have no business getting close to it, it becomes a pollutant. When animal blood or its representation by ocher is ritually painted on a stool or some other artifact, it enhances powers; if carelessly daubed anywhere else, such as on the ground or accidentally on a wall or furniture, it loses its aesthetic powers. If the seclusion of women is a question of hygiene and aesthetics,

---

[23]Early on, I came to this conclusion after an encounter with a maternal grand-aunt, Maame Akosua Adae, who lived in my ancestral home, Amakom, now part of Kumosi. I had reached 21 years and had no marriage plans, which shocked my grand-aunt. As I left, she said, "My grandchild, I hope you know that with every menstrual period you are signifying that you refuse to give life to the ancestors." It was my turn to be shocked.

then women today have been somewhat freed from these concerns by modern science and technology. Unfortunately, however, in the conservative arena of religion, the situation of customs regarding women remains unchanged.

Traditional religion undergirds and permeates all we Africans undertake—being born, healing, worshipping, living, dying. In everything, the Akan separate women from men, but in the end, though, it is the women who are given the burden of making life happen and keeping it healthy. And so they frequent the shrines. Although there are women priests and women healers,[24] the priests are primarily men (who have no monthly cycles to worry about) who tell women what to do to ensure that life is abundant. Without question, women devotees outnumber men, as any Protestant congregation in Africa will demonstrate. Is this a case of "mystifying" religion being uncritically swallowed by women in order to numb the sharp pains of reality?

WOMEN AND WITCHCRAFT

To my mind, this combination of the mystification of religion and the guilt created in women by their responsibility to bear and sustain human life is closely associated with the phenomenon of witchcraft in African society. In African Traditional Religion, human beings are possible hosts for the evil that diminishes the quality of life for an individual or the whole community. People possess and can be possessed by the forces of witchcraft. Among the Akan, witches are described as anti-social, self-seeking beings who stop at nothing to achieve their aims. They will kill, if necessary, so that they, their children, and close relations might get on in life. It is not difficult to blame witches for the many insecurities and hardships of life in Africa.

Although witchcraft has to do with *people* who possess extraordinary powers, it should be noted that the term wizard, used for a male witch, has dropped from use; its present connotation is quite different. It is also interesting to note that most authors writing on witchcraft, knowing that there are men who do possess powers which in women

---

[24]Kofi Appiah-Kubi, *Man Cures, God Heals: Religion and Medical Practice among the Akan of Ghana* (Totowa, NJ: Allanheld Osum Publishers, 1981) describes women's initiatives in establishing healing houses (pp. 27-31, 42-46).

would be labelled witchcraft, almost always begin with women.[25]

As witches have become known and hunted, women (and especially old women) have fallen victim to the spasmodic appearances of anti-witchcraft cults. Growing up in the Asante region of Ghana in the 1940s, I recall the panic spread abroad by the Tigare and Aberewa cults, which claimed to diagnose witches, to exorcise and neutralize their powers, and to protect people from their machinations.[26] Although one of these anti-witchcraft cults was called *Aberewa* (old woman), all of the witch-hunters were men. The Akan believe that only a witch can detect witch-craft in another person. While these male witch-hunters could be said to be witches themselves, they were seen as benevolent witches who could rid society of the influences of their female counterparts who used their powers for selfish ends. Male witches were said to walk normally, while female witches, "perverse" women, were said to walk on their heads.

Witches are women who work against the unity and coherence of community, and who do not seek the good of others or actively care for others. Since women are expected above all to give selfless attention to the needs of others, women who prosper are often suspected of not having been conscientious enough about their duties to others. On the other hand, if certain women are not successful, then perhaps it is witch-craft in themselves or emanating from others that frustrates their efforts.

Not too long ago, a Ghanaian colleague of mine, Elizabeth Amoah, conducted interviews of women accused of witchcraft or those whose circumstances could be attributed to witchcraft that they either practiced or fell victim to. Some women were suspected of witchcraft for no reason other than their high level of educational attainment. If a woman was well-off economically, unmarried, and had no children, the situation was all too clear—either she was a victim of witchcraft or she was herself a witch who had sacrificed the sense of community and posterity for her own gain. A woman who was successful in business and who had prosperous and or numerous children was also suspected of witchcraft: her comfortable circumstances were undoubtedly the

---

[25]See, for example, Michael C. Kirwen, *The Missionary and the Diviner* (Maryknoll, NY: Orbis, 1987), pp. 49-51.

[26]See H. DeBrunner, *Witchcraft in Ghana* (Accra: Presbyterian Book Depot), 1959.

cause of someone else's hardship, usually someone close to her, perhaps her husband.[27]

If a woman has many children when those around her—especially sisters or sisters-in-law—have none, she is a witch, calling attention to herself alone. If a woman is childless, she is a witch or a victim of witchcraft; others close to her may have sold her ovaries for money or tied up her womb out of vindictiveness. Unmarried women who are independent of male support are also likely to be accused of witchcraft. Widows, especially multiple widows, are often accused of causing the death of their husbands through witchcraft. Even a woman who is considered quarrelsome or who may have been plagued with constant ill-luck is considered a possible witch. If a woman cannot succeed in any economic enterprise, she may be a witch; if she prospers too obviously in it, she may also be a witch. If a successful woman has been cleared of witchcraft, she is often suspected of being prodigious with sexual favors.

Some women accept these accusations and live with the risk of being ostracized or treated with mistrust. Others truly suffer from false accusations. Elizabeth Amoah cites an example of a woman who sold *tatare*, a pancake made of ripe plantain and fried in palm oil. Once she was accused of witchcraft, everyone refused to buy from her, saying that the palm oil (palm oil is red in color) she used was blood. Accusations of witchcraft are rarely evaluated in a scientific way, or often in any way at all.

Scarcely ever does one hear of men accused of witchcraft and being made to suffer because of such accusations. What I want to highlight is that there seems to be an endemic societal aversion to women who are successful or women who are not dependent on men. Women must not call attention to themselves or be outstanding in any way. Obviously, breaking with traditional roles and prospering in that choice is a sure sign of strength, but the least misstep or mistake in the traditional role of wife and mother can undo a woman completely and identify her as a

---

[27]Elizabeth Amoah, "Femaleness: Akan Concepts and Practices" in Jeanne Becher, ed., *Women, Religion and Sexuality: Impact of Religious Teachings on Women* (Geneva: WCC, 1990), pp. 129-53. See also Elichi Amadi, *Ethics in Nigerian Culture* (Ibadan: Heinemann's Educational Books Ltd., 1982), pp. 22-31. Under "supernatural crimes," he writes: "A wife who was a witch was, people believed, quite capable of sucking her husband's book at night. In such a case the husband would waste away, while the wife grew fatter and more robust."

witch. While I do not know any woman who consciously avoids success because of the possibility of facing such accusations, I despair of the subconscious effect this may have on us African women.

WOMEN AND THE AFRICAN INSTITUTED CHURCHES (AIC)

Christianity in Africa has been institutionalized in an abundance of ways ranging from the older churches (mission or western churches, such as the Methodist Church Ghana; historical churches, such as the Coptic and Ethiopian Orthodox churches) to more indigenous expressions of Christianity. This latter category—variously called African Instituted Churches, African Independent Churches, or African Charismatic Churches—includes a range of groups from the praying (*Aladura*) churches of Nigeria to the Zionist groups of South Africa. These popular expressions of African Christianity were founded in Africa as a result of particular African charisms.[28]

In these churches, which I shall refer to by the generic name of Aladura, Christianity has evolved from a combination of teachings from the Hebrew Bible, traditional African spirituality and practice, and a theology that focuses on the victory of Jesus Christ over evil and death, arising from the gospel narratives. These church bodies demonstrate a flexible ecclesiology that follows the African traditions of hospitality and respect that enabled Christianity and Islam to thrive on the continent. Even today, new Aladura congregations spring up literally overnight.

The flexible "ecclesiology" of traditional African religion also has allowed believers to establish shrines after participating in an initiation ceremony commanded by the particular divinity. The call may come either directly from the divinity or indirectly through a third person. As such, it is not surprising to find many women-founded and women-headed Aladura churches and congregations.

---

[28]A brief overview of the development of these churches may be found in Lamin Sanneh, *West African Christianity: The Religious Impact* (Maryknoll, NY: Orbis Books, 1983; London: C. Hurst, 1983), pp. 180-209. See also Harold W. Turner, *Bibliography of New Religious Movements*, Vol. I: *Black Africa* (New York: G. K. Hall, 1977).

In structure, they often exhibit a symmetrical organization of men and women with the whole church headed by a prophet or prophets. One well-known Aladura church, the Cherubim and Seraphim, has two sections headed by a Baba Aladura and a Mother Cherubim, respectively.[29]

In the Aladura churches, the male hierarchy generally follows the order described in Paul's Letter to the Corinthians, "And God has appointed in the church first apostles, second prophets, third teachers; then deeds of power, then gifts of healing, forms of assistance, forms of leadership, various kinds of tongues" (1 Cor. 12:28) and Paul's Letter to the Ephesians, "The gifts he gave were that some would be apostles, some prophets, some evangelists, some pastors and teachers, to equip the saints for the work of ministry, for building up the body of Christ" (Eph. 4:11-12). The female leadership is based on other biblical themes, primarily from the Hebrew Scriptures. Popular role models are Miriam, Rachel, and Lydia.

Throughout West Africa, such popular Christianity tends to absolutize the Bible to such a degree that any historical-critical approach is viewed with suspicion or simply dismissed. While some African biblical scholars may mouth contemporary hermeneutical approaches to the Bible, they often accept or hide behind "paradoxes," refusing to draw conclusions. Because non-canonical material contemporary to the New Testament is generally ignored, statements on the position of women are usually taken from Genesis, Leviticus, or the New Testament Epistles; such texts tend to constitute a "man's Bible." Here are a few typical expressions resulting from such contemporary "theologizing":

1. The Gospel of Christ has created a new unity in the one Body of Christ. However, the modern philosophy of women's liberation is not biblical; rather, it is a threat to world peace and a rejection of defined role expectations of each sex within the created order.

---

[29]Akin Omoyajowo, *Cherubim and Seraphim: The History of an Independent Church* (New York: NOK Publishers, 1982), p. 200. *West African Christianity: The Religious Impact* by Lamin Sanneh contains an interesting account of the development of these churches (p. 143).

2. Here in Africa, particularly in Nigeria, both indigenous and established churches *allow* women's participation in their organization (emphasis is mine).

3. Paul established the equality of man and woman before God, but such equality does not remove the physical distinctions given at creation, which have a divine purpose. The modern call for the liberation of women is a replica of the Corinthian women's libertarianism. For women to aspire to become like men and reject their womanhood is not a genuine form of equality. Hence modern women's liberation is not biblical, and is not African.

4. As St. Paul silenced such women, the antinomian libertines (women liberationists) of today should not be encouraged in the church.[30]

These excerpts could have come from any pulpit or scholarly article. In Africa, the debate on sexism in the church has hardly begun.

Women in an Aladura Church

Although women play a more prominent role in the African Instituted Churches, we should inquire if these churches have in fact succeeded in incorporating women's insights into the will of God for human beings. It is generally asserted that the Aladura churches give women more room to express leadership abilities than do the churches that have grown out of the Euro-American missionary enterprise.[31] This can also be said of the African Instituted Churches of West Africa. Because the Aladura and the Zionist churches follow closely the prac-

---

[30]Excerpts from O. O. Obijole's seminar paper on "St. Paul on the Position of Women in the Church: A Study of Gal. 3:28, 1 Cor. 11:1-14 and 34-36: Paradox or Change?" at the Department of Religious Studies, University of Ibadan in May 1985. The lecturer was a Ph.D. candidate in New Testament Pauline Studies. He has graduated and is a bishop of the Anglican Church in Nigeria.

[31]Bengt Sundkler, *The Christian Ministry in Africa* (London: SCM Press, 1960), pp. 66 and 71; *Bantu Prophets* (London: SCM, 1961), pp. 139-44. Sundkler concluded that leadership exercised by women in these churches ran parallel to that of men. However, a church that followed the Euro-American model tended to have

tices of African Traditional Religion, many adherents of the religion are office bearers. It is not surprising, though, that while women are found in the hierarchy of the Cherubim and Seraphim as *Iya Alakoso* (superintending mother), few such churches have women heads. The case of Captain Christiana Abiodun Akinsowon, co-founder with Moses Orimolade of the Cherubim and Seraphim, has been well documented. In 1986, Captain Abiodun, as she is known, finally won the headship of the entire Cherubim and Seraphim movement.[32]

The sections of the Cherubim and Seraphim that have rejected Captain Abiodun's leadership have done so "on the sole reason that she is a woman."[33] When a prominent traditional ruler, the Alake of Abeokuta, was called in to arbitrate a leadership dispute between her and Moses Orimolade, the Alake agreed to support Captain Abiodun only if she would agree to accept the title of supreme *head of all the women* in the Cherubim and Seraphim societies of Nigeria (italics mine). This, the Alake thought, was a prestigious enough title and one which "any reasonable worker in the Lord's vineyard should gladly accept."[34]

Some observers have noted the similarities of these Christian women leaders not only to the prophetesses of African Traditional Religion, but also to the Montanist movement of the early church, which gave positions of authority to women. It has been pointed out that the discriminatory attitude of the western churches toward women is, in matters of religious tradition, quite alien to Africa.[35] My reading of the women founders and leaders of the African Instituted Churches leaves me convinced that African women like Captain Abiodun reflect the leadership of women in African Traditional Religion. They are recognized by their followers as divine agents. Churches in Africa cry for the richness of this empowering and caring ministry.

Throughout most Christian churches in Africa, I believe, we can safely say that women's organizations, where they exist, are more effi-

---

a male head, while a church in the "Zionist" tradition might be headed by a female. See also John D. Y. Peel, *Aladura: A Religious Movement among the Yoruba* (London: Oxford University Press, 1968), pp. 26, 183-84.

[32]*Sunday Times* (Lagos), June 22, 1986, records her magnanimous response to the entire struggle; however, the controversy persisted with some dissenting men continuing the battle through the press.

[33]Omoyajowo, *Cherabim and Seraphim*, p. 202.

[34]Ibid., p. 201.

[35]Ibid., 200-1.

ciently and energetically run than their male counterparts. It would not surprise any African woman to read that it is dangerous for a church leader to fall out with the women of the congregation. This follows societal patterns, and many a politician and traditional ruler can bear witness to this.[36] One issue to consider, however, is whether women in the Aladura churches have a sacramental role that differs from that in Western churches.

The status and involvement of women today in both church and society have closely followed women's traditional roles. It has been shown that while the Cherubim and Seraphim churches have encouraged women's participation, there is a keen awareness of the limits of this participation and its impact on the total community: "Yet, there are still traces of traditional male superiority in the Cherubim and Seraphim arrangements . . . most members are women—but men have more opportunities to lead." This is seen in practice by the possibility of nine "ranks" for men and only five for women.[37] I would maintain that this is not a mere trace, but rather a replica of what happens in both church and society.

Women's participation is curtailed even more by the application of "levitical laws," which, like traditional menstruation avoidances, exclude women in their menses and those who have just given birth. The latter are excluded from all meetings for forty days if they have had a male child and eighty days if they gave birth to a girl (as if the birth of a girl makes one doubly powerful/impure). Such restrictions seriously limit the spiritual service a woman can give to a church.[38] It is not surprising that the restrictions on participating in religious rituals are much more severe than those governing the daily running of a church. Menstruating women are simply excluded from the main church building. They cannot wear their white church uniform, but they may sing, read a text, and send in their offering. This situation led one secessionist leader to say, "If they [women] were clean in spirit and their money was acceptable in the house of God, why should they themselves be excluded?"[39]

---

[36]Sundkler, *Bantu Prophets*, pp. 139-44; see also Victor Hayward, *African Independent Movements* (Geneva: World Council of Churches, IMC Pamphlet No. 11).

[37]Omoyajowo, p. 194-96, 201.

[38]Ibid., pp. 106, 201-2.

[39]It is worth noting that in some Anglican churches in Nigeria women are advised

Adopting the practices of African Traditional Religion, the Aladura churches have often chosen to ordain into the ministry of sacraments mostly women who have reached menopause. Women still of child-bearing age must appoint delegates during their period of menstruation. The teachings of traditional religion are very clear in this respect.[40]

As I have already pointed out, women are rarely involved in the rituals of Traditional Religion. Among the Zulu no women are involved in magic or ritual generally, and they seldom become war doctors, rain makers, or other types of magicians, but a large majority of the possessed are women.[41] We find the same phenomenon in West Africa: most mediums are women and spirit possession is generally found among female *akomfo* (mediums) in Akan traditional worship.

The prophets and visionaries in the Aladura churches are preponderantly women. As a male colleague of mine has said, "They are simply being used by the male church leaders just as their sisters in traditional religion have always been."[42] Be that as it may, although there is no lack of women visionaries, healers, prophets, exhorters, and preachers, one is hard put to find women administering the Christian sacraments even in these otherwise "very African" churches. On the contrary, their very Africanness has meant that some of the taboos of African Traditional Religion have been transferred into Christian practices. Women who have attempted to do away with these traditional practices have received little encouragement. For example, when one early charismatic leader, Prophetess Taiwo, moved from Lagos to Ibadan to start a church with her brother-in-law, she was refused entrance into the sanctuary. In protest she established her own church, calling her group the "Light of Christ (Jesus) Church."[43]

---

not to take communion during their menstrual periods (Ogbu Kalu, ed., *Christianity in West Africa: The Nigerian Story* [Ibadan: Daystar Press, 1978]).

[40]Kofi Abrefa Busia, *The Position of the Chief in Modern Political Systems of Ashanti* (London: Oxford University press, 1951), p. 20; Harold W. Turner, *History of an African Independent Church: Church of the Lord Aladura* (Oxford: Clarendon Press, 1967), p. 43; C. G. Baeta, *Prophetism in Ghana* (London: SCM Press, 1962), p. 134.

[41]Sundkler, *Christian Ministry in Africa*, p. 139.

[42]Interview with Dr. M. Y. Nabofa, a lecturer and researcher on the Isoko traditional religion of Bendel State, Nigeria.

[43]Turner, *History of an African Independent Church*, pp. 49, 59, 90. It seems striking that even in the charismatic churches it is only when Jesus Christ, the Light

One exception is the Christian Catholic Apostolic Stone Church in Zion of South Africa, which actually ordains women, giving them authority "to preach the gospel of Jesus Christ, to pray for the sick, to bury the dead, to consecrate children, to administer the Lord's Supper, to baptize believers, and to solemnize marriages."[44] It should be noted that the sacrament of the Lord's Supper does not play as crucial a role in the Aladura churches as it does in the Western churches. The Aladura churches celebrate the sacrament but infrequently: "The mystique of the ministry is not attached to authority to celebrate the sacraments or to theological education, but is present in the anointed man of God who can perform the rituals of the church and lead its worship—healing, revelation, interpretation and discipline."[45] Nonetheless, only an apostle (a male) can celebrate the Lord's Supper or give authority to do so to ministers down to the rank of prophet.

The 1954 Constitution of the Church of the Lord (based on that of 1938) recognizes women prophets and gives them the staff of office (an iron rod) used by ministers. Yet, women prophets have been excluded from the altar and condemned to silence except in the absence of a male minister or lay leader. In 1959, the primate of the Aladura church declared that as long as the church exists the ministry of women shall not cease. It was decided that a married woman minister is to be stationed where her spouse is; an unmarried woman minister is to work with a trustworthy senior male minister. Only female ministers past the age of child-bearing are allowed to have separate churches. Some members of the church argue that if women preach, they also ought to have access to the sanctuary and be allowed to pronounce the benediction. In 1958, during these debates, the Church of the Lord gave one woman dispensation to enter the sanctuary and to pronounce the benediction.

It is difficult to escape the conclusion that even in the Aladura churches sacramental ministry is guarded jealously by African men. A review of the involvement of women in these churches shows that the traditional African views of male superiority and male privilege have been reinforced by both traditional religious biases and the Western

---

of the world, reappears that the ministry of women again becomes part of Christian tradition.

[44]Sundkler, p. 20.

[45]Harold W. Turner, *African Independent Church: The Life and Faith of the Church of the Lord Aladura* (Oxford: Clarendon Press, 1967), p. 33.

churches' exclusion of women from ministry. This has been somewhat eroded by the successful leadership of women like Captain Christiana Abiodun Akinsowon of the Cherubim and Seraphim. Fortunately, there is opportunity for self-expression and leadership in various African churches so that women can become more than simple clients. Because women do constitute the majority of worshipers today, the battle for ordination to "professional" and sacramental ministry must be fought by all Christian women, with the support of Christian men.

More often, the ambivalence, tension, and uncertainty of church teachings on the nature of woman prevails over any demonstration that a pastor's success is not dependent on the pastor's gender. This ambivalence is present in the Aladura churches as well. Bishop Ore Banjo of the Church of the Lord has been quoted as preaching, "Menstruation and fornication are deadly enemies to the angels, they fly away at the slightest smell of them."[46] Given that both menstruation and fornication cause ritual uncleanness, it seems ludicrous that while fornication might be washed away through ritual, menstruation cannot. One cannot help but ask why the Creator God would object to the power of procreation.

In summary, it appears that the bifocal organization of African society overrides most other religious considerations; women are asked to devote themselves to the divinities so that the community is guaranteed abundant life. Once again, the women with these responsibilities are placed under the direction of a few men, who appear to establish structures that ensure that their position in the "service to God" is one of directorship.

---

[46]Ibid., p. 43.

6

Marriage and Patriarchy

By nature, dominion is maternal for two reasons—the identity of a child's mother alone is certain, and power over a child is initially in the hands of the mother who nourishes and trains it. . . . Marriage is the contract which brings about patriarchy.[1]

Domestic affairs are not rags to be washed and hung outside (*Afisem nye ntamago na yasi ahata abonten*). (JGC 1136)

Patriarchy exists wherever one finds systemic and normative inequalities and subordination.

If the rags of domestic affairs were intended to be hung in public, we might consider not getting them so tattered in the first place. Having seen something of women's roles in political and economic structures in West Africa, we turn now to the family, the base of all societal organization in Africa. This world of secrets often hides a multitude of wrongs. Group solidarity is so strongly emphasized that "telling it as it is" stamps the teller with terrible labels, like traitor to the family or traitor to the nation. This is important to bear in mind when analyzing responses to questionnaires or surveys concerning family life; therefore, we should retain a margin of suspicion, especially when all seems faultless.

African women's priorities begin and end in relationships. While

---

[1]Rosemary Agonito, *History of Ideas on Women: A Source Book* (New York: Thomas Hobbes, 1977), p. 97.

the Ɔhemaa can publicly tell off the Ɔhene, she is most unlikely to do so, not because he is a man, but because he is a human being whose soul (life force) can be killed by disgrace. She would rather find a way to cope with his stubbornness or his refusal to see a different perspective than to resort to destroying him whom she mothers. Similarly, a market woman drives a hard bargain, but however it turns out, both buyer and seller will feel good and many times buyer-seller relationships in West African markets develop into long-lasting friendships. It is the quality of *relationships* rather than power or prestige that informs the daily encounters of the traditional African woman and that places a high premium on kinship.

To pursue my quest of "What is woman," I intend to look at the African woman within marriage, the transitional rite that establishes and solidifies relationships that enable her to function as a channel by which the ancestors can return to the community. My interest here is to look at how women function as members of their kin group and that of their husbands: what roles do they perform and what rewards do they obtain? A study of the male-female relationships within marriage indicates the changes brought about by colonization and the challenge of weaving national identities out of diverse kinship ideologies. It is in these social arrangements that differences between matrilineal and patrilineal structures seem most trenchant. The priority of matrilineal groups is the birth of female infants, for without them no blood can be transmitted and no ancestors can return to life, dooming the clan to perdition. Male children are accepted and welcomed because there are trees to fell and wars to fight.

TRADITIONAL MARRIAGE

The many types of traditional marriages among the Asante have become further complicated by Western secular forms of marriage as well as the religious forms enjoined on their adherents by Christianity and Islam. The co-existence of these forms of marriage and the increasing number of marriages across groups—both social and religious—have made the modern situation a veritable maze of hidden obstacles and barriers.

Traditional marriages are political alliances between groups instead of between two individuals and, as such, the issue of choice on the part of the prospective husband and wife plays a minor role. Royal marriages among the Akan were quite often political alliances that united two groups of people. In marriage, therefore, the private and the public meld together.

The Exchange of Nuptial Gifts

During the initiation of a marriage, an exchange of gifts and services takes place at several stages between the two groups. These nuptial gifts, for instance, the *ti nsa* (a drink, often alcoholic) and the *aseda* (thanks offering), are not seen as economic transfers in the way in which one would buy a slave. Rather, they are part of a religious and spiritualizing ritual, similar to that represented by the Golden Stool, a symbol that binds together the soul of the whole Asante nation. The *aseda* serves as a seal, a record for all involved that a deed of gift has been made and has been accepted, so that in the future there can be no argument as to whether a transaction has taken place. The *aseda* itself is distributed among the witnesses to the transaction. The nuptial gifts hold both parties of the covenant of marriage to the terms of contract. It has been suggested that a legal term, "consawment" be used for this gift-giving and receiving process;[2] I prefer the term "marriage securities."

The *ti nsa* and the *aseda* embody the exclusive sexual rights of the male over the female. Their significance is well illustrated by the marriage of the *Ɔhemaa*. Like all Akan women, she must perform her primary function of ensuring the posterity of the *abusua* and of the whole nation. For her marriage to be valid, nuptial gifts are given to eight pots representing the original ancestors of the Asante. The *ti nsa* is not to be expended as it is the security of the woman who may change her geographic locus to live as a stranger among her husband's people. If there is any dissolution of the marriage, the *ti nsa* is to be refunded to the givers. It is these refundable nuptial gifts that have sometimes been

---

[2]John Mensah Sarba, *Fanti Customary Laws* (1897; reprinted, London: Frank Cass, 1968), pp. 45-49. See also Robert S. Rattray, *Religion and Art in Ashanti* (1927; reprint, New York: AMS Press, 1979), pp. 81-85; E. A. Ajisafe Moore, *The Laws and Customs of the Yoruba People* (Abeokuta, Nigeria: Fola Bookshops, n.d.), pp. 47-55; and R. Olufemi Ekundare, *Marriage and Divorce under Yoruba Customary Law* (Ile-Ife: University of Ife Press, 1969), pp. 14-22. For a religious interpretation, see Buchi Emecheta, *The Bride Price* (New York: Braziller, 1976).

interpreted as a commercial transaction.[3] In my opinion, these marriage gifts more accurately represent a bonding factor that binds two families together. It should be noted, however, that the *aseda* or the *ti nsa* are not reciprocal gifts: they are always given by the husband's family to the wife's family.[4]

Marriage, then, locates a woman in a socially validated relationship that enables her to procreate to the advantage of either her matrikin or her affinal kin. Not much attention is paid to a woman's personal biological or psychological need to be the locus of life. This has resulted in disproportionate attention being given to the processes of initiating and validating marriages and little attention to the seeming imbecility of staying in difficult or impossible relationships—relationships into which a woman might be placed (somewhat like an investment) either by the family into which she was born or the one into which she married.

STATUS OF WOMEN IN MARRIAGE

A woman's status in marriage can be evaluated to a great extent by the degree of independence she enjoys in her affinal relations (those of her husband's family). A wife's status in a viri-local marriage, one in which the family locates in the husband's village or compound, remains unenviable, even in a matrilineal context. The position of a new Akan wife is one of complete isolation among strangers and independence from them. Her children belong to her and not to her husband. She herself is not bound to her husband by *ntorɔ* (spirit), although she must observe the *ntorɔ* taboos of her husband as well as those of her own father. It is in her interest to observe the taboos of her husband's clan because the welfare of her children depends on their subjection to their father's *ntorɔ*. By getting married, the Akan woman has acquired a double dose of male domination and may be in fact worse off than her sister in a patrilineal marriage.

Although a wife in a patrilineal marriage has no political power, she

---

[3]Joyce Nwaeze, "The Blackwoman: Suffering and Smiling," *Daily Times* (Lagos), May 12, 1985.

[4]Ibid.; Rattray, *Ashanti* (1923; reprint, Westport, CT: Greenwood/African Universities Press, 1969), pp. 137, 238.

belongs and is involved because her children belong to their father's group. While both Akan and Yoruba wives live in their affinal homes as facilitators, the Yoruba wife works both to better her status as mother and to ensure the future security of her affinal family while the Akan wife works for children whose fortunes and future security lie *outside* their patri-home.

Marriage simply transfers the Akan woman from one suzerain (her maternal uncle) to another (her husband) in order that she might serve the interests of both kin groups: she provides children to the one (her matrilineal family) and physical service to the other. Whereas marriage confers full responsibility and a measure of autonomy on a man as a member of the community, the woman remains a "subject."

In the playful bantering that goes on in these joyous transactions there is a point at which the groom is teased:

> Fool! You want to go away with this girl, go away with her then; but if she is fruitful and prosperous, she is so for us; and if she fails, she fails for you. If she finds a fortune, it is for us; if she incurs a debt, you pay.[5]

The marriage contract between a woman's kin group and her husband's kindred group absolves her from responsibility for debts and torts incurred by her while the marriage contract remains. This is seen as an equitable solution because her own kin group has lost her services. She now serves her husband who must be responsible for her debts because he benefits from her labor, which consists mainly of housekeeping. He is also responsible for her maintenance and that of her children. But even this position of apparent weakness on the part of the husband is, in actual practice, offset by the strength of his *ntorↄ*. It is important to point out that although the source of authority in an Asante kin group is matri-potestal, the actual well-being of the female is not enhanced. And the ultimate power remains in the hands of her maternal uncle.

---

[5]Note that Sarbah modifies this common understanding as follows: "While a husband is living with his wife, or is providing for and maintaining her, he is not liable for her contracts, debts or liabilities, except for any medical expenses she may be put to for herself or child by him" (p. 39). If, however, the wife goes into debt maintaining herself or her children by him, the husband is liable (p. 136).

The Asante culture provides no more equality of status for women than does the Judaeo-Christian cultures of the West or the Yoruba culture, which is patri-potestal as well as viri-local and patriarchal. The woman is not responsible as a "subject": she is expected to labor in exchange for "protection" and maintenance. The Yoruba and Asante communities have no room for the single woman who is responsible for the creation and disbursement of her own wealth as well as the liquidation of her own debts and other liabilities. A woman is not expected to be autonomous. In fact, in Africa no person is, but society ensures that women feel particularly dependent.

It is interesting to note that an Akan man can recover certain expenses incurred on behalf of his wife if the marriage should break down because of her "mischief." Because she receives no credit for her labor, she continues to be "in debt" to her husband. She is indebted for life to the husband's clan and the marriage still endures even after the death of the husband. As a widow, she continues to render services and to be cared for.

We Africans often protest vehemently against Western misinterpretations that we sell our daughters and buy wives. We say that whatever changes hands is a testimony to the marriage and that is why it must be returned when the marriage ends. If that is so, then all means of exchange—cows, gold, money—should be dissociated from the transaction and a piece of paper with signatures should suffice. Gifts should be treated as gifts, and loans as loans; no refund should be demanded of used articles.

The very idea of "giving away" a human being needs to be expunged. In days of old, we are told, young people of both sexes could be pawned to save families. We are past that. Girls are said to have been "married off" to men to pay off debts. We are past that, too. We are assured today, as we have always been, that an Asante bride is not a commodity to be sold. However, she is a gift. The fact remains also that it is the female who is given to the male and the male who produces material things in appreciation of "the gift." The explanation that the nuptial gift, the *aseda*, is a thanks offering is unsatisfactory. This is a cultural practice that dehumanizes a woman, placing her in bond to culture. Without the *aseda* a man cannot claim damages in the event of adultery, nor is he liable for his wife's debts and torts. The *aseda* is, then, a transaction between men over a woman. The *aseda* is given to the father of the woman by the father of the man; it is never given to a woman.

If the father is dead, his heir receives it. As the proverb says: *Obaa nnye aseda* (A woman does not receive the nuptial gift). In the end, the marriage ceremony symbolizes the transfer of the control of a woman's sexuality from her father or maternal uncle to her husband.

Although an Asante wife is not chattel, she *is* a gift with strings attached, and these strings are held by her maternal uncle. This is seen more clearly in two other traditional marriage practices: the *aysεte* and *kunawadiε*. *Aysεte* is a form of marriage that effectively exposes the subordination of a woman in marriage by substituting another family member for a wife who has died. Usually it is the dead wife's sister who becomes the replacement. A family may even replace an old wife with a young one. To demonstrate that this is not considered to be a new marriage, no additional *aseda* is given for the replacement wife.[6] It is as if wives were cars that were being traded in for new models. The fact that this is a relatively rare practice does not belie the principle it reveals.

A second traditional practice equally belittling to women is the reassignment of widows within the husband's patrilineage. This form of marriage, called *kunawadiε* in Asante, makes widowhood a temporary label for women. A widow is inherited by the heir of the deceased husband as part of his estate. This operates in patriarchal and patrilineal systems as well. If a widow refuses to stay married to the family of the deceased husband (his heir), then her family must return the *aseda* to the husband's family. If any children have been born, however, the *aseda* is given to them. A widow might be sent away without the refund of the *aseda* (given "a divorce") if the heir refuses to marry her or if the heir is a woman. Among the Yoruba, a widow who is very old stays on in her husband's house as an honorary wife and can expect the protection and means of sustenance justly due her for having spent her youth serving her husband and his family.

Despite this implied benevolence toward widows, the fact remains that the woman is imaged as a minor who must be protected and provided for by males, be they from her maternal relations or her husband's house. While the concept of *kunawadiε* as a way of preventing the destitution of widows sounds quite noble, it does not always work that way in practice: if a widow wants to leave, the *aseda* would have to be

---

[6]Robert S. Rattray, *Ashanti*, pp. 137, 238; and Rattray, *Religion and Art in Ashanti*, pp. 81-85.

refunded and widows who cannot afford to refund the *aseda* have no further options. Occasionally, the refund of the *aseda* may be waived by the husband's family to enable a widow to leave, usually if she is elderly, childless, and does not want to stay. Only the meanest of the mean would insist on a refund of old securities in such a case. Later I will take up the implications of these practices for inheritance laws.

These customs give some indication of the complexities in defining and describing marriage in the West African context. Marriage is fraught with pitfalls for the well-being of women and their dignity and worthiness as "autonomous" beings. John Mbiti has described how male anxiety over progeny and their desire for exclusive "possession" of their wives has led to a system of surrogate fatherhood among the Maasai of East Africa who may designate a sexual partner for wives in their absence.[7] It is not surprising that there is no evidence of consultation with the women involved as to their preference. On the other hand, there was an ancient tradition among the Birom in the Plateau State of Nigeria that enabled a married woman to be sexually related to men of her choice. If a child was born, it belonged to her husband.[8]

Location of Partners in Marriage

The inflexible Western formula for a family of one man and one woman plus their children living together under one roof runs counter to Africa's idea of how the human community should be organized. Among the Akan, where one chooses to live is quite flexible. In the late 1930s, for example, I myself experienced the viri-locality of Fante kinsmen in a *pramado* (men's quarters).[9] My mother Maame Yaa Dakwaa (known in the church as Mrs. Mercy D. Yamoah), who came from a matrilineal and flexible-locality background, married into a viri-local group. My paternal grandfather and his brother settled at Asamankese, a town in an Akan area of Ghana and built adjoining compounds. In these *pramado* each patriarch lived with his sons. With

---

[7]John S. Mbiti, *African Religions and Philosophy* (London: Heinemann, 1969), p. 147.

[8]See Toyin Willoughby Muyi, "The Plateau Women: Forging Ahead," *The Guardian* (Lagos), July 2, 1986.

[9]The *pramado* has been described by George Hagan in "An Analytical Study of Fanti Kinship," *Research Review* (University of Ghana Institute of African Studies) 5:1 (1968), pp. 50-90.

the exception of one older woman who lived in the *pramado*, all the other wives, daughters, and other female relations lived in other compounds around one hundred yards away called either *gyaadze* (kitchen) or *mmaamu* (women's quarters).[10] For us grandchildren, the difference between the *pramado* and the *gyaadze* was that if we wanted tidbits between meals we stayed in the *gyaadze*, and if we wanted tidbits from our grandfather we followed the grown-up girls carrying food to the *pramado*. Boys stayed around the *gyaadze* until they began to hear themselves called *okponn okotobonku* (a man who hangs around with women, especially in the kitchen). Girls played in the *pramado* and received tidbits from all the fathers until they began to hear from both the *gyaadze* and the *pramado*, "You won't learn to cook hanging around in the *pramado* as if you were a man."

When I returned home on family business in 1985 the arrangement was the same. While discussing family matters, I sat with my uncles only in the very lounge that had been my grandfather's. A male cousin my age lived in what used to be my father's room. (Even today I find it difficult to tell which cousins belong to which of the three uncles in my grandfather's *pramado* and the relationships in his brother's *pramado* are even more mysterious.) Yet, this is the situation in which some African women find themselves. All wives are the community's wives—except in the conjugal bed, and all children are simply children. There are no aunts, uncles, or cousins, only mothers, brothers, sisters, and fathers.

Another group of my matrikin lived in the same part of town and a third group lived in another area of town, but with similar housing arrangements. Both maternal granduncles were polygynous Asante, who had been brought to those parts by their mothers. In the true Asante fashion each granduncle was *fie-wura* (owner of the house; head of the family) and had his first wife living in his compound. The rest of the wives either had houses built for them as gifts or lived in their maternal compounds. Today, not much has changed. My aunt (Maame Akosua Esuaa—sister to my mother) "presides" over the women's compound where women of three generations still live. A male cousin of my mother lives in the *fikɛse* (the big house, the name usually given to the residence of the male elder) as head of our family.

---

[10]Gender-based housing also operates among other groups, such as the Ga of Accra, Ghana.

But things have changed as well. Viri-localities no longer house all males, as men become patriarchs and move, building literally anywhere in Ghana. Relatives are scattered throughout Accra in a variety of situations. Some occupy rooms in a compound or a block of flats, while others live in detached bungalows set in gardens; however, no home will contain just one mother, one father, and their children. Building a nuclear family takes place amid relatives and household help who live with the family. In practice, the contemporary Western understanding of family rarely occurs in Ghana.

I have told the story of my family in a personal way because reports in research studies often have a tendency to sound like ancient history. The family situation I have described is contemporary. My niece Ataa, who is the latest addition to our matrilineal compound, is an example of a contemporary Ghanaian woman. She is a young mother whose husband lives in another part of Asamankese, and she commutes between our ancestral home and her husband's house. An elderly woman, too weak to go regularly to the farm, baby-sits for the younger women. Single-parent homes are not necessarily an indication of a non-marriage or the breakdown of marriage. They are often dictated by choice or by the necessity to be close to one's wage-earning work. In West Africa, an intact marriage does not necessarily depend on cohabitation.[11]

These flexible housing arrangements are very important for a woman's autonomy. Even the patriarchal Yoruba have viri-local marriages where the actual geographic location of spouses is determined by economic activity and the matrilineal Ohaffia Igbo have a patrilocal arrangement. These marriages recognize the possibility of separate housing arrangements and are not incompatible with the independence of the African woman. This is an important factor for African women today, as marriage (and motherhood) remains the only acceptable state for them.[12] We must also note that it is possible today to have a "Westernized" African man insist that his wife resign her employment to follow him as he is transferred and also his counterpart, the

[11]See Audrey Chapman Smock, "Impact of Modernization in the Women's Position in the Family in Ghana," in Alice Schlegel, ed., *Sexual Stratification, a Cross-Cultural View* (New York: Columbia University Press, 1977), pp. 162-191.

[12]Deborah Pellow, *Women in Accra: Option for Autonomy* (Algonac, Mich.: Reference Publications Inc., 1977), pp. 46-51.

modern African woman, who would not dream of not doing so. If these two modern people marry each other, they will have no problems. The problem arises, however, if the African woman prefers customary practices and insists on not being part of what is moved. "Culture's Bondswoman" can be a two-edged sword, both liberative and oppressive.

CHILD-BEARING

Procreation is the most important factor governing marriages in Africa. This is true whether marriage is matrilineal, in which the woman's duty to the clan lies in procreation to ensure a link between the two realms, seen and unseen, mystery and matter; or patrilineal, in which the man's duty lies in procreating to perpetuate the family names, the only public sign that males are partners in peopling the earth. The situation for the married partners is the same: their positions as husband and wife are secured only by their ability to procreate. At a family naming ceremony I once heard a new father wax eloquent on how lucky his wife was: "It is only a foolish woman who stays in a childless marriage." However, there are a few such women, including myself. Because "the ability to produce a child is a necessary factor for the continuance of marriage,"[13] there is a tendency to turn a blind eye to infidelity, especially by matrikin, if the goal is procreation. One proverb says, *Wosum borɔde a, sum kwadu nso bi, na wonnim da ko a borɔde kɔm bɛba* (When you stake the plantain, stake also the banana, for you do not know when there will be a scarcity of plantains).[14] In these matters, a word to the wise has always been sufficient. It is interesting to note that women's wisdom in these matters is sometimes referred to as "foolishness."

The fertility of the woman is the biological foundation of marriage and it governs male-female relations within the institution. Motherhood is a highly valued role open only to women but desired by both men and women as well as society as a whole; it is the channel by

---

[13]Kofi Antubam, *Ghana's Heritage of Culture* (Leipzig: Koehler and Amelag, 1963), p. 23.

[14]Aboagye J. Gyekye, *Wosum Borɔde a sum kwadu bi* (Accra: Bureau of Ghana Languages, 1984). The English equivalent is "Do not put all your eggs in one basket.

which men reproduce themselves and continue the family name and it is the channel by which women actualize their psycho-religious need to be the source of life. Often, procreation is described as if women are simply "objects of genetic and social transmission."[15] Other researchers have made the point that the actual prestige of reproduction goes to those who "own" or control the reproductive capabilities of women; to this extent, women are not valued in themselves, but only as valuable objects or means to an end.[16] Another negative outcome has been sociological studies that have focused on women's fertility, as if women alone are to blame for the so-called over-population of the planet by their unregulated fecundity.[17]

This revering of women *only* as mothers is shown clearly in African folktalk. By example, a popular Akan saying states that "The wealth and pride of any man are his nephews," not his wives, sisters, daughters, or nieces. A further illustration is a story that appeared in a Nigerian paper some time ago. The wife of an Igbo man (for whom he had paid what he described as an exorbitant bride-price) had run away. His reaction to this crisis in his life was that he was not too worried, because at least for the bride-price paid she had left him with four children. He showed no regard at all for the woman's deep satisfaction at being a mother or acknowledgment of her being a part of the miracle of turning "a helpless thing" into a confident self-naming adult. A mother is often more thrilled to be an active participant in this on-going work of creation rather than in simply giving birth.

When a baby dies, even at birth, a mother grieves, contrary to what some anthropologists say about African women. If babies are not long mourned, it does not mean that the African woman does not feel the loss. Instead, the mother sets about having another baby as soon as

<hr />

[15]Schlegel, pp. 1-40. See in particular the essay "Towards a Theory of Sexual Stratification" (pp. 5-9) for a discussion of rewards, prestige, and power.

[16]Some research, work undertaken in South India by Ullrich, for example, belies these generalizations. Ullrich shows evidence that in communities where South Indian women work outside the home, their productive work adds to their own self-esteem and their value for society. Often the gains of such productiveness are at their own disposal (Helen E. Ullrich, "Caste Differences between Brahmin and non-Brahmin Women in a South Indian Village," in Schlegel, pp. 94-108). For more on this debate, see Schlegel, pp. 15, 245, and 319.

[17]Helen Ware, *Education and Modernization of the Family in West Africa* (Canberra: The University Press, 1981), pp. i, x.

possible for her own psyche and she is supported in this by the whole community, which devises means to ensure that she does not give way to depression. Motherhood for the African woman is not an arena ruled by calculations of reward or power or prestige, categories into which some Western researchers would like to cast it. That approach is a male-centered view of procreation. Motherhood may bring reward, power, and prestige when the children do well, but even if it does not, a woman's psycho-religious achievement is complete in itself: "Personal gratification" of motherhood will ensure that children are born.[18]

African children greatly esteem their mothers. Asked who they trusted most, Nigerian students placed mother first, father second, and wives third.[19] African male students abroad talk a lot about "doing something for mother." Their "talk" has been delightfully captured by Aidoo:

> For most, it was the mother thing. Everybody claimed that he wanted to make sure he did "something" for "me Mother"—"because," they would add, "my Mother has suffered." Awo, Mama, Ena, Maeta, Nne, Nna, Emama, Iyie.... Of course she has suffered, the African mother. Allah, how she has suffered.[20]

Indeed, the agony and smiles that intermingle in the birth chamber never leave a woman. At the deep center of a woman's being, uncontrolled and unknown by any other human being, lies motherhood.

POLYGYNY

If procreation is the essence of being a husband, then polygyny, having more than one wife, is distinctly advantageous. This psycho-religious force seems to me the primary need, more than any other, that keeps polygyny going in Africa. It is likely to continue as long as this

---

[18]Eleanor Burke Leacock, "Introduction," to Friedrich Engels, *The Origin of the Family, Private Property, and the State: In the Light of Researches of Lewis H. Morgan* (New York: International Publishers, 1972). See also Schlegel, p. 36, for a discussion of the importance of ideology and religion to determination of sexual status.

[19]Ware, p. xi.

[20]Ama Ata Aidoo, *Our Sister Killjoy, or, Reflections from a Black-Eyed Squint* (New York: NOK Publishers, 1979), p. 123.

need remains unchanged. My opinion in this area is continually confirmed by various sociological reports relating to population questions.[21] Yet, Westerners and westernized Africans, mostly women, and increasingly rural women, speak disparagingly about polygyny. The disputable nature of the benefits of polygyny were demonstrated in the results of a survey published in the *Sunday Times* (Lagos), February 24, 1985, in a piece captioned, "Madam and the Other Woman." A few replies:

Group A: Contra-Polygyny

1. I have told my husband that any day he decides to bring in another wife I will move out.
2. Our religion says that a man is entitled to four wives. . . I think there is something wrong with that religion.
3. God has designed it that a man should have one wife.
4. I do not want my husband to keep a woman outside our matrimonial home or marry another wife. Since we are Christians we have to stick to the Bible which stipulates one man, one wife.

Group B: Pro-Polygyny

1. I now have children and I have resolved not to have any more. My husband is free to marry a second wife if he chooses.
2. I would like my husband to have a second wife instead of a girlfriend outside.
3. I would not object to my husband having a second wife if he was prepared to maintain both of us.
4. There are too many women outside [marriage] now and I would like someone to help me in my domestic duties which are daily increasing, as long as he does not bring in an illegal structure.[22]

---

[21]See Christine Oppong, ed., Papers of the 15th Seminar of the International Sociological Association Committee on Family Research, Lome, Togo, January 1976; and Papers of the Colloquium on the Impact of Family Planning Programmes in Sub-Saharan Africa: Current Issues and Prospects (Addis-Ababa, 1987).

[22]*Sunday Times* (Lagos), February 24, 1985.

Women of all ages were queried in this survey. All except one were already married and all except four were in monogamous marriages. One of the pro-polygyny respondents had a mother who was a happy first wife in a polygynous marriage. Of the thirty-three women interviewed, none was from the rural area, so this survey reflects the opinion of women "professionals, traders, civil servants, and full-time housewives."[23]

The debatable nature of polygyny is demonstrated by the small margin of difference between the pros and the cons, with some women grudgingly tolerating "the other woman" in the matrimonial home and others rejecting the idea altogether.[24] One Muslim woman (A-2) who could have quoted the Qu'ran (Sura IV:29)[25] argued instead on psychological grounds and from her own experience that polygyny brought such horrendous burdens to a woman that she could only suspect that any religion that allowed it had tampered with God's will for marriage.

In the end, a thin majority accepted polygyny because they recognized its usefulness. Some of these women stated that it was not the best solution, not even for men; they added that if the men wanted to have their way on polygyny, they could go ahead but they must be willing to face the consequences. Those who supported polygyny often dream of traditional structures where everything is done properly and junior wives know their place. They believe polygyny will help reduce housekeeping hours and enable them to follow their own economic pursuits more efficiently. Women supporting polygyny also maintain that it provides "more children for the man" and that polygyny is better than a husband's having extra-marital relations with girlfriends. One woman said that if monogamy is going to drive her husband into keeping a girlfriend, which would be dangerous to the "physical and psychological well-being of the husband," instead let him take a second wife.

[23]I could not find a comparable source for rural areas. The generally depressed state of the African agricultural economy would mean that there are more to feed and less to share in a polygynous family.

[24]It is interesting to note that a number of respondents referred to a "girlfriend," an informal male-female relationship that has no standing in either tradition or modern legislation.

[25]See Azizah Al-hibri, ed., *Women and Islam* (Oxford/New York: Pergamon Press, 1982), p. 216.

One Islamic argument, the only religious support for the system, cited how selfless and pro-life women can and generally are:

Islam forbids keeping offspring from a marriage not well instituted [legal]. I want my husband to keep a second wife with all its attendant problems rather than keep a girlfriend whose offspring will be accepted neither by Allah nor man.[26]

There was also a variety of reasons why women opposed the practice of polygyny, yet only one woman felt polygyny to be grounds for divorce. Some women opposed polygyny on economic grounds because the men could not afford it, and others described difficulties in sharing and the resulting rivalry. Since jealousy and selfishness cannot be ruled out of these relationships, they felt it better in the first place to avoid a structure that would generate them.

A few women blamed other women for pushing men into polygyny. Many of the women were well represented by Mrs. Eunice Nwaosa, a trader, who said,

God forbid this bad thing! I cannot stand any of the two [second wife or girlfriend]. I married my husband fifteen years ago "for better, for worse" and I do not think he has ever had any serious complaints against me. I take care of him well and satisfy him in every way. I therefore see no reason why he will want to marry another wife or keep girlfriends outside our marriage.[27]

Not one woman noted that if women can be monogamous men can also! The women seemed quite prepared to cope with the apparent contradictions of the situation. Only one woman, a Muslim, centered the issue on the demands of religion and the "legitimacy of a child before Allah." Legitimacy guarantees not only one's final destination, but one's inheritance here on earth and one's sense of belonging.

The question of polygyny has occupied more time and space than I feel it merits.[28] The challenge for me lies in a critical assessment of the

---

[26]*Sunday Times* (Lagos), February 24, 1985.
[27]Ibid.
[28]For more on polygyny, see Ogundipe-Leslie Molara, *Recreating Ourselves* (Trenton, N.J.: Africa World Press, 1994), pp. 74-75, 211-212.

meaning of marriage, not only in Africa but throughout the world where the institution is in crisis. Both churches and governments are unable to regulate this most intimate yet public of institutions. It is not whether a marriage is polygynous or monogamous that defines the status of women; rather it is the dependence and domination mentalities of the women and men sharing marriage that need transformation. Above all, I feel that real change will come about when women can say—with or without husbands, with or without children—that the most important fact is that women are human and will find fullness in reaching for goals that we set for ourselves.

DISSOLUTION OF MARRIAGE

Among the Akan or Yoruba, the voluntary dissolution of marriage in terms of divorce is neither wished for nor even contemplated. In theory, the marriage contract is for a life-long partnership—as long as the couple bears children—that brings benefits to both sides; otherwise, no amount of social pressure and tradition could make it endure.[29] The Akan male sees marriage as a means of obtaining continuous service and warmth from his wife and children during his lifetime, burial by his children when he dies, and mourning by his wife or wives at his demise. Marriage enables the Akan woman to channel the ancestors back to life, to continue to obtain spiritual protection for her children (which is said to be provided by males only), and to acquire property (through gifts) to aid her matrikin.

I feel the need to point out that, although the psycho-religious element is paramount for both spouses, the economic gains (service) primarily profit the man. Even the economic gain (property) of an Akan woman is meant to benefit her kin-group rather than her personally. In any case, marriage continues to hold sway over women even if economic security is no longer provided. A key factor in the marriage—parenting—will continue to hold the psyche of the African. We need people of "our own blood,"[30] and even the very idea of an old age among strangers, however benevolent, is abhorred.[31]

---

[29]Antubam, p. 117.

[30]"A hen dies on its eggs," quotes a proverb (*Sunday Times*, Lagos, May 12, 1985).

[31]See A. K. Ajisafe, quoted in T. O. Elias, *Ground Work of Nigerian Law*

Dissolution by Divorce

For an individual woman, the proverb says, divorce is not a disgrace until it becomes a habit (JGC 18). For the matrilineal Akan as well as other peoples who maintain low or non-refundable marriage securities, divorce is not necessarily a crisis, either of family or of finances. For matrilineal peoples, it is the woman and her children who are all important and, after all, they belong only to the matrilineage. The Asante have an adage: "Marriages dissolve, but matrilineages remain."[32] Another proverb maintains that divorce does not bring about the demise of a town (JGC 3435).

Nonetheless, a traditional view of marriage is presented by an 81-year-old rural Ibibio wife, a member of a polygynous marriage, who had been quite fortunate in her entire married life. She said, "Divorce could never be thought of in my day. The wife was regarded as the life-long property of the husband. . . . After all, I gave him nine children." In addition to the entire range of attitudes that lies between these two approaches to divorce—one that shows a certain tolerance and the other that dismisses divorce—is the contemporary and existential situation that divorce and, increasingly, Western-style "separations" are becoming more common.

Customary marriages could be dissolved only under specific conditions, but, as we might suspect, these were not necessarily reciprocal for husbands and wives. For instance, adultery or lack of respect for the spouse was grounds only for a man to divorce his wife, as was a pregnancy from someone other than the husband. On the other hand, impotence or infertility and insanity are valid conditions for divorce

---

(London: Routledge and Kegan Paul, 1954): "Under ancient customary law, marriage was almost always indissoluble as it was looked upon as a permanent social and spiritual bond between man and wife on the one hand and their respective families on the other" (p. 280, n. 1). See also E. A. Ajisafe Moore, *The Laws and Customs of the Yoruba People* (Abeokuta, Nigeria: Fola Bookshops, n.d.): "Divorce is not permissible in native law" and "To the Yoruba woman especially it is beneath her dignity to marry a foreigner, a non-Yoruba. . ." (p. 54).

[32]Christine Oppong, *Middle Class African Marriage* (London/Boston: G. Allen & Unwin, 1981); see the Foreword by Meyer Fortes for confirmation of this traditional Akan attitude toward marriage (p. x). Also see Audrey Chapman Smock, "Modernisation and Women's Position in the Family in Ghana" in Schlegel, pp. 205-211.

for both parties.[33] Significantly, however, to protect paternity, Nigeria's Marriage, Divorce, and Custody of Children and Adoption By-Laws Order of 1958 refused to entertain divorce suits from women nursing a child under three years old or from women with three or more children by the husband.[34] It seems that this was in response to the plight of men who would have difficulty looking after young children and who would want to retain the wife as a child-minder instead of letting her take the children away. In general, the Yoruba frown upon guardianship. Any thought of a wife in charge of his children would be simply too depressing for a Yoruba man; he would rather let the woman stay with him even if other wifely duties had ceased.[35]

The meaning of the "marriage security" was also considered in this legislation. Provision was made for a situation whereby any "dowry" was refundable although it was discounted by the number of children produced and the number of years that the marriage had lasted. This served to acknowledge a woman's past services to her spouse. But does it not seem that this refund turns the dowry into an advance payment for a woman's "service" during an entire marriage, which could last over fifty years?

Dissolution by Death

Severance of a marriage by death, though worked into the Western or Christian marriage rubrics, has no real meaning among the Akan or Yoruba peoples. The ritual of traditional marriage knows no death; this is true for both husbands and wives, although, again, this applies more to the woman than the man. In order to put an end to the relationship established in marriage, the two groups involved in the marriage must undertake the appropriate rituals. The categories of widow and widower are not permanent, but rather describe transitions in the lives of women and men. In any case, the surviving partner is expected to remarry as soon as all rites have been duly completed and they have been freed from their previous ties to a particular person.[36]

---

[33]R. Olufemi Ekundare, *Marriage and Divorce under Yoruba Customary Law* (Ile-Ife: University of Ife Press, 1969), p. 28.

[34]Ibid., p. 31.

[35]Ibid., pp. 41-42.

[36]Anthropologists and missionaries have often given readers the impression that

Although it has been suspected at times (usually by men!) that a wife with weak marital bonds or a difficult situation might have wished to see her husband dead,[37] the unhappy fate of African widows makes this unlikely. The following are traditionally required of a widow:

> When a man dies his wife mourns for him for three months. She must not plait her hair and if already plaited she must loose it. She must not take a bath for three months. She must not change the clothes which she was wearing at the time of her husband's death. She must sleep on rag mats. She must keep indoors for the three months, and if she cannot help going out, it must be in the evening. But such a case is very rare.[38]

What woman would wish to be a widow after she has observed or participated in the treatment given to widows?[39] This experience alone is deterrent enough to any lurking desire to seek freedom from marriage through murder. After the death of a spouse, a widow may not even be allowed to remarry.[40]

Widow rites are intended to separate the spirit of the deceased husband from the surviving wife or wives in preparation for transfer of the wife or wives to another male in the affinal family.[41] The woman does not always actually assume conjugal relations with the new husband,

---

only men die, leaving behind widows. This is obviously not true. Because rites for widowers tend not to be exotic or as lurid, demanding, and demeaning as widow rites, they have been less frequently reported. My concern here is not so much the rites themselves as what they say of woman's being.

[37]Because the kitchen is off-bounds to men, as pointed out earlier, men's imaginations have often run wild as to what goes on in the kitchen. Stories are often told of men (who have good reason to believe they deserve it!) who fear their wives are slowly poisoning them.

[38]Ajisafe Moore, p. 75.

[39]For more on the difficulties of widowhood see Daisy N. Nwachuku, "The Christian Widow in African Culture," in *The Will to Arise: Women, Tradition and the Church in Africa*, Mercy Amba Oduyoye and Musimbi R. A. Kanyoro, eds. (Maryknoll, N.Y.: Orbis Books, 1992), pp. 54-73.

[40]Men have been known to bind their wives with traditional oaths from remarrying when they die or when the wife obtains a divorce. See Kofi Abrefa Busia, *The Position of the Chief in Modern Political Systems of Ashanti* (London: Oxford University Press, 1951), p. 78, and Iris Andreski, *Old Wives' Tales: Life Stories from Ibibioland* (New York: Schocken Books, 1970), p. 90.

[41]Women are never married twice; after the severance of their first marriage, no

but provision is made for a man to look after his immediate relation's wives and children just as he cares for the rest of the deceased man's property.

Although the intentions of this provision are benevolent and humanitarian, some other ramifications begin to appear in the consideration of property rights and inheritance. In a patrilineal system, even widows who escape re-assignment may stay on in affinal homes and even if they could afford to return their marriage-securities on demand. They often do this to protect their children's interest in the deceased husband's family.[42] In any case, a widow, whether Akan or Yoruba, does not stand to inherit her deceased husband's property. The Yoruba woman benefits from the spouse's estate through her son, and is taken care of by either her daughters or her daughters-in-law. If she is childless, though, a widow falls to the bottom line of the litany of the African wife's woes, with no one to care for her.[43] However, this will happen only if she opts for a divorce; otherwise, tradition stipulates that she be taken care of by her husband's relations.

INDEPENDENCE AND AUTONOMY

Practices involving marriage—its validation, the flexible location of marriage partners, childbearing, and severance of marriage contract—have all been impacted by Westernization. None has been simplified by this incursion and in none of the areas has national governments been able to regulate practices at the national level by legislation. In all of these areas, however, one aspect draws my attention—the outcome of these practices on the independence and autonomy of women. Traditional norms are enforced whenever they serve to silence women, reduce or eliminate their voices. My observation is that these traditional systems have been strengthened by Western patriarchal structures as national governments and institutions have been formed.

---

elaborate ceremony is due them (Samuel Johnson, *A History of the Yorubas* [1921; reprinted, Lagos: Church Missionary Society, 1960], p. 116).

[42] Andreski, p. 146; Ajisafe, p. 62. See also Daisy N. Nwachuku, "The Christian Widow in African Culture" in Mercy Oduyoye and Musimbi Kanyoro, eds., *The Will To Arise: Women, Tradition and the Church in Africa* (Maryknoll, N.Y.: Orbis Books, 1992), pp. 54-73.

[43] Andreski, p. 90.

At a time when women globally are struggling to bring about an inclusive anthropology that emphasizes the contribution of all human beings and the diversity of experience, the foundation of laws are being laid in many African countries without the participation of women. While some women are trying to deconstruct the whole patriarchal way of running human community, it is a well-known fact that some women would rather cling tenaciously to the "golden chains" of the past. Patriarchy is not the same as androcracy; as a system of domination it also offers some women privileged positions.

Modernization has had a debilitating influence on marriage and on human relations generally. Customary housing arrangements have been altered by mobility, and few women have a resident parent-in-law to curb the excesses of young husbands. Yet child-bearing continues to be the sole focus of marriage, and is used to rationalize polygyny and divorce. Property and inheritance regulations seem to become more and more intent on marginalizing women except the few who can "go to court." And today, the category of woman called "widow" is often a disinherited species, sharing no part of the legacy of her father or her husband, and unable to have saved or acquired property because she was busy being a traditional wife spending on spouse, children, and extended family.

Faced with such injustice, polygyny may be viewed as a system with the potential to ensure the independence of women in decision-making and to secure for them more time to manage their own economic and social affairs, if indeed they must be married. African women who are ready to accommodate polygyny obviously do not see their men's propensity for plural relations as anything to envy or admire.[44] In my opinion, such an ideology held by men may well be a sign of the underdevelopment of men's sensitivity to the other. Self-aggrandizement cannot be a sign of superiority among humans.

It seems to me that the key to women's graduation to autonomy and majority is tied to law-making, from the local government level to the national parliaments. It must be based on proportional representation

---

[44]Such a polycoitus ideology does not make men great even if they think it does. I find the following proverb right on target: "*Mmaa pɛ mu wo biribi a anka ɔpapo da apakan mu*" (The goat would be king if the display of coital energies were what it takes). It is also interesting to note that Europeans and Americans often think that the African women's response to polygyny should be polyandry; this is simply not true!

all along the line; tokenism will not do. If a local governor can find only one wise woman, then let the local governor form a panel of only one wise man and one wise woman. It has been shown that men and women do have divergent positions on the direction of change, as seen, for example, in reference to the registration of marriage, power, and money.[45] Who should make decisions on questions of inheritance and the management of finances? In the meantime, it is the women, and especially poor women, who suffer, as the feminization of poverty and increasing instability of marriage clearly demonstrate.[46]

During my school days I received a copy of *The Subjection of Women* by John Stuart Mills. Although I read it, at the time it made little impression on me; I am confident now that I did not understand even the half of it. Since that time, though, I have never forgotten its title and have often returned to study it. No other book from my school days made such an impression on me—with the exception of the Bible. Both sources—Mills and the Bible—have convinced me that a more critical approach to women's studies is needed. Closely binding a woman's sense of being to marriage and child-bearing has been a traditional means of marginalizing women from political power. Regaining political power requires the voices of all women: mothers, widows, divorced women, wives, single women. The framework of patriarchy is constructed on many pillars. Each requires scrutiny, but patriarchy itself is defective and must be torn down.

---

[45]Christine Oppong's research in Ghana has unveiled several conflict-loaded elements in modern marriages among Westernized Ghanaians who are formulators of new legislation. See Christine Oppong, *Female and Male in West Africa* (London: George Allen & Unwin, 1983), pp. 144-155.

[46]Ibid., pp. 118-20.

The Third Cycle

Dreams

Bi Nka Bi
None bites the other

The Adinkra symbol for justice, fair play, peace,
forgiveness, unity and harmony.

7

To Deal Justly with African Women

The language used in describing women in both traditional and modern social structures and the position of women in the economy and the society belie the statement of African men that African women are not oppressed. When I look at the mold in which religion has cast women, the psychological binds of socioeconomic realities that hold us in place, our political powerlessness, and the daily diminution of our domestic influence by Western-type patriarchal norms, I call what I see injustice. No other word fits. I do not wish to be pushed to the point where I must bare my breasts, throw off my clothes, or beat pots and pans in the streets, but as an African woman I do want to be given a hearing.[1]

Among the Akan, traditions that melded psycho-religious and politico-economic needs formerly generated a parallel scheme of female power (blood) and male power (semen). Today, this scheme has been all but abandoned in favor of a typically monolithic patriarchy that has been reinforced by colonialism. Our contemporary language has created a mindset in which male and female are rigidly opposed to each other and our religious myths show a bias toward rigid limits for women and mobility for men.

The older understanding of God as both female and male, as shown

---

[1]I've chosen these words carefully. According to folktalk, a curse falls on any child who hurts her/his mother sufficiently for her to "bare the breasts" that fed the child. "Throwing off clothes" refers to a famous women's march in Nigeria in 1929,

in the language of the Ewe people of Ghana, Togo, and the Benin Republic, has been lost in modernity.[2] Today, it is the Western idea that man (the greater) contains woman (the lesser) that has captured the African mind. Western feminism, which is attempting to appropriate the androgynous ideal for language about God and has made strides in this area, does not transfer readily or effectively to the African context. To my mind, Western feminism has had the effect of masking African women's concerns under the rubric of Westernization rather than naming them as oppression.

I have tried to show that there is no archetypal African woman: neither the Yoruba nor the Akan has an Eve. Instead, our creation stories show a communal ideal in which people emerge on earth in groups or pairs. Not even Osun, the only woman among the first set of Yoruba divinities, can be viewed as an Eve. Nor do the portraits of women in African mythology serve as models for us of women's being—what any woman or all women ought to be. A woman is simply a human being; she does not have to prove that her way of being is as human as that of a man. Her destiny as a woman is not derived from a man's destiny.

SO MUCH WORK TO DO

We must look squarely at the realities. We must examine why some African women feel a lack of balance, mutuality, and reciprocity in male-female relations in Africa. We need—at the very least—to begin to study this situation seriously. While I have focused on my reflections on a limited ethno-geographic area, the society of the Akan and Yoruba, we always need to look further and go beyond our own boundaries, as no people or culture today can be self-contained.

To better understand what is happening to African women we should pay attention to the economic factors that affect their lives but also be aware of cultural undercurrents that determine their status. The results of five-year development plans and a decade of emphasis on women's

---

and "beating pots and pans" refers to a women's protest in Ghana against introducing legal categories of "registered" and "unregistered" wives.

[2]The Ewe used Mawu-Lisa as the name of God to represent a God who is both female (*mawu*) and male (*lisa*).

development programs have shown clearly that women's development needs go far beyond economics. Religion and cultural understandings must also claim our attention. Consider motherhood, for example, which is the focal image of "the African woman" in the cultural arena. Church programs can emphasize "mothers' unions" and African artists can augment Christian art with madonnas. Yet to deal justly with the motherhood of African women, the African community must consider how motherhood is expressed and what motherhood entails for the personhood of each woman. Motherhood that is truly satisfying for a woman also works to benefit the society as a whole.

It is important to remember that few African women are expected to resist child-bearing and motherhood, not even if they must die to fulfill this drive. As the proverb says, *Animuguase mfata Ɔkaniba, sɛ wo bɛrɛfere de ɛfamin Owu* (An Akan must not live with disgrace; better to die than to face embarrassment). While we in Africa do not believe in controlling birth, we surely do want healthy mothers with robust, well-cared-for children, and in today's world that means planning. A successful plan must be crafted with the people who will implement it clearly in mind; their worldview cannot be circumvented.

Unfortunately, a communal view of women's being, one which focuses on the community's well-being and coherence, often breeds a cultural sexism that rigidly positions a woman even though it leaves a man mobile. A woman takes her place and begins to work from the time she takes her first steps until she can no longer move about; then she continues to work with her hands and tongue. Her work usually revolves around childbearing and -rearing, but she is never exempted from the economic activities expected of all women in the community.

Any "equality" African women have gained in the past by being co-contributors to the traditional economies of family and nation has deteriorated as a result of Westernization, a system that has introduced the idea of "maintained" women, housewives who "do nothing," meaning women whose labors in the family are not rewarded with paychecks. Formerly, titles that distinguished married women from unmarried ones were not part of African culture. By some strange logic, while an adult unmarried male graduates from "Master" to "Mister" as he ages with no connotation of his marital status, the change from "Miss" to "Mrs." for a female indicates that she has passed from the authority of her father to that of her husband. Whether a man is married or not seems immaterial.

Although the Western logic of "maintained" women is alien to Africa, it has been used to justify unequal pay for equal work and to reserve certain jobs for males. It has undoubtedly been a cause of the feminization of poverty in Africa. The myth of equal opportunity is just that—a myth that does not serve the best interests of African women. Playing fair with women demands that we look critically at women's multiple roles and possible oppression; playing fair with women means that we not take it for granted that women are content with their situation.

Homemaking, for example, is treated as if it "simply happens," as if a fairy godmother does the actual work. She simply speaks or touches and the home is healthy and happy; no physical energy or time or intellectual activity is involved. But this is not the case, not by any means. Since a woman's work in the home is not quantified in terms of money, it is simply not registered at all. Yet it *is* work as understood in a man's world. Moreover, the woman stretches all her faculties and muscles to the breaking point while bringing forth and raising the generations.

The conventions that govern women-men relations, both customary and legislated, are extremely resistant to change. These models of patriarchal hierarchies (economic, religious, political, and social) defy any change—short of completely dismantling the whole system and then re-imaging and re-modeling it. This seems highly improbable because resistance in so many areas prevents acting justly toward women.

Marital Law

Attempts to regulate marital laws have not yielded much fruit since a British attempt in Lagos in 1864, nor have the national governments with their spasmodic and piecemeal efforts achieved much impact on what people *choose* to do. Traditions are disparate; although not formally codified and often presented in folktalk, their clearly understood meaning is determined by those who hold power through tradition and customary law. In rural areas, government ordinances that could have deep social consequences are virtually unenforceable. In urban areas, the context of a body politic governed by three religious codes (Christianity, Islam, and African Traditional Religion) and ethnic diversity provides ample loopholes that are exploited at every turn. Civil law stands helpless before the many customary regulations, and because civil law, put in place by colonialism, has not anticipated their resilience or made any provision for them, it is often totally ineffective. If civil law does not fit the customary structure, it is simply discarded.

The colonial marriage ordinance passed in Lagos in 1864 by the British, who attempted to introduce Western matrimonial laws into what is now Nigeria, illustrates the situation. The law, which applied only to "Lagos and its dependencies" (an ill-defined political unit, to be sure), provided for monogamous marriage without specifying how parties would contract for such a marriage if a traditional marriage already subsisted. As a result, an amendment was passed in 1884 that prohibited the addition of a traditional marriage to a Western one or the contracting of a Western marriage while a traditional one subsisted. However, this regulation was immediately and consistently ignored in Nigeria and in Ghana where this colonial edict was also promulgated.

Marriages in these countries are validated primarily by customary law; great embarrassment could result if one were to contract a Western marriage before going through the customary rites. These customary forms of marriage vary widely. The Akan alone have at least twenty-four varieties,[3] and Akan tradition normally confers the title of "wife" on a woman for whom some nuptial security has been received.[4] Modern Nigerian law, however, stipulates no such security; any "security" may be waived without invalidating the marriage.[5]

British attempts to interfere with Akan customary marriage provisions were usually insensitive to the existence of polygyny, the absence of a common budget between spouses, matrilineal inheritance, and other understandings that were quite antithetical to what the British were attempting to impose.[6] Even to the present time, for instance, the idea of financial cooperation with a spouse has been actively dis-

---

[3]Dorothy Dee Vellenga, "Legal Expressions of Heterosexual Conflicts in Ghana," in Christine Oppong, ed., *Female and Male in West Africa* (London: George Allen & Unwin, 1983), pp. 144-45; Robert S. Rattray, *Ashanti Law and Constitution* (1911; reprint, New York: Negro Universities Press, 1969), p. 23.

[4]R. Olufemi Ekundare, *Marriage and Divorce under Yoruba Customary Law* (Ile-Ife: University of Ife Press, 1969), pp. 1-10.

[5]See T. O. Elias, *Groundwork of Nigerian Law* (London: Routledge & Kegan Paul, 1954), p. 287, for a description of various marriage securities. See in particular Chapter 16 on Family Law.

[6]Dorothy Dee Vellenga, "Legal Expressions of Heterosexual Conflicts in Ghana," in Oppong, *Female and Male in West Africa* (London: George Allen & Unwin, 1983), pp. 144-45.

couraged not only by traditional norms but by experience. From 1884 through 1995, efforts made to deal with this maze have simply failed. One outrageous fiasco took place in Ghana in 1961 when the members of parliament could not define who a wife was because the members knew of various "wives" whose children would be disinherited by any law passed in this respect. They settled on a rubric of "one registered wife" with subsequent "unregistered" wives, which was roundly rejected by street demonstrations of Ghanaian women.

Inheritance

The definition of exactly who is a wife is important because of issues of property and posterity. During Ghana's second republic (1969-1979), when there were women members of parliament, a maintenance bill was passed to provide financial security to wives.[7] This became necessary when the matrilineal system began to break down as land was sold to "strangers" or was acquired by the government. Women wanted the conjugal bonds strengthened so that fathers would be responsible for their own children. However, it is not surprising that none of this has indeed benefited the majority of women. On the other hand, men do gain the usual advantages: they still seek to claim tradition if they want to evade responsibility for their children or to cut their wives from their property, even if their wives have spent their whole lives in conjugal service.

Authorities on Yoruba customary law agree that a Yoruba woman has a right to own property before and after marriage and that whatever she acquired before marriage, including marriage presents, is exclusively hers.[8] However, if during the period of the marriage her husband wants to give her a gift, he must follow recognized procedures; other-

---

[7] The National Councils of Women and Women Lawyers have been instrumental in obtaining reforms that protect women and children from destitution related to marriage. See Arthur Philips and Henry F. Morris, *Marriage Laws in Africa* (London, 1971), pp. 38-66; and Florence Abena Dolphyne, *The Emancipation of Women: An African Perspective* (Accra: Ghana Universities Press, 1991), pp. 26-29.

[8] Ekundare, pp. 24-25. What happens to property when a marriage ends presents a legal tangle, given the varieties of understandings under customary law and further complications ensuing from western divorce laws. See Philips and Morris, pp. 176-180.

wise anything passed from a husband to a wife is intended "for use only." A Yoruba wife cannot make use of anything of her husband's without his explicit permission. Such an understanding makes it impossible to accommodate the Western phrase of sharing "all worldly goods" with a spouse. That provision in marriage law remains unenforceable to this day.

Among the Akan, the property of an Akan husband passes to his matrikin and not to his wife and children. Even within the matrikin there are quite specific provisions as to who will inherit. For instance, whatever a wife helps her husband to acquire becomes the sole property of the husband.[9] Generally, neither a husband nor a wife is obliged to pay the other's debts. (The British colonial government had a riot on its hands one time when it attempted to confiscate Igbo women's property to pay for taxes their husbands could not afford.) The matrilineal Asante exclude men from trying to gain access to women's property with shaming devices to ridicule men who sit around waiting to take over women's property; such devices have no standing in customary law, but as "folktalk" they have a certain weight. (I have long suspected that some of this folktalk eventually becomes established as customary law, especially if it is pro-male.)

Neither Akan children nor wives have any claim to their father's property. It becomes increasingly clear that marriage does not improve a woman's chances of owning property and may in fact stand in the way of her doing so, unless a husband has specifically transferred a property to her during his lifetime and observed all customary processes for making a deed of gift. There is also a curious silence over women's property, except for the Akan stipulation above about property a woman helps her husband acquire. Does the law not expect women to acquire property and to dispose of it by an act of their own will or by law if they should die? The implication of this silence is devastating for women's autonomy.

One researcher expressed her deep abhorrence of these limitations. African societies, she maintains, have not shown any awareness of such

---

[9]John Mensah Sarbah, *Fanti Customary Laws* (1897; reprint, London: Frank Cass, 1968), pp. 6, 60. (Quoted in Oppong, *Marriage among a Matrilineal Elite: A Family Study of Ghanaian Senior Civil Servants* (London: Cambridge University Press, 1974), pp. 31-32. See also Chapter 2 of Oppong for more on the necessity of hearing women's voices.

factors, but yet they determine a woman's potential for autonomy. Concerning the African woman, she writes, "She cannot provide a roof over the family's head. If she does, it is a curse for the man to live under it."[10] Such a curse could be forestalled, however, by simply preventing the woman from owning land.[11] In the end, women are still often labeled as property. When they die, they themselves are unable to leave anything to be inherited (except the clothes on their backs!).

In a newspaper article in 1985, Janet Dowyoro pleaded with women to be agents of "the right type of progress." While holding on to traditional sex role differentiations, she wrote, women can object to their stratification. No hierarchy of "responsibilities and respect" is to be deemed justifiable. Women have to call for "equal treatment, fairness, and justice in the handling of women's affairs." The fact that customary practices are clung to tenaciously in the midst of dramatic social change indicates that some powerful groups benefit from this state of flux. Dowyoro argued that women must know "when and where to draw the line" in the "women's struggle." However, she warned that the struggle would continue until the last vestiges of suppression are eliminated. She concluded, "When the women's plea is acknowledged, women's liberation will then become 'women appreciation.' "[12]

Of course, African women would appreciate it if African men would voluntarily empty themselves of their privileges so African women could begin afresh to build together and to invest one another with equal value. Although voluntary divestment of privilege would be unique in human history, perhaps the African man *is* unique.

Violence against Women

Let me underline that socio-cultural norms generally demand submissive and subordinate behavior of women; this, in turn, makes them easy victims of violence and predisposes them to accept the violence done to them. For example:

> The wife is part of the family, a co-partner in a unit. She dare not lay a finger on her husband although he may beat her. She cannot

---

[10]Joyce Nwaeze, *Sunday Times* (Lagos), May 12, 1985, p. 9.
[11]Elizabeth Obadina, *Guardian* (Lagos), July 14, 1985.
[12]*Sunday Times* (Lagos), December 5, 1985.

take him to the local court unless there is unfair, excessive and repeated *punishment.* . . . As a woman is completely dependent on him she respects her husband.[13]

The use of italics is mine, and I do so to emphasize the assumption that a husband is entitled to discipline his wife. Although I am extremely conscious of violence against women in Africa, it is difficult to find statistics to illustrate its prevalence. Conversations and observations, however, leave no doubt in my mind as to how widespread it is in practice.[14]

The first conversations I heard about female circumcision left me in awe of the dignity that exuded from women whose culture demanded the surgery. When I began to read and to listen to more voices, I realized ever more intensely that one must refrain from definitive statements and certainly from arrogant prescriptions on socio-cultural issues. African women who are studying or challenging such practices tread lightly in their desire to learn and to participate in what they see as a necessary transformation of the practice. Here, attitudes count more than knowledge, and legislation is but an impotent tool.

For the moment, we ask why women affirm a practice that they know has at times been injurious to women's health. A dominant strand in the practice responds to men's needs and women are socialized to meet these male needs. To be a real woman is to be married and to produce children. In some African cultures, without circumcision there is no marriage, so mothers will ensure that their daughters undergo the surgery.

Other bodily modifications like fattening (or in the case of Western women, slimming) are disciplines imposed on women by socio-cultural expectations. Narrow hips, it is said, cannot easily bear children, and in Africa, a marriage without children is an unmitigated disaster. As reproduction is not only a socio-cultural but also a religious duty in Africa, women's bodily discipline takes on a theological dimension. Beauty becomes a key factor in women's lives as a prerequisite for "catching and holding a man." Ornaments in nostrils, in the earlobes,

---

[13]Michel Gelfand, *The Genuine Shona* (Harare: Mambo Press, 1973), p. 34.

[14]Mercy Amba Oduyoye, "Violence against Women: A Challenge to Christian Theology," *Journal of Inculturation Theology* (I:1, Port Harcourt, Nigeria), 1994.

elongated necks, anklets that can only be called manacles and are fitted by metalsmiths show to what extent women will go to please men.

In Africa, wife-beating is one aspect of domestic violence around which a heavy cloak of silence is drawn. Worse, some men see wife-beating as a duty and are proud to declare their compliance. Even worse still is to hear women talk about the beating they receive as a normal part of their marital relations. When this battering is made public or resisted by a woman, she is viewed as disloyal or unwomanly.[15] One other socio-cultural form of violence against women that is even more pernicious than battering by husbands is the verbal violence in speech and particularly in the lyrics of songs. These types of violence against women need to be resisted and transformed as they tend to pervade all facets of human life.

A VARIETY OF PERSPECTIVES

African men are unique, of course, in their open practice of a plurality of wives, even if they have sworn to a monogamous contract and know that the state of bigamy is "legally culpable." These painfully honest, truth-telling African men simply confirm my reading of the power of traditional folktalk and, by extension, the regulations that have to do with women and men. Could it be that men—as the architects not only of their own lives but of the whole community—are above such talk?

It is common knowledge that few cases of bigamy reach the law courts. Few African women would choose to see the father of their children (and their children's spiritual protector) queried in public about his sex life because they (the mothers) have complained. The reluctance with which women conform to the demands of polygyny indicates the reluctance of their sacrifice on the altar of the male ego and their fatigue with playing the "prophet" to the African man. Seventy-year-old Bolanle Oyewunmi expressed this bluntly: "It is not good for a man to have more than one wife . . . when he gets old, he is the one to suffer." She explained that at that stage the wives and children simply melt away, each leaving him to the care of the other, but she added, "If

---

[15]It is important to point out that in some African societies women are more ready to leave abusive marriages than in others.

my husband insists on having other women he must follow traditional procedure and do it properly."

Most African men feel that the status quo suits them fine. For some women, however, it is less than satisfactory and they too must be heard. Although there are many strategies for coping with the situation, in Africa they are well summed up by Folake Solanke, a state attorney in Nigeria: "Ladies and gentlemen, there is no need for confrontation." If Africa seems quiet over issues of the autonomy of women, it is not for lack of awareness of the gravity of the situation nor, as the men say, because "African women are not oppressed." The situation has deteriorated and some men have even become aware of the "barriers to women's progress."[16]

There are numerous obstacles to women's search for an enhanced status in Africa, with a chief obstacle being public attitudes toward women's role in society. In a blatantly sexist and misogynist article in the *Sunday Times* (Lagos), a writer enumerated a list of women's non-achievements, ending with: "They did not even use their greatest and most effective weapon, which is to starve men of sex to achieve their heart's desire."[17] While this writer (hopefully) is not typical, he is part of the "folktalk" and received more newspaper space than did the interviewers of sixteen women. Attorney Solanke is right: it is futile for women to embark on a collision course with men, as one never wins using weapons invented and perfected by the opponent. The opponent who perfected the weapon is bound to be one step ahead of you in violence.

However, frontal attack is not the only means to achieve power over decision-making. Working for the repeal of laws that perpetuate discrimination against women is also possible.[18] In West Africa, this means not only the customary laws but also the colonial ones and the religious ones (Western, Christian, and Islamic). Even more important for women is being present where and when the groundwork is being laid

---

[16]See, for example, Pius Isiekwene, *The Guardian* (Lagos), July 14, 1985, in which he mentions illiteracy and the widening gap between women and men in economic, social, and political spheres.

[17]C. O. Dureke, "Counting Women's Gains in a Decade of Emphasis," *Sunday Times* (Lagos), May 12, 1985.

[18]Christine Obbo, *African Women: Their Struggle for Economic Independence* (London: Zed Press, 1981), p. 147. Rose Muguta, a Zambian, agrees with Attorney Solanke that "men do not have want to have pressure put on them by women."

for new laws. Women who seek change through the political process must exhibit great perseverance because they are continually ridiculed in African newspapers. The flags of culture and religion can always be raised to prevent formulations that are just to women, and the psychological weight of religion and culture cannot be ignored. Both women and men must be present to encode the culture.

There is real fear on the part of some Africans, particularly men, that feminism is bound to result in a traumatic disruption of family life. But this is the last thing any African woman would advocate, because, in the last resort, "people is all people have."[19] People are both female and male. Yet to suffer and smile and say with resignation that nothing will ever change is to maintain that male-female relationships are beyond redemption and that women alone are lovers of life. Such a position does not lead to community building and I submit that whatever does not create community is not in the best interests of humanity. It has been observed that Ghanaian women often seem to prefer the status quo in order to safeguard their own interests and that they do so by helping to keep "the façade of male dominance," if indeed it is a façade.[20] Why, then, do African women rarely say anything threatening? It would seem that deference to male domination is one of their most effective tools for manipulating men. This manipulation of the symbols of obedience lets "the women make men feel like they are still masters."[21]

The only difficulty with this approach is that, indeed, men are not stupid: they often accept the sham adulation for what it is and continue to use their dominant positions to get more power over women's lives. Concrete evidence of power, such as a piece of sexist legislation that disinherits a woman, cannot be countered by lowering the eyes, little knee-bobs, or soft talk. While such actions might get some things on the home front, they will certainly not make a difference in the general scheme of things. On the other hand, South African women, who have been faced not only with patriarchal structures but also with the triple yoke of oppression, racism, and classism, have made progress in prof-

---

[19] Ama Ata Aidoo, *Our Sister Killjoy*, p. 28.

[20] Nimrod Asante-Darko and Isaak Van Der Geest, "Male Chauvinism: Men and Women in Ghanaian Highlife Songs" in Oppong, ed., *Female and Male in West Africa*, pp. 248-51.

[21] Christine Obbo, *African Women*, p. 120, n.1; see also Helen Ware, ed., *Education and Modernization of the Family in West Africa* (Canberra: The University Press, 1981), pp. xiv-xv.

iting from traditional property laws that did not exclude women from ownership and inheritance.[22]

Ghanaian "highlife" songs, one of the most popular types of music, are full of Akan proverbs that bolster the theme of male dominance and the anomaly of "women without men." This absorption of folktalk by popular music to belittle women is not a modern invention, but rather an integral part of the drama of story-telling. As a young girl, I sat with others and sang, "*Kooko aben, nkanfoɔ aben, nea mmaa pɛne apɔtɔnsu*" (the delicacies are ready/all that women want is a good meal), while the boys cast teasing glances and gestures at us. This chorus embodied the whole image of women wanting to be fed with a soft life. Today I see the irony—that a song about cooking and food that women labored to prepare should be used against women.

The positive aspects of male-female relations in marriage that, in the past, enabled women to treat such negative imagery as "good-humored teasing" are fast disappearing. Humor seems to be fading as materialism grows. Women are gradually facing sexism and male domination that, stripped of humor and good intentions, become hurtful. In the face of this, traditional feigned submissiveness no longer works. Conditions have changed; we are not dealing with good-humored, benevolent overlords. In describing some of the characteristics of the new middle-class African marriage, Christine Oppong spells out the new litany of woes.[23] Similarly, Dorothy Dee Vellenga shows how progressively powerless Ghanaian women are becoming in their own lives and in supporting those people they help to nourish.[24]

Nigeria is not so different. In general, women are growing to recognize their marginality in politics and their need to work toward becoming an integral part of the development. Many factors, though, converge to isolate women from the centers of power: their inequality of access to the modern sectors of the economy, the persistence of an ideology of male dominance, an increase in the costs of domestic labor, an inability to pay hired hands or acquire modern technology, the

---

[22]Zanele Dhlamini, "A Black South African Woman's View," *World Student Christian Federation Journal* (1979:1). A special issue, "Women in the Struggle for Liberation," of this quarterly journal.

[23]Christine Oppong, *Middle Class African Marriage* (London: George Allen and Unwin, 1981), p. 209. (Also published by Cambridge University Press in 1974 as *Marriage among a Matrilineal Elite*.)

[24]Vellenga in Oppong, ed., *Female and Male in West Africa*, pp. 144-48.

progressive breakdown of cooperative efforts in the traditional sector, and the conflict in being both wife and employee. Indeed, this is true throughout Africa.

BREAKING THE SILENCE

Any strategy to achieve greater power must be accompanied by "voicing," for if we ourselves do not deliberately attempt to break the silence about our situation as African women, others will continue to maintain it. As we began to raise our voices during the last decade, we heard of the young prostitute who would have remained a wayward girl instead of the product of the regional as well as global mishandling of women's affairs; we also heard of homes in Nigeria where patriarchs who have four wives summon those wives with a system of four separate buzzer signals!

But we must not let our voices grow quiet. Simultaneously with our cries, a vigorous campaign *against* change is being waged by both men and women. In the same issue of the *Sunday Times* of Lagos (May 12, 1985) to which I have already referred as a source of contemporary "folktalk," two photographs were published, the first of two women and a man condemned to death for possession of cocaine and the second of a woman who collapsed when facing the same charges. These were not new photos; they had been reprinted to make a specific point and were accompanied by an editorial that focused on how women had "changed." A short story in the same issue entitled "I Will Never Forgive My Mother" completed the picture of women's stubbornness and misbehavior.

An earlier issue of the *Daily Times* (Lagos) presented an editorial column entitled "Improving Women's Image" that included the following statements (among others):

1. Far from being oppressed or treated with levity as many feminists would have us believe, Nigerian society has always recognized and respected the "God-ordained and cultural roles of our women. Society places no obstacle on their path to self actualization."

2. In what appears their determination to secure equality with men . . . [women] have been engaged in ignoble pursuits and negative tendencies which were once thought the exclusive preserves of men . . . in utter disregard to their being seen as symbols of "morality."

3. Deluded by the mistaken notion that because they are women— the supposed weaker sex, society and the law will be lenient and more forgiving of their crimes. The recent conviction [for cocaine] puts paid to this wrong notion.

Dealing justly with African women must begin with taking seriously women's questions and concerns about their status. Trivializing women's concerns—as is done regularly in our newspapers—does far more harm than good. Women's voices should be listened to when they speak about the God-ordained dignity of every human person and the consequent need of each person for respect. To expect women to uphold all that is humanizing in African culture and yet deny their participation in the politics of family and nation is like asking them to make bricks without straw. In the end, even if this means challenging much that is ingrained in our religio-culture, we need to acknowledge that women are not mere symbols of morality, but that they are equally human. Perhaps, then, we can remove the obstacles in women's paths to self-actualization and moral being and continue on our path to democratization based on the full participation of all women and men.

8

Calling the Church to Account

Saying that God is male does not make the male God.

Because Christianity succeeded in establishing a European image of womanhood in Africa due to the fact that their first converts were slaves, outcasts, and servants, a people without status in the community, the true embodiments of the African image had no chance to influence the new faith and the new system.[1]

There is a myth in Christian circles that the church brought liberation to the African woman. Indeed, this is a myth, a claim glibly made and difficult to illustrate with concrete or continuing examples. Yet, what actual difference has Christianity made for women, other than its attempt to foist the image of a European middle-class housewife on an Africa that had no middle class that earned salaries or lived on investments? The system of wages created by Westernization has produced an elite, a class that serves and upholds Western Christian attitudes and a church that continues to mirror pre-1914 Europe. For many Christians, this description of Western churches is hard to stomach, but it is a view shared by many African Christians who see and experience Africa's present predicament of religious, political, economic, and social chaos.

The way Western churches that have been implanted in Africa look at women mirrors their Euro-American predecessors. As transplants

---

[1]Zulu Sofola, unpublished lecture given to the Conference of African Theologians, University of Ibadan, 1979.

that have never firmly taken root, they have not yet grown free of the attitudes of their "mother churches," nor have they been able to cope with reforms that have taken or are taking place in those churches. Issues such as the ordination of clergy and ecumenism are prime examples, as is their firm attachment to nineteenth-century evangelical theology. Faced with the vastly complicated, hydra-headed challenges of living in today's world, Africa finds little sustenance in the continuing importation of uncritical forms of Christianity with answers that were neatly packaged in another part of the world. These churches, which most often take the form of patriarchal hierarchies, accept the material services of women but do not listen to their voices, seek their leadership, or welcome their initiatives. One African spokeswoman has said: "It is an indictment on the Euro-Christian world that African church women have no significance in the Church."[2]

My criticism of African churches is made to challenge them to work toward redeeming Christianity from its image as a force that coerces women into accepting roles that hamper the free and full expression of their humanity. As with class and race, on issues of gender discrimination, the church seems to align itself with forces that question the true humanity of "the other" and, at times, seems to actually find ways of justifying the oppression or marginalization of "the other." Although nineteenth-century missionary theology has been revised or discarded in most areas of the world, the Western churches in Africa continue to disseminate neo-orthodox theology from pulpit and podium, in academic journals and religious tracts. This continued dependence on Euro-American modes and hopes is no substitute for working out our own salvation as Christians who have a particular culture and history.

WOMEN AND SCRIPTURE

In African churches, it is not unusual to hear reminders of what "the Bible says" about women.[3] African churches, with their many varia-

---

[2]Ibid.

[3]In Africa, generally, the historical-critical method of biblical scholarship has remained within the universities. Biblical models of human relationships, which fit well with the African traditional worldview, have been accepted as unchanging norms for all times and all peoples. It is not surprising, then, that anything other than a literal reading of the Bible is unacceptable.

tions, have not produced a body of official dogmatics hewn from the African context; however, they have developed a theology of folktalk on what God requires of women. Instead of promoting a new style of life appropriate to a people who are living with God "who has made all things new," the church in Africa continues to use the Hebrew Scriptures and the Epistles of St. Paul to reinforce the norms of traditional religion and culture. In the same way that the folktalk of Akan proverbs delineates cultural norms for women, so the theology of "the Bible says" defines accepted norms for African Christian women.

Growing up in Mmofraturo, a Methodist girls' boarding school in Kumasi, the focal point of the Ashanti nation, I remember clearly our morning ritual assembly for prayers and announcements. Each girl, in turn, was required to recite a biblical text. It was our tradition to quote from the Book of Proverbs, Ecclesiastes, or the Sermon on the Mount; Proverbs was our favorite. Proverbs were already a part of our culture and we school girls could easily get away with converting Akan proverbs into King James language and then simply inventing chapter and verse numbers. Many biblical pronouncements that have direct parallels in our traditional corpus of proverbs, such as those that deal with relations in the family, acquire a universal character, which in turn is cited to reinforce the traditional socialization of African young people. (Perhaps the morning ritual in our Methodist boarding school accomplished goals other than those sought by its leaders!)

Throughout Africa, the Bible has been and continues to be absolutized: it is one of our oracles that we consult for instant solutions and responses. Although Nigeria has a budding Association of Nigerian Biblicists, biblicist seems to me to be interpreted as someone who feels that "whatever is in the Bible is true." This norm of biblical usage among African Christians is problematic to me as it seems highly dependent on one's interpretation of "truth." I also question any uncritical reading of biblical texts, knowing something of the fluidity of their many translations.

The Bibles Africans use today are either older versions in English, French, Spanish, or Portuguese, or translations in local languages of these outdated versions. Few Africans, even those in religious studies, read the biblical languages of Greek or Hebrew. Among the faithful who read the Bible, the King James translation with its heavily androcentric language or local-language translations based on it have become the standard. The familiarity of these texts is a veritable opiate that will not be easily or willfully discarded.

To speak to African Christians on feminism, or rather woman's be-ing, I find it necessary to begin where the majority of us (Africans) stand as a people. We keep the wise sayings of the Bible and our African traditions in our hearts with pleasure; we have them always ready on our lips because we believe it is for our own good and, by extension, the good of the whole community (Prov. 22:17-18). It is most important to note that, whatever their religious persuasion, Africans take God seriously. When an eminent Nigerian lawyer was invited to speak about the legal rights of women, she quoted the Bible, interpreting Ephesians 5:28-31. She instructed preachers to: "Place emphasis on love, honor, and care . . . rather than subjugation, for love means security for both parties—in love there is no loss of face."[4]

The expression "no loss of face" raises the serious matter of cultural influences in biblical interpretation. In both Yoruba and Akan, the expression refers not simply to physiology but to one's whole being and personality. In this sense, it is like the Hebraic "face," which goes beyond one's feature to one's countenance. Hence, Folake Solanke was pointing out that just and loving human relations can survive only when the equal value of all persons is upheld. It is the oft-announced Christian principle of *imago Dei* that ought to be operative.

Unfortunately, biblical interpretation and Christian theology in Africa have had the effect of sacralizing the marginalization of women's experience, even in traditional African religions. It is painful to observe African women whose female ancestors were dynamically involved in every aspect of human life define themselves now in terms of irrelevance and impotence. This distorts the essence of African womanhood. Yet, it is generally admitted that the large dose of Christianity that has been part of the socio-cultural Westernization of Africa, especially in terms of women's education, vocations, and the interpretation of marriage, has oriented women to accept the meaning of helper as subordinate.

Although the Christian heritage of the biblical, prophetic denunciation of oppression has served Africa well, oppressive strands of the

---

[4]Folake Solanke, address given at the Religious Studies Conference, University of Ibadan, 1976. A selection of the papers was published in *Orita, Ibadan Journal of Religious Studies* 10:2 (1976). This journal is a particularly rich source of information of African Traditional Religion.

same Bible do reinforce the traditional socio-cultural oppression of women. At this point, prophecy resumes its original character as a voice crying in the wilderness, ignored by the powerful and the respectable. On the whole, we can say that Christianity has converted the African people to a new religion without converting their culture. It has simply appropriated parts of that culture and attempted to blot out other parts without understanding how the total culture functions as an integrated worldview and system of human organization. One can understand how Western missionaries in their eagerness, unfamiliar with African culture and clothed in ethnocentric pride, snatched converts from an unconverted culture. Today, though, must this continue? Must the church continue to base its theology on an alien terminology, using out-dated exegetical methods that enthrone an uncritical use of biblical texts against women?

ON WORSHIP

Visualizing God as male and experiencing leadership as a male prerogative have blinded the church to the absence or presence of women. It has made it difficult—and indeed, in some churches, impossible—to conceive of women priests and women leaders.[5] In the Judeo-Christian tradition, announcing the word of God or witnessing to the "finger of God" was never a strictly male prerogative. One factor that seems to have prejudiced the tradition against women is the primal role of blood in religious sacrifice. In Africa, a collaboration between the traditions of Hebrew Scripture and aspects of traditional religion has effected the nearly total exclusion of women from rituals; this naturally militates against women priests. Even worse, significant exceptions in Africa's religious practices that validate the contributions of women have been overlooked because they do not confirm Judeo-Christian perspectives.

A scholar of African Traditional Religions has remarked that it would appear all religions agree in principle that men and women are equal in

---

[5]Modupe Owanikin, "The Priesthood of Church Women in the Nigerian Context," in Mercy Amba Oduyoye and Musimbi R. A. Kanyoro, eds., *The Will to Arise: Women, Tradition and the Church in Africa* (Maryknoll, N.Y.: Orbis Books, 1992), pp. 206-220. See also papers of G. T. Ogundipe ("The Ordination of Women in the Methodist Church Nigeria") and Mercy A. Oduyoye ("And Women, Where Do They Come In?") published in 1977 by the Methodist Church Nigeria.

spiritual matters, but that women's "religious sense and strong spiritual craving has been utilized to make her yield implicit obedience to her menfolks, father, brother, husband"; thus, a woman surrenders herself to the man-made world in which she finds herself.[6] Rather than admitting that the exclusion of women from the priesthood is unnecessary (obviously here I am not referring to the Roman Catholic church), there is a constant effort to evolve "forms of ministry" to utilize the women's talents developed in mothering, motherhood, and the management and organization of homes.[7] Given the range of varying policies on women's ministry, why do not the churches seek a more visible unity?

For some women, seeking ordination to the priesthood is asking to be co-opted into the ranks of the oppressors: for until the concept and purpose of the ministry change, they argue, women's creative energies are better employed elsewhere. If the church that claims to be doing Christ's work among the people actually repels people baptized into Christ, then we do well to ask questions about the "Christ-likeness" of that church. If the ministry appears bankrupt in any way, it is an indictment that should not be taken lightly.

In assigning roles based on gender, the theory of complementarity plays a negative role for women in domestic organizations and in the church. In practice, complementarity allows the man to choose what he wants to be and to do and then demands that the woman fill in the blanks. It is the woman, invariably, who complements the man. Generally, the woman has little or no choice in the matter—she has to do "the rest" if the community is to remain whole and healthy. This leads some Christian women (and the number of Africans among them is growing)

---

[6]This point was made at a Religious Studies Conference (1976) at the University of Ibadan by Professor J. O. Awolalu. See *Orita, Journal of Religious Studies* 10:2 (1976).

[7]See, for example, the Sheffield recommendations to the Faith and Order Commission of the World Council of Churches in Lima in 1982 in Constance Parvey, ed., *The Community of Women and Men in the Church* (Grand Rapids, Mich.: Eerdmans and Geneva: World Council of Churches, 1983). For a discussion of how the World Council of Churches has "managed" the discussion of the participation of women in the church, see Marga Bührig, *Woman Invisible: A Personal Odyssey in Christian Feminism* (Valley Forge, PA: Trinity Press International, 1987) and Mercy Amba Oduyoye, *Who Will Roll the Stone Away?* (Geneva: World Council of Churches, 1991).

to say that women should be given the same opportunities as men: women should be allowed any vocation in the church that they believe God has called them to.

Some women have awakened to the fact that they have surrendered not only to a "man"-made world but also to a "man"-made God who has decreed their isolation from public life and sentenced them to serve in obscurity and silence. In debates on the ordination of women to the priesthood, it has been argued that the maleness of Jesus of Nazareth and his twelve disciples precludes women from representing Christ at the eucharist. (I've always found it curious that the ethnic factor has not been similarly used against Gentiles.) Maleness, however, has not been used to hedge the table from women. Women can receive the ministrations of men, but they themselves cannot "serve at the table." Does the fact that men serve "at table" in church (spiritual) and women serve "at table" in the home (material) mean that the church has succeeded in making motherhood incompatible with priesthood? Why are spiritual needs separated in this way from material needs? This docetic Christianity goes against any integrated worldviews, whether they are African or theological. If—and, indeed, many African women suspect this is true—it is menstruation that still poses a problem, then the church has a responsibility to deal with this biological function rather than to hide from it or to use it as one more weapon of mystification.

ON GOD AND GENDER

As few African theologians talk about women outside of marriage or family life, there is little awareness or interest in on-going theological reconstructions of the "feminine nature" of God. While some of us women theologians have had and continue to have lively debates in this area, many theologians, including Africans, have only reluctantly come to terms with the fact that to be relevant they have to discard the "lofty" idea that theology is theology—universal and objective; they have begun to take seriously how context shapes what one says about God.

Although the gender of God does not have a big role to play in African religious language, questions of a gendered or non-gendered understanding of God have become a crucial point in the global theological dialogue, and the African religious experience can contribute to the discussion. However God is named in any African language, in the traditional African experience God is not transferred directly or indirectly onto human beings as the *imago Dei*. While the African myth of "destiny" is related to God, it is not said to mirror God in any way and, if it does, the relation is with the individual woman or man and not with the abstract of gender.

If anything, the African mind contains an image of a motherly Father or a fatherly Mother as the Source Being. Individuals are directly responsible for their destinies and they are accountable before God and the ancestors and before history and posterity for how they function in the community in which they find themselves. In the Source Being, there is no question of male preceding female or appearing simultaneously in the collective memories of the peoples whose concern is with the unfolding of individual destinies.[8]

For African Christians, African religio-cultural presuppositions have meant that the fatherhood of God in the Bible does not confer any special priority on human fathers; in the tradition the father's role is carefully balanced by a mother's counterpart. So, calling God "Father" or using a masculine pronoun in relation to God does not unsettle women in Africa. One could say the same is true for Christ, whose historical maleness in Jesus of Nazareth has yet to be interpreted in Africa as excluding women from associating with Christ's role or from being children of God.

However, here is where, for me, the dynamics of the interplay of words and functions begins to give the lie to Christianity. When theologians and preachers begin to argue that priesthood is barred to women because Jesus was a male, I see the argument begin to fall in place and "things" for me begin to fall apart. Why is this clan of male priests being created? Did not baptism replace circumcision? Does my baptism make me less a child of God because I do not have the physiology with which Mary's child was born? Absurd! The church in Africa cannot afford this logic, not in cultures where women are named after men (as I was after my paternal grandfather) and men are named after women. Unable to sustain the menstruation pollution argument—we do talk

---

[8]Barthian anthropology, for example, founded on 1 Corinthians 11:3, Colossians 2:9-10, Philippians 2:68 and 2 Corinthians 5:21 and on the logic of the biblical creation myth is utterly irrelevant vis-à-vis the African worldview.

after all about being washed in the precious Blood of the Lamb—we are turning to abstruse arguments as to the gender of the risen and exalted Christ, our only priest and mediator before God. This is either cultural captivity, in which God's loving intentions for life ("Increase and multiply") become tied to the idolatrous worship of blood, or we have simply decided—by whatever logic we may call it—that women should not touch the ritual of the eucharist—the blood and body of our Lord.

In such an atmosphere the church in Africa must participate in the Western debate on the exclusive masculine language of Christianity. We need to share our traditional African understandings of democracies in which Ruler-in-Council is not an individual acting alone, but one who pronounces "what is good" after consulting on all levels and reaching a consensus showing the road the whole community ought to travel. It may be that we might redeem both King and Kingdom. Surely it is better to join the debate than simply to continue mouthing what we were taught a hundred or more years ago by European and American missionaries.

ON WOMEN

Sometimes African theology, African God-talk, seems no more than a pretentious smoke screen that dissipates on close examination. Apart from South Africa, where apartheid has dramatized what it means to class people according to physical traits, African theologians have not related their God-talk to issues of justice. Hierarchical and oppressive terms like Omnipresent, Omniscient, Ruler, or All Mighty translate into race relations as racism and into gender relations as sexism. Being non-white or non-male imposes a penalty simply for not being born into the group that defines true humanity. Being "non-anything" excludes a person from being fully human. The power to define—to enable a group to name itself the representation of true humanity—is truly an awesome power. The person or group defined is then in a position of non-being that is only active to the extent that it is allowed to be. This is how structures of injustice develop.

African theologians who have used the liberation paradigm to express the church's faith have taken up these structures of injustice, analyzing class (economics) and race (skin color); they usually ignore gender. This has happened, to some degree, because in the rhetoric of the construct, as in African languages, one does not need to single out women.[9] It is the English language (and gendered European languages) that has had adverse effects on the presence/absence of women. It would help if African Christian writers and preachers were more faithful to their African languages, ending any ambiguity in this area by translating what is intended to include both women and men with humanity.

God cannot be said to have brought into being one variety of humanity that is inherently not up to the mark. Our cardinal human sin has always been that of broken relations with the source of our being, God. The result has been brokenness in human relations and in our relation with the rest of creation. It is this brokenness, this inability to touch the other without transmitting death instead of life, that the church must deal with if it is to be able to empower women and men to celebrate each other's being and thus spread love and life. Theology is essentially a reflection on our human experience that begins with our belief in God, the Source Being. In Christian scripture as in the traditional religio-cultural corpus, what salvages all brokenness and leads to salvation—wholeness, well-being, *shalom*, healthy living   is what is inspired of God.

The credibility of the church is not enhanced by any exhibition of sexism in its beliefs and practices. Either women and men are of equal value before God, both created in the image of the one God, or else we declare Genesis 1:26 a lie. If we stand with the text, then the male alone cannot stand for God if the female cannot also do so. We cannot use scripture to legitimize the non-inclusion of femaleness in the norm of humanness. To be authentic, Christian theology must promote the interdependence of distinctive beings and stand by the principles of inclusiveness and interdependence.

The African church needs to empower women not only to speak for themselves and manage their "women's affairs," but to be fully present in decisions and operations that affect the whole church, including the forming of its theology. Only then will the church become a home for both women and men. Since for generations women have attempted to enable relationships and promote life, God-talk and theological educa-

---

[9]When African theologians use the term "man" in a generic sense, they use words like *Nipa* (in Akan), *Enia* or *Aratye* (Yoruba). All these names are generic, like humanity or humankind.

tion remains deficient as long as their life experiences continue to be excluded or marginalized. Male blinders have turned the African church's seminaries into male-run theological factories where the ecclesiastical organization (whichever church it may be, Catholic, Protestant, or Independent) imprints its stamp on all who pass through. (Occasionally, there may be a female member of the faculty.) In this world of rising expectations, few people will continue to take the church seriously if it persists in preaching Christ but does not live Christ. A church that consistently ignores the implications of the gospel for the lives of women—and others of the underclass—cannot continue to be an authentic voice for salvation. Not until we can say that what hurts women also hurts the entire Body of Christ, will we in truth be able to speak of "one Body."

THE SPIRIT

Whatever is keeping subordination of women alive in the church cannot be the Spirit of God. The church is intended to be the ecclesia of all people, women and men, across all social barriers. In the church we expect to experience "reciprocity and mutual respect, support and protection of each person's freedom in continuum with our freedom as the children of promise."[10] When we find patriarchal hierarchies enthroned in the place of all this, we must begin to wonder if we are not closing our eyes and ears to the truth revealed by the Spirit of God.

We see the visible manifestation of patriarchal structures and hierarchies, whether in the church or in African cultures, wherever we encounter the subordination of women's services or a refusal to listen to women's voices. Where leadership and initiative are seen as contrary to the female spirit (or are viewed as characteristics only of rebellious women) and are not encouraged or supported, we can suspect the Spirit of God is being ignored. The pyramids of power that exist in African culture have found companions in Christianity.

The tension these attitudes generate is a barrier to unity and community, yet this does not seem to bother the church or worry the people in the pews of Africa's churches—as long as the hierarchy *seems* to serve the church's interests. "Good" church women, who continue their

---

[10]Parvey, p. 3.

work and service only to see their men and the church hierarchy content, sacrifice their leadership abilities at the altar of the church's unconcern for women. This is a tragedy. Participation in the ministry of the church should be an exercise of responsibility and of full personhood. Inclusiveness as a principle of community building is severely curtailed if women are limited in their exercise of initiative and authority to women's groups, where they meet to decide, to plan, and to work to contribute to the unified budget of the church, a budget in which they may have had absolutely no input.

In my opinion, it is still debatable whether or not the influence of Christianity has been beneficial to the socio-cultural transformation of Africa—and I am most concerned with its effects on women. It seems that the sexist elements of Western culture have simply fueled the cultural sexism of traditional African society. Christian anthropology has certainly contributed to this. African men, at home with androcentrism and the patriarchal order of the biblical cultures, have felt their views confirmed by Christianity. The Christian churches have not encouraged or even accommodated women who have raised their voices in protest. Indeed, some African women endowed with strong voices and leadership abilities have followed their calls to ministry by founding new churches. By and large, it would appear that African women have remained dependent on male exegesis and male theology; they have accepted male interpretations of biblical events as universally and historically normal. Thus, they simply maneuver as best they can within these confines.

Ecumenical experience has taught me that Christian churches in the West are at least willing to examine and discuss these issues. African churches, on the other hand, declare that no problem exists. This must change. The place of women in the church is perhaps the most crucial issue in our century for the total work of evangelization. In the words of Teresa Okure, a well-known African theologian: "The Church cannot afford to continue to preach the equality of all human beings and races in Christ and yet allow its practices to be in living contradiction of this truth."[11] While the preaching of the church proclaims that the "old things" have passed away, the practice of the church clings to these "old things" instead of searching out the "new."

---

[11]Teresa Okure, unpublished papers, Seminar of Women Theologians of Nigeria, Institute of Church and Society, Ibadan, 1981.

The imagining and visualization of God as male has created an authority in the church that wears blinders to all but male needs and ear plugs to all but male voices. Interpreting biblical myths and stories to suit socio-cultural preoccupations, the church continues to absolutize the world of generations long gone. This is not to say that the church in Africa is not conscious of the ethics that accompany salvation in the Bible. Biblical ethics demand that all who would be moral agents, responsible to God, have to be on the side of the poor, oppressed, and the marginalized; God calls all people to defeat the enemies of the *imago Dei* and of wholesome community by a concerted effort.

The fragments of human separations are diverse yet connected. They go beyond the clear-cut pairs of slave-master, Hellenist-Hebrew, metropolis-suburbs, urban-rural, or male-female. All human separations need mending and we must choose a place to begin. The challenges to the churches in Africa are many. In the past, by and large, the church has stood by impotently, unable to remonstrate clearly with God's word. The church in Africa has not always accepted that brokenness exists and this has been shown, for example, in its refusal to see the hurt of women.

Christian feminists call the church to open up its structures to unmask the thinking that sets up patriarchal hierarchies and to enable the divine plan for full human relationships between women and men to develop. The linear, non-participatory way of looking at human community of such hierarchies conceals with a tragic negative mask the beauty and connectedness with the divine which Jesus' naming of God as Father should give us. Christian feminists remember that our Christian church grew from a religion that survived because its earliest adherents were willing to die to obey their God rather than to live in obedience of fellow human beings.

A CALL FOR CHANGE

In Africa, as in other areas of the world, the churches often wait for political crises to make statements, civil wars to work on reconciliation, natural disasters to provide humanitarian aid. The church in Africa tends to be a "rear-action" church, rarely visible on the front lines, and often delayed in arriving on the scene afterward to pick up the pieces. In terms of being with the people in crises, the church in Africa, with the significant exception of some clergy and lay leaders, has usually stood aloof and remained mute.[12]

In spite of the pain and the ugliness of brokenness, there often seems to be a lack of concern in the churches in Africa on issues of woman's being. The church has not joined in the search for a new value system; rather, it has suggested that there is no issue, thereby demonstrating its complicity in the structures of injustice that Western feminist and womanist thinkers are uncovering.[13] This position should be abandoned. The church should enable all people to enter in hope into the struggles of others, to seek creatively to suffer our way through contradictions, to cope joyfully with diversities and with the varieties of being human, and to celebrate them. Liberation must be viewed as men and women walking together on the journey home, with the church as the umbrella of faith, hope, and love. The church must shed its image as a male organization with a female clientele whom it placates with vain promises, half truths, *and* the prospect of redemption at the end of time. Wider vistas of human living are needed here and now.

Since the report on women by the World Council of Churches in 1948,[14] the ecumenical movement has been trying to establish guidelines by which Christians can build a community of women and men based on the vision of cooperation. Although many African Christians are associated with this movement, either by belonging to member churches of the World Council or other Christian movements and associations, little has happened. The literature is vast and yet it seems as if nothing has happened before. Attitudes and hierarchies die hard. When women have made progress, it has usually been by their sheer efforts and against all the odds. One thing is clear: sisterhoods (whether of

---

[12]See Daisy Obi, "The Uninvolved Church," *The State of Christian Theology in Nigeria 1980-81* (Ibadan: Daystar Press, 1985). See also Jean-Marc Éla, *The African Cry* (Maryknoll, NY: Orbis Books, 1986) and Margaret S. Larom, ed., *Claiming the Promise, African Churches Speak* (New York: Friendship Press, 1994). Particularly informative about the current more dynamic involvement of the church is André Karaamaga, ed., *Problems and Promises of Africa: The Mombasa Symposium* (All Africa Council of Churches, 1991), which addresses the challenges of structural adjustment programs and the scare of AIDS/HIV.

[13]"Womanist" is a term African-American feminist theologians use. See, for example, the essays and books by Jacqueline Grant, Marcia Riggs, Emilie Townes, Delores Williams among others.

[14]"Life and Work of Women in the Church" (Geneva: World Council of Churches, December 1948).

market women, church women, or professional groups) have been the backbone and source of energy for women's economic and social change. The very least the church can do is to make a conscious effort to promote and support women's study meetings as well as refresher courses for clergy and lay preachers on women's issues in order to enable the church to understand and to take effective steps against sexism.

To begin with, we Christians who form the visible church must boldly identify as sin the suppression of the full humanity of persons by the use of generalities that in actual practice do not apply to them. In fact, generalities often hide basic inequalities. Part of our search should be for new forms of being together. Most African churches with Western roots have thriving women's groups; although some also have mixed young people's groups, men's groups are rare. I have wondered why Christian men seem to have little need to talk to each other in organized groups. I know from my own experience that the "clients" of the church—women and children—need supportive groups to survive. I can only conclude that the men of the church do not need "to group" because *they are the church*: they sit on the official boards to direct the affairs of the body. The "men's group" really does exist: it is the church's decision-making body to which women and young people must be represented so their presence in the pews will not be ignored altogether.

We must remember that we are talking about more than half the membership of the church. Talking to and hearing one another (more than just listening) will go a long way to uncovering the hurts, healing them, and developing understanding of what is at stake in the feminist demand for a new and higher anthropology. We Christians who form the church will be judged by how we relate with one another as human beings, how we relate as human beings to our environment, and to the Source Being.

To make a difference, joint groups of women and men might study the Scriptures, guided by historical-critical methods that take into account both the circumstances of the original writers and readers/hearers as well as our own cultural, political, and economic situation. By doing so, we may move not only to a better appreciation of women's issues but also of what the church should be about in Africa; with its economic quandaries, political instability, poverty, oppression, and pretended innocence of sexism. Then we shall begin to build a community of interpretation, breaking our old habits of treating the Bible as an oracle used by priests and preachers who tell us "the will of God." Small mixed groups studying the Bible and the issues of our society will work to transform hard-crusted attitudes in a far more effective way than preaching, pronouncements, or protests. Their very existence will demonstrate the community of women and men that is the church.

Women, it seems to me, have survived the oppressive notions of the church by looking on the brighter side. Sometimes we must laugh to keep from weeping. Other times, we can do no more than weep. Yet, women have stayed in the church against all odds. Women continue to be the clients of the church because of their unsuppressible hope that the Christian community will bring liberation from brokenness. Women continue in the church in order to appropriate the healing powers of the Christ who cared so much for community that he died for it. Living in community before God keeps alive their hope that the church will become a living community of women and men relating to one another and to their Source Being.

In August 1998, the member churches of the World Council of Churches will account to one another for what they have accomplished during the Decade of Women. What transformations have occurred in congregations and synods to demonstrate the churches' solidarity with women? The target areas agreed upon in 1987 were church teachings about women, women and poverty, women and racism, and violence against women. Will 1998 (which coincides with the jubilee of the founding of the World Council of Churches) bring a morn of song or will the night of weeping continue?

9

Acting as Women

Hey, Maria, be stationary!
No! My sister, keep moving.

A popular cartoon strip in a Nigerian newspaper once featured the following episode between Big Joe and Maria, two characters created by Cliff Ogiugo.

Big Joe (coming behind Maria): Hey, Maria, be stationary! (Maria stops and turns to face Joe and he continues.) There is an eclipse! If you've any reflective pieces of metal like coins in your pockets, better drop them or you're dead.

(Maria stands and looks on as Joe empties her pockets of all her money and lines up the coins in two rows of five on the ground. He then turns Maria to face the direction she was originally going and with what looks like a "loving" push from the back, Big Joe explains to her):

Big Joe: OK. You're all right. (Meanwhile as an aside): Thanks to the eclipse.

This particular cartoon strip is typical of the relations between Joe and Maria. Good natured but slow, Maria always loses out in her encounters with Big Joe. In this episode, Big Joe, no taller or bigger than Maria, robs her of all her pocket money by showing fake loving concern. As I stand in solidarity with Maria, as a woman with other women,

I can do no other than to warn her: Next time Big Joe asks you to stand still, give the matter serious thought. Watch to see that he *also* drops his "reflective pieces."

THE CHURCH IS US

The African church is a human community in which women are commanded to be stationary. The baptismal creed of the church at Corinth and the Tridentine decision to grant women souls demand that women assert and put into practice their intrinsic worth before God as being equally human with men.[1] We women must take our lives into our own hands, as men have always done. To be able to give an account of ourselves, we must respond to God with our own voice. It will not do for us to say to God (or ourselves), "The men you gave me dictated what my talents ought to be or what I did for your church." As the first Jews who followed Christ's way declared, their obedience was to God instead of to humankind. We women must insist on having the opportunity to participate in the church according to our God-given talents rather than according to the dictates of men. We must offer the church what we feel able to, so that we might conscientiously work out our own salvation without any gender-based constraints imposed on us by a particular culture. Theocracy should be salvific *and* liberating. Any theocracy, however, can be distorted by a patriarchal lens to oppress or dehumanize women. When this happens, men are also debased and sexism rears its head even among men otherwise committed to freeing the oppressed and searching out the humanness of "the other."

READING THE BIBLE

Our lifestyle as Christian women is shaped not only by traditional imagery of religion, culture, and society but also by the incorporation of Western colonial norms in the teaching of the church. In Africa, Pauline language has been used to set the tone for a theology of order

---

[1]It is significant to point out that men admitted this fundamental principle not so that women might have as much human value as men, but so that women might equally stand before God's judgment and answer as persons.

and of gender. Because of its widespread treatment of the Bible as an infallible oracle, the church in Africa is slow to change its attitudes, and this is particularly true of its attitudes toward women.

Africans, so adept in our culture of orality, have a prodigious memory for what "the Bible says" just as we do for our myths, tales, and proverbs. With our finely tuned ears and memory, prooftexting can be an easy but nonetheless lethal tool as we pull passages from our memory and recite them at will. This lack of *contextual* reading of the Bible has meant, for example, that we misinterpret passages from Genesis 3 or that we are able to ignore studies that show that Paul's language about women is not part of an exclusive revelation to Paul, nor is it exclusively or specially "Christian." It follows that if most learned writers of Paul's time used the same language, Paul's words on women are not necessarily a direct message from God to the church. Similarly, problems of same-sex love, which made Paul clamp down on women's freedom in Christ, were also discussed by his contemporary Jews, Greeks, and Romans.[2]

Another factor that African women should not overlook is that, generally speaking, those who advocate ideas that are initially liberative often revert to more conservative positions. This is shown in the way in which Paul contradicts his original message of freedom in Christ Jesus (Gal. 3:28) and reverts to a language of subordination of women, which conformed with that of his contemporaries. Similarly, after the death of Muhammad, Islam turned away from his visions for women's humanity and personhood.[3]

It is crucial that Christian women be aware that what men *claim* the Bible and other sources of religious teaching, for that matter, say is not necessarily definitive. Wide variations in translations and the facile manipulations of those translations are sufficient reasons for us to listen very carefully and to continually raise questions.[4] Women cannot leave Bible translation, study, or interpretation to an all-male clergy.

---

[2]See Bernadette Brooten, "Paul's Views on the Nature of Women and Female Homoeroticism," in Clarissa W. Atkinson, Constance H. Buchanan and Margaret R. Miles, eds., *Immaculate and Powerful* (Boston: Beacon Press, 1985), pp. 61-87.

[3]Azizah al-Hibri, ed., *Women in Islam* (Oxford: Pergamon Press, 1982), pp. vii-x.

[4]Compare, for example, translations of Jeremiah 31:22 in the Jerusalem Bible, the Revised Standard Version, or the New English Bible; or study men's manipulations of the Eve story in the Qur'an and Hadith. An example in African tradition may be found in the story of Anowa. Anowa's childlessness was due to her

We have Bible scholars who are women and they are increasing in number. We must support them and listen to them.[5] But most important of all, we must begin to question and to do our own thinking. Each of us has a duty to contribute to theological thinking. Leaving theology in the hands of an all-male caste whose pronouncements on the Bible are hardly ever questioned—not by men, and certainly not by us women— is to be content to respond to God through others.

We have to study the Bible ourselves with our own life experiences as the starting point. That is what the authors of the Bible did. Indeed, the Bible gathers together theologies made up of experiences of individuals and whole communities over hundreds of years to answer the questions: What is God doing? or, What is God saying to us? Even though biblical times are removed from us by nearly two millennia, we believe that God continues to work and to talk to us through the Bible, a human story with events, scenes, and beliefs, some of which we feel very close to as Africans. As we review and record our own experiences of God, we begin to write a "new book" of how God deals with today's world and its peoples. Nothing lies beyond the scope of this "African Testament."

We women must reread the Bible to seek guidance on how to listen to God and to recognize where God is at work in our world today. Although today's issues may at times appear different, they are nonetheless the same fundamental human dilemmas, such as the meaning of marriage, the value of human relations, the nature of sin, the functioning of grace. As women, we need to engage in a continuing synthesis of our past experiences and present possibilities instead of simply accepting the dogmas and lifestyles imposed upon us by religion or culture. So we read the Bible, remaining always open to the voice of God and knowing that what works in one situation or time period does not necessarily or always work in another.

Take, for instance, the women we meet in the Bible. Study them as individual women who lived in a particular place at a particular time. There is no one image of woman, just as we found no single image of

---

"restlessness" rather than to Ako's impotence, which remained a secret between him and the Diviner.

[5]See the work, for example, of Teresa Okure (Nigeria), a New Testament scholar specializing in the Gospel of John, or of Musimbi Kanyoro (Kenya), Joyce Tzabede (Swaziland), or Bette Ekeya (Kenya).

woman in the Akan-Yoruba folktalk. Some we will admire, some we will not. And, if we study in a group, then we must honor the choices and interpretations of other women. Dialogue informs any vision of society. If we conclude that we women have little in common except that we are all female and thus the center of new life—the potential of being the "mother of all life," we still share a biological gift that makes women life-affirming and life-loving.[6]

We do not, of course, always find women in the Bible who provide answers for the problems of today. But we do find women who inspire *us* to devise the answers. Although Hebrew women could not be priests, they could be prophets. African Christian women today can be both prophets and priests. In the past and today, our presence as mediums with therapeutic powers and our powers of dreams, visions, and prophesies have been interpreted as attempts to exercise power over others. Such an interpretation is detrimental to the work of priest-healers of Africa, a number of whom are women.[7] This could lead to our religious roles, such as they are, becoming further demeaned, suspect, marginalized, or even outlawed by future legislation. But if women appropriate both our Christian and African heritages, we can be social commentators on behalf of justice and true religion as well as cultic functionaries. We can be prophets in our churches like Anna, who saw in the baby Jesus the vision of a New World (Lk. 2:36-38), as well as prophets like the *Ahemaa* and the *Iyalode* who stood for social justice and women's participation in political decisions.

WOMEN AND RELIGIOUS RITUAL

When women seek to participate at the Christian communion table, a fundamental problem surfaces that seems to go back to the sacrificial rituals of primal religions, including those of Africa. The Holy Table

---

[6] I always think of the women in Exodus, the Egyptian midwives, the mother and sister of Moses, the princess of Egypt. These typically nameless women were God's chosen ministers in bringing about the Exodus liberation. And so many other women made decisions that affected Hebrew history: Tamar, Rahab, Deborah, Ruth, Esther, Elizabeth, Mary of Nazareth, to name a few.

[7] Kofi Appiah-Kubi, *Man Cures, God Heals: Religion and Medical Practice among the Akan of Ghana* (Totowa, N.J.: Allanheld Osum Publishers, 1981), pp. 35-71, 81-125.

was reserved in the early church for an exclusively male priesthood, a community that obviously excluded women. Yet, the Holy Table attempts to become a communion table of the entire Christian community by the generous invitation made by priests at the altar, which enables women to come forward to share the meal. In some churches in Africa, the synthesis of Hebrew Bible teachings with the traditions of African religion prevents women who are life-giving—those who are menstruating or those who have just given birth—from participating in this life-giving table. Why do women need a rite of purification after birth? Why does Christianity not celebrate this life-givingness? Should not African women in the church question this ritual and seek to demystify the patriarchal ideologies that tend to marginalize women?

Akan myths of *ntorɔ* incorporate some of this same identification of what is spiritual with what is male. Two different myths of origins tell of how an animal (a python or a crocodile) teaches human couples how to copulate and then the myths associate that animal with the engendering of life and with semen. In this way, a patriarchal psychospiritual power is established. Both the child and the mother must submit to the father's spiritual power and oversight in order to have a stable life.[8] So although we can quibble about whether or not the Supreme God has a genderless imagery, the immediate spirit that guides one's life is male, what I am prone to call a literal case of "phallocracy."

As Christian women we do have a precedent. Jesus once asked his followers, "Who do you say that I am?" Asked such a question, we have no need to echo anyone else's findings about God: we can raise our own voice. For me, Jesus Christ as Lord does not permit *any* priest, man or woman, to lord it over the church. Jesus specifically excluded oppressive hierarchies that were operated by a self-serving leadership. In the same way, the phrase "God is Father" means that God is like the male spirit that "made my head" and guards it. But the source of my being is *abadae* (womb compassion) and no man or woman can represent God to me who does not exhibit what I see of God. It is the man or woman who acts to set things right, who fills the poor with good things

---

[8]Rattray quotes an Asante proverb, *Die wahye wo ti sene ono na obo no* (The person who puts a pot over your head is the one who breaks it). The proverb is interpreted to mean that the father makes the child's personality and protects or even molds the child's head; if a child gets on the father's wrong side, the father can also destroy the child. (*Religion and Art in Ashanti* [1927; reprint, New York: AMS Press, 1979], p. 51.)

and sends the rich away empty-handed who is God-filled; such people create "good" from chaos and ugliness. People who respect my person enough to call me to the responsibility of being about "good" are the people who are godly.

For me, therefore, the grammar of the gender of God is not the heart of the matter. It becomes so only when the male imagery of God is used as a tool of patriarchal oppression to dampen the spirits of the sisterhood or to draw boundaries around women's participation in the church's ministry. If our imagery of God continues to be that of a male and father, then we must remember that God safeguards our autonomy as persons and our freedom to live as responsible human persons.

African society is organized in such a way that all able-bodied persons work almost as soon as they can walk; when they can no longer walk, they still function as a source of wisdom and as the storehouse of the collective memory of the family. Because of this, it was not easy to marginalize (and thus control) any group of people. While women were obviously neither physically nor intellectually weak, their one distinctive physical characteristic was the biological factor of menstruation and parturition. Historically in Africa, as communities became more and more centralized and gravitated to increasingly larger units, women were left behind in the homes, and control through the "government" moved into centralized administrative facilities. It is interesting to observe the same process in church development: the earliest churches were in homes with women presiding; eventually, they gathered together under an all-male curia in Rome.[9] This is true of other patriarchies as well.

In the history of our Akan communities, menstruation became a focus of mystification and played a negative role in women's participation. It continues to function this way in African Christianity. If the church dares to label God's chosen creative process as unclean, should not women work to strip menstruation of this mystification? The church has set up an idolatrous system around a god of "purity" who does not seem to have anything to do with justice and right-doing and who lacks respect for baptism and all that it means in the Good News of Jesus Christ.

---

[9] Elisabeth Schüssler Fiorenza, *In Memory of Her: A Feminist Theological Reconstruction of Christian Origins* (New York: Crossroads, 1983), pp. 288-294 (on the patriarchalization of church and ministry) and pp. 309-315 (on the genderization of ecclesial offices).

When we examined African Traditional Religion, we questioned why women must wait until their creating fountain dries up before they can participate in life-seeking and life-affirming rituals. Perhaps what I have called the god of "purity" is instead the god of male being, establishing norms of being human. Traditional Akan thinking matched and balanced the bloodless semen power of *ntoro* with the female blood power. Does the church have a female-counterpart to provide balance for its all-male clergy? Instead of being oriented toward what is love and all that we think of as godly and god-ward, we women await men to tell us just what limits to observe. We have allowed patriarchy to breed and thrive unchallenged in the church. At this point, I begin to understand why some women have argued that using male language to talk about God has in fact made God male and as a result excluded women from full humanity. We should ask why widows and celibate women were accepted in the ministry of the early church. Do men claim the most active years of women's lives for *their* service and leave the residue for God? Should women accept this scheme for our service in the church? We need to do a thorough job of filtering Christianity to determine what really liberates us to be the church.

ON LOVING OTHERS

Women have begun to see women's complicity in the situation. They have surrendered not only to a man-made world but also to a man-made God who has decreed the isolation of women from public life and sentenced them to serve in obscurity and silence.[10] If, indeed, we are accomplices to our own marginalization, we have to find out why. We African women have been brought up, and folktalk has been part of our education, to be devoted daughters, sisters, wives, and mothers, to always love others more than self. It seems to me that in this process we have also learned to vote against the self, always preferring others and loving them more than we love ourselves, doing for them what we decline to do for ourselves because we consider ourselves unworthy of such attention. We have been content to work for, rather than with, children, spouse, and other relatives. We have declined to exercise power

---

[10]Walter Davis, *Orita, Ibadan Journal of Religious Studies* 10:2 (1976), pp. 122-46.

over others; this in itself is just as well, but in the process we have also given up power over our own lives. The result is that we are in the process of losing our voices, even though, as the proverb says, our tongues are stronger than other muscles.[11] We have reduced ourselves at times to moving to the streets in protest or to employing "power" in other ways; it is disturbing that we seem to glory in these situations. In my opinion, such ploys are demeaning. Instead we should seek to accrue dignity and respect for our persons and personalities. I often ask myself why women should be placed in positions where we have to feign submission to men. Where are dignity and respect for oneself and for others?[12]

This abdication of autonomy is exalted in many cultures as a hallmark of "the virtuous woman." Even if our divestiture of self or power and our acceptance of the need to have a male as the head have been voluntary, we should still question why gender is the ultimate distinction between human beings? Other qualities—those that determine how we interact with other human beings and with our environment—seem far more significant. Instead of congratulating ourselves for knowing how to "get our way," we should seek ways of achieving our common goals while being true to ourselves and to others; if we cannot achieve our goals without pretense, then perhaps we should take another look at our goals.

We desecrate our life-giving function if our kitchens with their pots and pans or our sexuality become arenas for exercising control over others, rather than ways of sharing and participating in life. Instead of prostituting our kitchens or profaning our bodies, church women would do well to loosen our tongues and raise our voices telling aloud our real hurts and seeking redress. Using the kitchen or the bedroom is simply playing the man's game. When market women have been really pushed by unrealistic taxation or price control, they have taken to the streets in protest. We must ask, though, why women were not present in the first place when these decisions were being made.

---

[11]The Akan proverb, *Tɛkerɛma bediɛ, ɛfa adiɛ sen ahoɔdenfo* (The female tongue achieves more than brawn can accomplish), recognizes the diversity of approaches to solutions (Robert S. Rattray, *Ashanti Law and Constitution* [1911; reprint, New York: Negro Universities Press, 1969], p. 16).

[12]For a discussion of women's "ploys for power," see Christine Obbo, *African Women: Their Struggle for Economic Independence* (London: Zed Press, 1981), pp. 144-151.

African women have always been sensitive to the coherence of the communities to which we belong; we have hidden the violence the system does to us even from ourselves. Our *afisɛn* (domestic affairs) are never washed and hung outside. Our preoccupation has been with the integrity of family life. We have been content to spoil our children, our husbands, and anyone else who has come our way. The result is that our services are now taken for granted and even demanded.[13] Yet, when we have carried on even under extreme hurt, we have often been rewarded with more sexist exploitation, a situation in which we are made to believe that it is even more blessed to love others more than ourselves. We forget then that being human is having and exercising a choice. Judged by traditional reciprocity, we are being most "*un*african" by loving people more than they are prepared to love us.

The existential situation of women in Ghana is one of gradually crumbling traditional social support systems that make it difficult if not impossible for women by themselves to be the custodians of tradition. While women, in their bondage to culture, have been working at the task of replenishing the communal bowl, men have often preferred to seek individual advancement. As custodians of communal land, men continue to move women off farmlands to sell the land to monied investors—hence, the continuing disintegration of the system.

As culture's bondswomen, we have tried to follow traditional principles within a world that is fast changing and among people who themselves show unwillingness to keep their side of tradition. Reflecting on a radio program urging women to stay at home, I said to myself that it is the professional women and salary earners who can afford modern institutions like childcare who go on the radio telling all women that their first duty is to their home, husband, and children. We create a situation of conflict if we do not see that the woman with one child on her back and perhaps another in tow as she peddles tomatoes and peppers throughout the day is also doing her duty. We Christian women, and particularly those of us who are part of the educated urban elite, might be creating a new African woman who will end up carrying the burdens of the Western woman on top of her traditional ones. As we re-image our womanness, we must remember that women need to stand

---

[13]I do grow concerned from time to time with one issue: Why, in the midst of this, do we seem to enjoy a perverse kind of power? Has our monopoly of caring turned it into a tool for seeking power?

by women and that, contrary to our proverbial sayings, all women are not the same. Celebrating both unity and diversity, women can stand together.

WOMEN SUPPORTING WOMEN

"If we do not know where we are going to, at least we know where we are coming from," says the Yoruba proverb. Our past, where we are coming from, did have ways of supporting women. Traditional society worked for women through networks of kindred, friends, wives of an affinal home, women selling the same commodity, or women passing on skills of pottery, weaving or beadwork. Whether it was a birth, marriage, or funeral, Yoruba women got together and worked. Women supported women, standing in solidarity as women. How can we adapt this traditional experience to help us in these changing times, knowing that its bifocal system (one male and one female) of community organization was partly responsible for the resilience and strength of women in traditional society? Its bifocal nature may help us discover or evolve aspects that will enable our effectiveness as women in modern structures and give us access to decision-making. With our collective strength—numerical, financial and cerebral—we can draw on this bifocal system to gain entry into political structures to help formulate laws under which we all can live as free and responsible human beings.

As church women, perhaps we should transform Mothers' Unions into Women's Unions to gain inclusiveness and a better representational voice in the assemblies of the church. We must remember that the ecclesiology that marginalizes us as women is built upon theories of exclusion. We cannot heal breaches within the Christian community if we ourselves operate exclusive structures. The African Instituted churches[14] have shown us a direction to follow as, for example, Captain Abiodun and others who have claimed the early and medieval Christian tradition of women leaders founding religious houses. By enabling and empowering women, women as a whole will achieve a

---

[14]These churches established and led by Africans have been variously labeled as Separatist, Prophetic, Indigenous, Independent, Charismatic, and so forth. Many of them have come together in an all-Africa body with the name "Organisation of African Instituted Churches."

stronger presence and a voice that will be heard. Standing as individuals our oppression readily weighs us down, one by one. But when we Christian women stand by other women, we are not only following traditional African structures and women in church history, we are also following Elizabeth, the cousin of Mary, the older woman who believed the pregnant virgin's fantastic tale. The bonding of Mary and Elizabeth was so liberative that it enabled a virgin with child to put away fear and shame to declare that God had done great things to her. Their bond of solidarity becomes ours.

This growing solidarity of sisterhoods around the world enjoins us to not allow a precious heritage to atrophy and die. West African women need to listen to their sisters from other parts of the African continent. We need to take on our share in enabling others to recover their own worth as women and to empower other women to survive and struggle against injustice. Asian peasant women and factory workers, the landless women of Latin America, and the lace makers of Switzerland all endure oppression peculiar to our gender. Their stories and ours are one. That women are an underclass is a global reality, for what is crucial is for us to be clear on the point that being universal does not make sexism a manifestation of the will of God.

Gender binds us together in many ways. The taboos of sexuality among Westernized Christian women in Africa continue to show up in our encounters in society. So intimidated have we been that we have not even asked the church to reevaluate menstruation and pregnancy in relation to eucharistic ministry. Yet our participation is crucial. During informal conversations we women have sometimes shown as much unease about pregnant women at the Holy Table. If we ourselves regard pregnancy as an unholy state, we can contribute nothing to the discussion of the ordination of women priests or pastors. If we continue to associate coitus with defilement or to accept the supposed double defilement that comes with bearing a girl, we hold on to traditional religious beliefs of pollution and see ourselves as the major pollutants. It is the women who must initiate rational discussion of these subjects in the church and the academy. Our responsibilities for community education are clear.

Another area in which our voices are silent is the treatment of single and childless women whose grim fate undermines the solidarity of all women and serves to uphold patriarchal norms. The easy labeling of women as prostitutes evades the whole issue of the defiling male. If we open up these issues we shall unmask the patriarchalization of the economy, the political structure, and the absence of effective educational structures for girls that collude to throw girls into the streets. Studies in other countries, especially in Asia, have uncovered the close link between prostitution and the burdens of young girls and women who have to support members of their family, often their parents. These are women who, like Rahab, are concerned not so much with their own survival and finery—as we very smugly judge them—but for the survival of others whom we do not see in the streets.[15]

Our sisterhood of concern must keep these issues of the unequal burdens of women in the public sphere in order to tackle the roots of the problem. These marks of patriarchal oppression are evident even in the transfer of northern Euro-American industries to southern third-world countries where profits are multiplied as factory hands—the majority of whom are women—receive paltry wages. The problems, religious, social, and economic, are complex, but this is no excuse to do nothing. We must be able to recognize and name patriarchal oppression.

Because we are human and participate in structures of class and race, there are oppressors and oppressed among us as well. Women in high positions, having strength of character and being loyal to tradition, can be either negative or positive assets in our liberation struggle. Similar to the *Ɔhemaa* or the *Iyalode*, they are close to the centers of power. Yet, if they become isolated from other women or, like Jezebel, are uncritical of the prevailing roles of women, then they are bound to hurt the women's cause. It was Jezebel's uncritical appropriation of her own culture, coupled with insensitive universalizing of that culture's demands that prompted her actions (2 Kings 21:1-29). Sarah was also a culture-bound woman in an authority role. Oppressed by a culture that put no value on childless women, she in turn became oppressor to Hagar, whom both she and Abraham exploited under the patriarchal provisions of their times (Gen. 16:1-16; 21:8-21). Cruelty between and among women is often cited to dismiss our just demands or to muffle our voices. We must continually struggle to transcend the structures of

---

[15]For a brief but comprehensive discussion of the causes of prostitution in Zaire, see "Human Sexuality, Marriage, and Prostitution" by Bernadette Mbuy-Beya in *The Will To Arise: Women, Tradition, and the Church in Africa* (Maryknoll, N.Y.: Orbis Books, 1992), pp. 155-179.

race or class and any forms of oppression when we relate to other women. The "suicide" of both race and class is necessary for effective solidarity among women.

An analysis of the patriarchal hierarchy shows that we have survived at the bottom of the pyramid by building our own pyramids of hurt within that sub-structure. Imagine patriarchy as a big conical structure within which several other conical structures of oppressive hierarchies fit. At the bottom of each cone will be women. In Africa we have a special cone, the "Ideal Woman," at the bottom of which is the childless prostitute and, sitting comfortably at the top, the wife who is the mother of sons and daughters. Church women's groups can begin here to break the silence around this women's patriarchally controlled valuation of themselves. Polygynous marriage seems to provide an obvious starting point as such a marriage visibly groups women together in a hierarchical order. Serious studies by women of polygyny as a system will uncover its strengths and weaknesses as a human organization. If we cannot find ways to work out conditions under which it can be life-promoting, then we should find ways of ending it in order to eliminate the psychological burdens it imposes on women, children, and men. Simply to acquiesce because men want this system in which women must marry and have children shows the extent of our domestication and alienation from our own humanity. Acquiesence to this form of patriarchy does not seem to me to work toward building a just and loving community.

As we search for solidarity, we should examine how solidarity among women in Egypt was God's instrument to bring about the Exodus as Hebrew mothers and Egyptian midwives collaborated to save baby boys. One specifically privileged woman (an Egyptian princess) collaborated with a slave woman (mother of Moses) to save and nurture one of the baby boys who grew up to become a leader of the people. The sister of Moses, perhaps the youngest of the women of that drama, showed a resourcefulness and intelligence that made her the catalyst in that unplanned but cooperative venture that had its source in women's love of life. It is essential that we Christian women celebrate such collaboration as we struggle for liberation from patriachal structures, political, ecclesiastical, and economic. Without these foresisters, those of Exodus and those of our own African tradition, we have no history; if we have forgotten where we are coming from and we do not know where we are going, we become easy prey. So we turn to our history of struggle, collaboration, and solidarity. We seek knowledge and we seek to free ourselves from the pre-eminence of men to work out new and life-giving ways of relating to others.

The image of the African Christian woman as wife and mother is modeled on Proverbs 31:10-31, which has close affinity with our culture. Womanhood in Africa is almost synonymous with motherhood. Woman's experience of being human is that of making space for others to grow, mothering, assisting at the "making of the human in others" and being simultaneously affected by that effort. Instead of Eve, the source of all sin,[16] we should bring to the fore Eve, the mother of life who is an intelligent educator and counsellor. She is not a super-human, but only a person who is very human and life-loving. We must study texts such as Proverbs 31 against their own background as well as ours, for biblical models also can grow obsolete.[17]

THE ROLE OF SELF-AFFIRMING LANGUAGE

We must refuse to cooperate in the devaluation of our persons or humanity. We were not born with any of the behavioral patterns called feminine and masculine and, as such, we owe them no honor; rather, we have a duty to nourish our humanity. If our bondage to culture means that we have accepted myths of womanhood, knowing full well ourselves that there is no such thing as *the* woman, it is incumbent upon us to review these myths and test all the language that says "It is not good for you." What is not positive imagery of women should die from disuse, or it will continue to hamper our desire to live as human beings who are female. I do not think it helps to be swallowed up in androgynous imagery that may end up as male as "man" or "men" always have been, in spite of their legal inclusiveness.[18]

The delicate task of evolving a new language, positive myths, and

---

[16]The image of Eve does not correspond with the Qur'anic image. See Rabiatu Ammah, "Paradise Lies at the Feet of Muslim Women," in Oduyoye and Kanyoro, eds., *The Will To Arise*, pp. 179-188.

[17]The images of mothering and motherhood I have raised up here are not intended to exclude other forms of being woman. But I believe that mothering is the closest that human beings come to the Compassionate God who makes us free.

[18]N. Ogundipe-Leslie, "Sisters Are Not Brothers in Christ: Global Women in Church and Society" (*Geneva: World Council of Churches*, 1995), pp. 179-188. A

dynamic icons that will project the humanity of women as partners in creation and in community is gigantic and exciting. Perhaps it even intimidates us African women. But we have the responsibility to begin, to do our part in our generation. We seem hesitant and apprehensive because we are aware of the delicacy with which the process must be undertaken. It is a task that must engage all our thoughtfulness, because it involves breaking the very chains we have been wearing and examining them one by one, link by link, gold and lead alike.

I was still in school when a friend, then in a co-educational teacher training college, told me the following incident. A tutor, frustrated at the seemingly nonchalant attitude of his students toward submitting assignments, was doing his best to impress on them the implications of this for their future careers. He knew what to say to men. At a loss as to what might motivate women, he gave up with a statement to the effect that the women did not need to worry about doing well in college: while men have to struggle for greatness, women become great by association. Living somebody else's life—even if that person is a husband, son, father, or even a daughter—is a fragile existence. Can such a frail image of self endure throughout life? That story greatly worried me.[19] How does one account for one's self using someone else's life? If we do not live our own lives, we shall continue to sing other people's songs.

We must also demand the opportunity to live as independent persons capable of participating in all areas of life, and to develop this model of woman's being in home, church, and country. Our quest for identity and recognition demands acknowledgment that our work and earnings constitute an indispensable part of what goes into the family's well-being and, beyond that, what makes us feel autonomous. We must be cautious with language that refers to us adult women as "dependents," even while we contribute to family budgets. Such language

---

report of a meeting of the WCC held in Japan in December 1988 to help focus the WCC's "Ecumenical Decade, Churches in Solidarity with Women."

[19]This story made a great impression on me, shaping my life and my relations to men. Before I had heard that story I had been made to stand on a desk during a mathematics class while the teacher told the class, "Look at her, she is not pretty, she is not going to find a husband, and she will not pay attention in math class." That year I won a prize in mathematics, the only one I won in school. Since I had nothing to do with how I looked, I was determined to show this teacher that I could stand on my own feet.

renders our participation invisible and makes us into perpetual minors.

We need to develop and use inclusive language for domestic matters. It is *our* family, *our* children, not *his* children; we had them *with* him and not *for* him and it is *our* home if we live there, not *his* house. This may sound trite but such language creates an entirely different set of images about women. We are not employees of the men we marry, we are partners. If a human being may be described as belonging to another human being, we both belong to each other. We ought to be able to say, "We had children for us."

The most difficult part of re-imaging ourselves and affirming our experience is to articulate our oppression. Our inhibitions are valid because we have been brought up to smile—even when suffering. Any collective hurts we identify are immediately personalized and particularized.[20] We must, therefore, find ways of acting not just as individuals but collectively.

Sources of protest are many. A woman may simply ask herself, "Why do I have to do this?" Another woman who is looking for the divine image in humanity may ask, "What does it mean for both men and women to be in the image of God?" The latter woman may protest against the church orders that seek to subordinate her humanity. Other women simply act in affirmation of their humanity and by their very style of life protest against the patriarchal ordering of the world. The life carrier, according to Eve's name and Akan beliefs, cannot sit by and watch that life demeaned, oppressed, or marginalized, least of all her own life. For such a woman feminism is the positive application of human culture.

The next time you might hear an African man rise quickly as a spokesperson for the African woman and say she has no need of liberation, do some reinterpretation. He has spoken so spontaneously because he expects her to be unable to speak for herself. If he says the women's liberation movement is an imported commodity, he is admitting that it has found a market (as do other Euro-American exports) in Africa. If he tells you that feminism is promoted by "unfulfilled" women, under-

---

[20]This becomes a serious problem for if a woman calls attention to the tensions of childlessness, it is immediately seen as *her* problem; if a woman seeks to talk about the abuses of prostitution, she is personally involved through her husband, son, or daughter; if she talks of domestic violence, *she* is being battered at home ("*Poo mmɔbɔ*"—Sorry, that's sad, that husband is a beast.) Yet these are public issues that involve all women.

stand that he means those women whom society has been unable to "socialize" and who therefore are not accomplished at being "docile doves." And if he tells you that feminism is middle class, listen most skeptically. Women who speak against polygyny, those whose sweat fertilizes the rural farms, those who petition for water near their kitchens without success, those who leave their wares in the market to march against arbitrary taxation, price control, and marital and inheritance laws—all are of one class, the female underclass.

MAKING THE WORLD OUR HOME

To make where she lives a home, an African woman is ready and willing to adopt the style of "putting up with," for her style of life is directed by working things out and smoothing over domestic conflict. If need be, she becomes the sacrifice.[21] In a crisis, she is the one who risks being thrown out to be replaced by another woman. This domestic picture is reflected in employment, in politics, and in the church. A woman's most creative role is to be a facilitator. Whatever will provide space for others to expand, she gladly provides, whether it is by her silence or her word, her presence or her absence. We daughters of Anowa put up with injustice to ensure peace and harmony and growth for others. We are the first to excuse those who walk over us or to take the blame for the failures of others.

Our desire to make a home is positive. The problem with our homemaking is the unilateral way in which we women appropriate the process, shielding men and male children from learning self-giving. Should we not examine this? If politicians cared for the needs of nations the way women run homes—putting the nation before their individual need to be "great"—and if the armed forces protected the people—as a hen gathers her chicks and guards her eggs with her life—rather than warred with them, we might see a new day in Africa. The spectre of armies raised and paid by nations to war against their own people militates

---

[21]A woman from Sierra Leone told of a couple who were desperate for a child. Told by the doctor that having a child might mean the death of the woman, the husband, a clergyman, is reported to have said, "If that is what it takes, let it be so." The wife went along with the decision. She died in childbirth, having had a son. The husband said, "Thank God it is a boy."

against the homemaking efforts of African women. We should not keep quiet in our opposition of death-dealing regimes. Militarism has got to be the most insane manifestation of patriarchy.

Several biblical models of homemaking can aid us. Eve explored her environment looking for what might be useful; a lover of knowledge, she was generous at giving. The princess who nurtured Moses nursed his sense of justice and holy anger at exploitation. Hilda the prophetess was a political and military consultant to kings anxious for the nation to remain a home to its people. Mary of Nazareth and her program for God's jubilee year show the reign of God revealed to her, an ordinary person visited by God. We women must stay sensitive to social injustice. We must listen to the voices too weak to be heard on political platforms, in parliaments, boardrooms, or military tribunals.

Women need to take stock of available resources. We need to place our oppression in the larger context of our country, church, and world. We have to recognize what demons are at work and name them. Whatever subjugates also dominates; whatever exhibits superiority divides and manipulates. Systems that are so well-ordered as to intimidate us are not for our good. Religious structures that leave us with little other than "the man says that God says" have to be suspected, even if the man is a priest.

Women's demand for fuller participation is therefore not a self-serving call. Our accumulated wisdom of mothering can serve the nation by community building. What African woman, having a chance to run from disaster, would leave children and relatives behind? If forced to do so, what African woman would not look back on the disaster? For women the figure of Lot's wife is a portrait of the cost of compassion, not the punishment for disobedience of a patriarchal injunction.

AT HOME WITH THE FUTURE

One empowering strand in the church's teaching enables us to live as if all the good we hope for is in fact already in our hands, giving us the courage to be what we hope to be. Writing the Book of Revelation in a period of extreme suffering and uncertainty, St. John the Divine had a vision of the New Jerusalem coming on earth and called attention to it. Look! The New is already here. We do not have to go up to heaven, heaven has come down to meet us. If only we have eyes to see, we can observe God walking among us. This dramatization of Christian hope in a new myth enables us women of Africa to live our future today. Our future as women is in living our true humanity in a world that we have helped to shape, and in which even now we have begun to live and to enjoy, conscious of our situation and seeking conscientiously to change structures and attitudes. Even the prospect of being a part of this calls for celebrating.

In this transformed world, our new home, life is not structured on a "me or you" mentality. With transformed relationships, we begin to see the whole earth as a home where hostility, hunger, and oppression are no longer our companions. With such a vision the world is our home. Even though the hurt of all our sisters has to be healed if we are to be whole ourselves, we praise God that we have sisters. Global solidarity on life issues like abortion, same-sex love, female prostitution, male prostitution, child abuse, and child care bind us together. We are open to share our experiences, to learn to deal with them, and to teach our strategies to others. In the understanding company of the global sisterhood, a home is created for women to be themselves, to assess and critically appropriate our various cultures.

With a frank turning to face the old world with its tangled web of oppression, we set about unraveling it. Each may pick a different thread. While doing this we learn to live in close proximity, interacting with people on the same project. While working together, we already live in the future as we sing new songs to one another and, together, promote our new imagery. New myths, tales, and proverbs evolve from our real lives, true stories that are stranger than fiction. As we unravel our oppression we weave new patterns of living from our boundless human creativity.

10

Beads and Strands

Time was when no "decent" Akan woman would be seen without her beads.

Beadwork is an art form I associate with my paternal grandmother Maame (Martha Aba Awotwiwa Yamoah). She participated in the fish trade in the Asamankese market and was happy nowhere else except in church. The market was her life and she clung to it until she could no longer see to get there. In the Methodist Church in Asamankese, she is remembered for her *Ebibindwom* (songs of Africa), the lyrics she wove together from Bible stories in church during sermons and sang at home while she made or threaded beads.[1] Beadwork and singing, that is how I remember her. She sorted beads out of an earthenware pot and threaded them for legs, waist, wrists, and neck. Some of these beads were traditional handcrafted ones whose names held worldviews and philosophies of life—precious black *bota* beads fashioned from solid rock, mixed in with mass-produced European glass trade beads made from sand.

I remember her drawing beads from old strings and remaking them for new uses, or simply replacing old string with stronger new string. The latter was fast and much fun, even a child could do it when the One Who Knows How (Maame) began the process by fastening the old and new strings together. Though apparently easy, if done absent-mindedly

---

[1] See Mercy Amba Oduyoye, *Hearing and Knowing* (Maryknoll, N.Y.: Orbis Books, 1986), pp. 45-49, for examples of *Ebibindwom* (Fanti Lyrics is the official translation of *Ebibindwom*).

or with too much pressure the stringer could easily lose an hour pick-
ing up scattered beads. I remember our bead-making sessions: new
patterns from old, beads moved from pot onto floor, onto lap; beads
chosen for stringing; beads drawn off to put back into pots; beads
chipped or split in half and so no longer usable; or beads that needed
just a little more polishing before stringing. Beads and beadwork are
an imaginative pastime, fascinating yet functional, like composing and
singing Fanti lyrics. All is flexible, all is renewable.

As I look at the world of African women today and reflect on that
life in these pages, I think of beadwork. When I look at the variety of
beads, I think of the changing being of the African woman: my grandmother, my mother, myself, my nieces, and my grandniece: different
beads from the same pot, different shapes, sizes, colors, uses, ever
changing patterns strung on new strings. I hear the deliberate, gentle
instructing voices of the older women evoke the rhythm of *sam-sina*,
the action of drawing a bead off the thread or pulling the thread through
a bead. Women threading beads. I watch the different colors and I see
a pattern emerge as they reject some beads and pick up others. Deliberate choices and delicate handling, for every bead is precious and
none must be lost. Even those not needed at the moment will go back
into the pot along with those we have not chosen. We appear only in
beads of our choice, strung on strong strings in patterns of our creation.

I also think of weaving, of the multi-colored, ever new patterns of
Kente and *Aso Oke* cloth.[2] In my reflections I hear the rhythm of weaving. I see a Yoruba woman, sitting straight-backed on a stool facing the
broad woman's loom. Weaving large and wide, she does not produce
narrow strips to be sewn together, but a whole universe of cloth—
several motifs and several colors, blending and clashing, but forming
one piece. I think of wholeness, a whole being who mothers a whole
universe and clothes it with love.

As I watch the world of women and see a Yoruba woman at her
loom, I see a time-consuming affair, a new challenge, and I see her
transparent joy. I see shredded lives being bound together by inter-
twining them. I see her, with her back straight and her eyes straining to

---

[2]These two types of hand-woven fabrics are highly prized by Akan and Yoruba;
used for special occasions, they are made of strips four or five inches wide that are
woven on narrow looms and then sewn together.

join two ends of a broken thread, creating a new pattern. Differently colored threads go in and out and some wait to be picked up from a nearby basket. The beading and weaving continue, as if in preparation for the puberty rites of our new woman beingness. As African women, Akan and Yoruba, we work to shape our new world. Like our weaving or our beadwork, we bring it into being as we create new patterns of life based on the old.

Our world is also renewed through our songs. I feel growing tension between our cultural axioms encapsulated in myth and proverb and the ever changing conditions that social science lays bare for us. But I am not distressed, for did not the drums say, *ɛsono biribi, ɛsono mmerɛbi* (different things, different times).

> Different things! Different times!
> Roll the drums
> Making stale what used to be fresh
> Breaking open the cracks into the future.
> The drum speaks,
> The Word rolls out.
> It is heard
> And things begin to change.

> Soon, soon! No! Now!
> All is transformed—that is creation.
> People hand craft,
> Nature gives birth.
> The Word transforms—that's creation.
> Different times! Different things.

My impression, now confirmed by the various studies, is that there have been areas of progress as well as areas of deterioration for African women. It is now openly acknowledged that two-thirds of the work necessary for human survival is done by women and in Africa that percentage could be higher. It is important to note that rural areas remain the most materially impoverished areas in Africa, and women, who comprise 80 percent of the farming and agriculture workers, are the most affected sector. Young men often move, seeking survival on the fringes of urban life. African women researchers need to give more attention to women's development, to arrest the feminization of poverty that is beginning to engulf Africa. Feminism and nationalism must work together in Africa, drawing on the resources of sociologists, economists, and legal experts to equalize benefits.

The traditional bi-focal structure—upheld fully in rhetoric but only partially in practice—produces a paradigm for the reintegration of African women into authority structures.[3] Few women have truly gained participation in the current structures devised by men following models of Western modernization. Such women are required to serve the system without questioning and to feel grateful and humbled that they have attained such heights. That the majority of women do ask questions and do seek change is the anchor that stabilizes African women's hopes. Although this is a sign that all is not well with the African woman, it is also a sign of hope: where pain is felt, life is still present. When the hurt of women is acknowledged, taken seriously, and responded to, then one can continue to hope in Africa's rhetoric of community.

Women in Africa have survived in large part because of their own empowering networks built on traditional culture. Some of these become specialized but marginal groups whose goals and priorities do not necessarily affect the rest of the community or any policy-making body. Organizations of church women tend to follow this pattern. Such marginalized assemblies of women become salvific only if they engender strength and solidarity in their members and they seek fair representation and adequate involvement in more central bodies. Groups of African women often get society's attention only through protest, which is stark evidence of the patriarchy that rules Africa. I believe that only through honest and serious debate can we begin to identify goals, if not reach a limited consensus.

I have felt a great deal of tension in writing this third cycle of tales. It is an acceptable academic exercise to dig up, describe, analyze, and categorize. One is encouraged to formulate theories to explicate the findings of research. But to e-*value*-ate, *pre*-scribe, and call for commitment is the job of the patriarch and pontiff, pastor and preacher, president and politician—those who are entitled to pontificate on human affairs and to call others to a life of sacrifice. These people's truth-

[3]See Kamene Okonjo, "The Dual-Sex Political System in Operation," and Judith Van Allen, "Aba Riots," in Nancy J. Hafkin and Edna E. Bay, eds., *Women in Africa: Studies in Social and Economic Change* (Stanford, Calif.: Stanford University Press, 1976).

claims may be born from power games or struggles where the position of the "winner" becomes the position of orthodoxy and thus the truth by which the community is governed. Yet, although I am not patriarch, pastor, president, or politician, I have gone ahead and called the church to put its house in order and I have called my sisters to stand together to enhance our being as women. I have called for commitment because life is dear. My call to my sisters tells of my dream; it is a plea for solidarity and a cry to be free of imposed subordination.

But we all remain free to tell of our dreams if we do not allow our imagination to be captive. The ability to dream, like the ability to feel pain, is a sign that we are still alive and in possession of what it takes to transform our lives—faith, hope, and courage. Dreams enable the affirmation of selfhood. They allow us to opt out of power struggles and to establish communities for ourselves that enable us to experience and to enjoy our own being. They are a call to the unknown, to the desert, but with a promise that there we shall find ourselves. It is our dreams that are the heart of Judeo-Christian apocalyptic art, as are the words of all people who struggle against injustice and for peace and community.

As we claim the prophetic heritage of Christianity, we begin to weave new myths for ourselves from the old myths. As we break the golden chains of our belongingness, we remember Anowa saying that none of us belongs, that we are all wayfarers. At the same time, even though we belong to no place, we can belong to ourselves. We may have to break taboos on our way to new life. We know that this entails risk, and that it promises but does not guarantee liberation.

Some of the strings of beads we wear feature some very ugly and uncomfortably rough beads. We need to untie our beads and restring them so we can draw off these beads. This exercise, too, entails risk, for we may find our beads scattered. Biological gender differentiation is usually the centerpiece of the very intricate beadwork that is our lives. Biological gender is a given we cannot escape, but gender as a base for building human relations and hierarchies is of our own making. Thus, we can draw it out of the center and find a less conspicuous position for it. As we have seen, in mythology as in experienced life, gender as a centerpiece creates ambiguities. Male and female creator divinities simply mirror our human relations and provide no normative paradigms for human relationships because they too are culture-bound.

Notions of the "ideal woman" fit poorly around most women's wrists and are certainly not for display around the neck and covering the breasts. Such beads have to be drawn off; the wearer must remove the threads that hold them together and examine each bead to determine its value. Take, for instance, the symbolism in Akan art that says that death is female. The same culture that says it is womanly to fear death and "a man does not fear death" also says, "fear woman." What do we make of all this?[4] We have to ask our own questions and seek our own answers. And we have to determine which questions are worth asking. I no longer ask who created the "ideal" woman; I know there is no such creature.

We cannot wear beads that suggest we are made by men. Such beads—like the Gabon creation myth in which man made woman out of a piece of wood—are simply impossible to wear; for the person who whittled you into being can make you whatever size he wants or make you disappear altogether.[5] The view of woman as a derivative being is oppressive. It underlies women's exclusion from power structures and marks the diminution of our full humanity. What we are given in its place is the solicitous care of paternalism, a force that isolates and insulates us, almost to the point of eliminating our presence altogether. Maleness is presumed to be the norm of human beingness. The same human traits receive approval or disapproval, depending on the gender of the person exhibiting them. Self-affirmation is admired in a man and called masculinity, while in a woman it is denounced as selfishness or egocentrism. "If, when it falls in one place it cools, but when it falls in another it burns, that is not good government" (JGC 3281).

The single, large bead I can string and wear all by itself is one that says, "The full personhood of the African woman (*all* women) is non-

---

[4]Kofi Antubam, *Ghana's Heritage of Culture* (Leipzig: Kochler and Amelag, 1963), pp. 62-92. Also of interest may be the videos "Fear Woman" and "She Shall Be Called Woman" from the collection of The Africa Studies Center, Michigan State University, and "Be a Woman" of the All Africa Conference of Churches, Nairobi (1992).

[5]Ulli Beier, ed., *The Origin of Life and Death* (Ibadan: Heinemann, 1966), pp. 18-22; George S. Lewis, *Black Heritage Unveiled* (Los Angeles: Spencer's International Enterprise, 1987), pp. 133-134. Lewis urges African-American men to return to their Yoruba roots in order "to break the tangle of pathology as it affects the Black family structure in America and Nigeria today." I am grateful that not all men feel the same way and recall that it was another man, J. B. Danquah, who introduced me in 1953 to John Stuart Mills's writings on the subjection of women.

negotiable and self-defined." Just human relationships can survive only when the equal value of all persons is upheld. One area we need to focus on in West Africa is that of unequal inheritance rights, which we are quickly legalizing. We women must join in structuring a fair system so we do not become the passive victims of a changing culture. African women need to participate in creating and choosing our social forms and in selecting the criteria to answer the question, "What is woman?" We need to challenge traditional gender-based dicta that tell us we must do this and we must refrain from doing that. These norms and taboos are not sacrosanct; they simply sustain the dominant view of life and do not benefit its victims.

PATRIARCHIES

All criteria for differentiation of human beings stand suspect when we discover that matri-centered cultures do no more to guarantee the identity and autonomy of women than overt patriarchies. In Africa, colonization did not create patriarchy; it only strengthened it. Before colonialism, the avuncular potestas of the Akan already served as a surrogate patriarchy. There is abundant evidence of the marginalization of the African woman and the feminization of poverty in Africa today. We must have the courage to challenge African men who refuse to acknowledge the threat that paternalism poses to the unity of humanity.

The dichotomies of dualistic thinking we Africans usually associate with Western thought begin to resemble male thinking: a scheme that enables those in power to legitimize their authority over those not in power and that sends the powerless scuttling for succor from the gods. Dichotomies enable the "distancing" of issues and challenges, while theorizing postpones action for change. We African women observe the divide-and-rule strategy of paternalism and we see a strategy we were formerly taught to denounce as exploitative and domesticating, part and parcel of colonialism. As women, we cannot join in when the African press smugly labels Western feminists "neurotic," and chastises African women, who are supposed to be spiritually and psychologically strong, for emulating them. Western approaches to feminism may differ, but the goal—an end to the marginalization of women—is sound. However, the calm dignity of the African woman, straight-backed, head high, carrying the continent on her back, should not be mistaken for contentment. While it may not show on her face or in her demeanor, she knows that the *ebonu*, the cloth that ties her baby to her, is old and threadbare and may give way anytime.

One of the earliest remarks that started me thinking about the situation of women in Africa was the notorious "The hand that rocks the cradle rules the world." I felt betrayed. I knew, I know, that women do *not* rule the world, that much is clear to me. Women are babysitters and teachers who run programs, usually (and in Africa nearly always) devised by men that do not give women any choice in how they rock the cradle. Children are brought up to fit into niches. No woman wants to experience the agony of "deviant" progeny. So, in the end, we usually become very effective agents in perpetuating our own marginalization. We effect socialization by gender. We train our children to be acceptable to their father.

To challenge this pattern, we need a new myth about becoming human that goes beyond scientific or biological origins. We need a myth that focuses on human interconnectedness as part of becoming human. Today, myths of human connectedness must mirror our new vision of the earth as a home for a single human race, interconnected and of equal value. We must recognize that social structures are created by human beings and, therefore, may be scrambled, reorganized, or discarded if they have become dysfunctional. No culture is fixed. Even precious elements of each culture must face re-evaluation and be consciously accepted by each new generation. Principles of reciprocity, mutuality, and complementarity have effectively served traditional African society; yet, in our context and time they have acquired ambiguities. Mothering, rather than parenting, has been our norm. Yet large doses of mothering ("smothering") have completed the flight to patriarchy. In Akan culture, our mothering has prevented men from seeing our real hurt.[6]

We must be careful as we work on tasks of self-definition. We must not become so busy defending positions or territories that we are un-

---

[6]One of the symbols of *Akunintam* or *Nwowabere* ("the cloth of real warriors" and royalty is decorated with appliques of animals and abstract symbols) represented female protection of the male. It is composed of a circle with four crescent moons shielding it. See Antubam, p. 152. See also the various interpretations of Jeremiah 31:21-22 from its obscure Hebrew original.

able to move from them when factors change around us. We must not become slaves to our own creations, worshiping idols made by our hands or imaginations of woman being crafted by our foresisters. We need an understanding of truth and of the role that power plays. Our grandmothers' pots still hold precious beads, such as the symmetrical structuring of authority, which ensured that women's voices were heard at home, in public affairs, and in religion. Now, more than ever, we need to expand and utilize this tradition for women's development and for the development of policies that shape the entire nation. We need to focus particularly on women's full participation in law making, a religio-cultural area that I see as the battleground of the coming decades. We shall remain marginal if we do not seek a share of the decision-making that goes into creating and running the central structures that control our lives.

Just as Christian theologians (mostly Western and mostly male) never took seriously the situation of oppressed people when formulating their ideas, so African male intellectuals, including theologians, have not given much attention to women in their various enterprises. What appears in print, however, confirms my fear that females are not only subsumed under the male but that whenever the female is differentiated, it is often as a focus of evil. The issue of language, where I began my cycle of story-telling, is crucial for women's development, self-perception, and integrity. The language of culture and religion, in particular, minimizes women's presence and creates a seemingly impenetrable crust for African women to break through. The approach with the most potential at the moment seems to be community-based efforts by women and, hopefully, by the church. How else can we usher in a life of liberating love?

I do not see myself participating in a world in which human relations progressively improve in a linear fashion. Rather, I feel caught up in a whirlwind going round and round, never touching ground but continually swirling, moving on to other places, sometimes higher, sometimes lower. While I spin, the whirling storm continues to move in different directions, carrying with it some of its acquisitions from previous turns and spins.

A symbol of this whirlwind could be a whorl. In Akan art, the whorl is said to represent femaleness—indecision, frailty, continuity of growth, peace, and mercy. Sometimes the whorl is portrayed as the coil of a serpent representing the interchange of life and death.[7] For me, the whorl does not represent indecision and frailty; instead, it is the *power* to turn and to move to different planes of life, while growing and exhibiting mercy and peace. In the whirl of women-men relations, we should avoid dogmatic truths, which become desperate attempts to turn creativity back into chaos. As the storm catches us up and spins us about, we watch carefully, we feel the movements about us, and we remember, always, what we are about. We seek to retain what is the heart of our African woman-beingness: that we be life-loving.

> May we have joy
> As we learn to define ourselves.
> Our world, our home, our journey.
> May we do so
> Telling our own stories and
> Singing our own songs,
> Enjoying them as they are or for what they may become.
> Weaving the new patterns we want to wear,
> We continue to tell our tales of the genesis of our participation.
> We gather the whole household and begin a new tale.
> *Nse se nse se o!*
> *Nse se soa wo.*

•

Once the theologians believed that the female sex as a whole was rather slow of understanding. One of the female sex, Hypatia—eloquent, beautiful, and modest (the first of the encomiums is not being exactly feminine!)—understood both mathematics and philosophy. Her existence did not suit this notion of the female sex as a whole, so men put an end to her existence by hacking her to death, naked, in the temple of their god. And so all wise mothers lulled their little girls into a stupor to save them from the fate of Hypatia.

---

[7]Antubam, p. 111.

And it came to pass in those days that a boy of six years sat with his mother, munching the bread she had baked, and watching her knead the dough for the bread he would eat in the evening.

"Mother," said he, "where does the grain come from?"

Mother (wiping the sweat off her forehead with the back of her left hand), "The Earth grew it."

"And who made the Earth?"

"Aha," said Mother, "that is a long story. Two gods were having a wrestling match; one was female, the other male. When the male god saw he could not win, he abandoned the rules of the game, picked up a machete, and hacked the body of the female god in two, and he put half up to make the sky and half down to make the earth. Quickly he went up, made peace with the upper half, and from there tried to control the lower half."

"But," began the son.

"No buts," said the mother. "I shall not continue the story until you wake your sister up and bring her here."

So off went the boy who soon returned arm in arm with his twin sister. They were the Male and the Female. The mother put them to work sifting flour for the third round of baking, which would be tomorrow's bread.

When he becomes a Father and she a Mother, perhaps they will have a new myth for their new age.

Myth, history, and faith agree: people can change.

Bibliography

Abimbola, Wande. *Ifa, An Exposition of Ifa Literary Corpus.* Ibadan: Oxford University Press, 1976.

_____. *Ifa Divination Poetry.* Translated, edited, and with an introduction. New York: NOK Publishers, 1977.

_____. *Sixteen Great Poems of Ifa.* Paris: UNESCO, 1975.

Ackermann, Denise. *Women Hold Up Half the Sky: Women in the Church in South Africa.* Pietermaritzburg: Cluster Publishing, 1991.

Addo, Nelson et al. *West African Seminary on Population Studies.* Accra: University of Ghana, 1972.

Ademola, Frances. *Reflections: Nigerian Prose and Verse.* Lagos: African Universities Press, 1962.

Agonito, Rosemary. *History of Ideas on Women: A Source Book.* New York: Thomas Hobbes, 1977.

Aidoo, Ama Ata. *Anowa.* London: Harlow, 1970.

_____. *The Dilemma of a Ghost.* Accra: Longmans, 1965.

_____. *No Sweetness Here.* New York: Doubleday, 1971.

_____. *Our Sister Killjoy, or, Reflections from a Black-Eyed Squint.* New York: NOK Publishers, 1979.

_____. "To Be a Woman," in Robin Morgan, ed., *Sisterhood Is Global.* Garden City, New York: Anchor Books, 1984.

Ajisafe, A. K. *The Laws and Customs of the Yoruba People.* New York: G. Routledge and Sons, 1924.

Ajisafe Moore, E. J. *The Laws and Customs of the Yoruba People.* Abeokuta, Nigeria: Fola Bookshops, n.d.

al-Hibri, Azizah, ed. *Women in Islam.* Oxford: Pergamon Press, 1982.

Amadi, Elechi. *The Concubine.* Nairobi, East African Educational Publishers, Inc., 1966.

Amadiume, Ifi. *Male Daughters, Female Husbands.* London: Zed Books, 1987.

Amoah, Elizabeth. "Femaleness: Akan Concepts and Practices," in Jeanne Belcher, ed., *Women, Religion and Society, Studies on the Impact of Religious Teachings on Women.* Geneva: World Council of Churches, 1991.

Anderson, Izett, and F. Cundall, eds. *Jamaica Negro Proverbs and Sayings* (2nd ed., revised and enlarged by Cundall). London: West India Committee for the Institute of Jamaica, 1927.

Andreski, Iris. *Old Wives' Tales: Life Stories from Ibibioland*. New York: Schocken Books, 1970.

Antubam, Kofi. *Ghana's Heritage of Culture*. Leipzig: Koehler and Amelag, 1963.

Appiah-Kubi, Kofi. *Man Cures, God Heals: Religion and Medical Practice among the Akan of Ghana*. Totowa, New Jersey: Allanheld Osmun Publishers, 1981.

Areje, Raphael. *Yoruba Proverbs*. Ibadan: Daystar Press, 1985.

Arhin, Kwame. "The Political and Military Roles of Akan Women," in Christine Oppong, ed., *Female and Male in West Africa*. London: G. Allen & Unwin, 1983).

_____. "Status Differentiation in Ashanti in the 19th Century: A Preliminary Study," Institute of African Studies *Research Review* 4:3 (1968).

Armah, Ayi Kwei. *The Beautyful Ones Are Not Yet Born*. New York: Collier Books, 1969.

_____. *Two Thousand Seasons*. Nairobi: East Africa Publishing House, 1973.

Atkinson, Clarissa W., Constance H. Buchanan and Margaret R. Miles, eds. *Immaculate and Powerful: The Female in Sacred Image and Social Reality*. Boston: Beacon Press, 1985.

Awolalu, J. O. *Yoruba Belief and Sacrificial Rites*. London: Longmans, 1979.

Ba, Mariama. *So Long a Letter*. London: Heinemann, African Writers Series, 1989.

Baeta, C. G. *Prophetism in Ghana*. London: SCM Press, 1962.

Barker, W. H., and C. Sinclair, eds. *West African Folktales*. London: George G. Harrap and Co., 1917. Reprint, Metro Books Inc. Northbrook, Ill. 1972.

Bascom, William. *Ifa Divination: Communication between God and Men in West Africa*. Bloomington: Indiana University Press, 1969.

Beier, Ulli, ed. *The Origin of Life and Death*. Ibadan: Heinemann, 1966.

Bernard, Jane. *Black Mistress*. London: Hodder & Stoughton, 1957.

Biobaku, S. O., ed. *Sources of Yoruba History*. Oxford: Clarendon Press, 1973.

Brooten, Bernadette J. "Paul's View on the Nature of Women and Female Homoeroticism (Romans 1:26)," in Clarissa W. Atkinson, Constance H. Buchanan, and Margaret R. Miles, eds., *Immaculate and Powerful* (Boston: Beacon Press, 1985).

Brunner, Charlotte, ed. *African Women's Writings*. London: Heinemann, African Writers Series, 1993.

_____. *Unwinding Threads*. London: Heinemann, African Writers Series, 1983.

Bührig, Marga. *Woman Invisible: A Personal Odyssey in Christian Feminism*.

Valley Forge, Pennsylvania: Trinity Press International, 1993.

Busia, Kofi Abrefa. *The Position of the Chief in Modern Political Systems of Ashanti.* London: Oxford University Press, 1951.

Caldwell, John et al., eds. *Population Growth and Socio-Economic Change in West Africa.* New York: Columbia University Press, 1975.

Christaller, John G. *Twi Mmebusem.* Basel: 1879.

Clark, John Pepper. *The Ozidi Saga.* Ibadan: Ibadan University Press and Oxford University Press, 1977.

Crane, Louise. *Ms. Africa: Profiles of African Women.* New York: Lippincott, 1973.

Cranmer-Byng, L., and S. A. Kapadia, eds. *Ancient Jewish Proverbs.* Wisdom of the East Series, compiled and classified by A. Cohen. London: John Murray, 1911.

Crowther, Samuel. *Vocabulary of the Yoruba Languages.* With introductory remarks by O. E. Vidal. London: Seeleys, 1852.

Daly, Mary. *Gyn/Ecology: The Metaethics of Radical Feminism.* Boston: Beacon Press, 1978.

DeBrunner, H. *Witchcraft in Ghana.* Accra: Presbyterian Book Depot, 1959.

Delano, I. O. *The Soul of Nigeria.* 1937.

Dolphyne, Florence Abena. *The Emancipation of Women: An African Perspective.* Accra: Ghana Universities Press, 1991.

Edet, Rosemary and Meg Umeagudosu, eds. *Life, Women and Culture: Theological Reflections.* Proceedings of the National Conference of a Circle of African Women Theologians, 1990. Lagos: African Heritage Research and Publications, 1991.

Edet, Rosemary Nkoyo. *The Resilience of Religious Tradition in the Dramas of Wole Soyinka and James Enettenshaw.* Rome: Città Nuova, 1984.

Ekundare, R. Olufemi. *Marriage and Divorce under Yoruba Customary Law.* Ile-Ife: University of Ife Press, 1969.

Elias, Taslim Olawade. *Groundwork of Nigerian Law.* London: Routledge & Paul, 1954.

Emecheta, Buchie. *The Bride Price.* New York: George Braziller, 1976.

_____. *The Joys of Motherhood.* New York: George Braziller, 1979.

Engels, Friedrich. *The Origin of the Family, Private Property, and the State: in the Light of Researches of Lewis H. Morgan.* New York: International Publishers, 1891.

Faith and Order Commission. *Minutes of Lima, January 1982.* Geneva: World Council of Churches, 1982.

Fitzjohn, Willie. *Chief Gbondo.* Ibadan: Daystar Press, 1974.

Frazer, Robert. *The Novels of Ayikwei Armah.* London: Heinemann, 1980.

Giovanni, Nikki. *Gemini.* Penguin Books, 1971.

Gleason, Judith, Awotunde Arinde, and John Olaniyi Ogundipe. *A Recitation of Ifa, Oracle of Yoruba.* New York: Grossman Publishers, 1973.

Gyekye, Aboagye J., *Wosum Borodee a Sum Kwadu bi.* Accra: Bureau of Ghana Languages, 1984.

Hafkin, N. J., and E. E. Bay, eds. *Women in Africa: Studies in Social and Economic Change.* Palo Alto: Stanford University Press, 1976.

Hayward, Victor. *African Independent Movements.* IMC Pamphlet No. 11. Geneva: World Council of Churches, 1963.

Idowu, E. B. *Olodumare: God in Yoruba Belief.* London: Longmans, 1962.

Isichei, Elizabeth. *A History of Christianity in Africa: From Antiquity to the Present.* Grand Rapids, Michigan: Eerdmans, 1995.

Johnson, Samuel. *A History of the Yorubas from the Earliest Times to the Beginning of the British Protectorate.* London: Routledge & Sons, 1921; reprinted, Lagos: Church Missionary Society, 1960.

Kalu, Ogbu, ed. *Christianity in West Africa: The Nigerian Story.* Ibadan: Daystar Press, 1978.

King, Noel Quinton. *African Cosmos: An Introduction to Religion in Africa.* Belmont, Calif.: Wadsworth Publishing Co., 1986.

Kirwen, Michael C. *The Missioner and the Diviner.* Maryknoll, New York: Orbis Books, 1987.

Klissou, Pierre. *La Polygamie au Bénin et dans la sous-région Ouest-Africaine.* Louvain-La Neuve: Université Catholique de Louvain, Institut de Démographie, 1992.

Konadu, Asare. *A Woman in Her Prime.* London: Heinemann, African Writers Series, 1976.

Landman, Christine. *The Piety of Afrikaans Women.* Pretoria, University of South Africa, 1995.

Leacock, Eleanor Burke et al., ed. *Women and Colonization: Anthropological Perspectives.* New York: Praeger, 1980.

Lewis, George S. *Black Heritage Unveiled.* Los Angeles: Spencer's International Enterprise, 1987.

Maimela, Simon S., ed. *Culture, Religion and Liberation.* African Challenges Series. Nairobi: All African Council of Churches, 1994.

Marshall, Gloria A. *Women, Trade, and the Yoruba Family.* Ann Arbor: University of Michigan Press, 1964.

Mbiti, John S. *African Religions and Philosophy.* London: Heinemann, 1969.

Meagher, P. K. et al., eds. *Encyclopedic Dictionary of Religion.* Washington, D.C.: Corpus Publications, 1970.

Merrick, G. *Hausa Proverbs.* 1905; reprint, New York: Negro Universities Press, 1969.

Meyerowitz, Eva. *The Akan of Ghana, Their Ancient Beliefs.* London: Faber, 1958.

_____. *At the Court of an Akan King.* London: Faber & Faber, 1958.

_____. *The Divine Kingship in Ghana and Ancient Egypt.* London: Faber & Faber, 1960.

_____. *The Early History of the Akan States of Ghana.* London: Red Candle Press, 1974.

_____. *The Sacred State of the Akan.* London: Faber & Faber, 1949; Ann Arbor, Michigan: University Microfilms International, 1979.

Mogekwu, G. C. *African Society, Culture and Politics.* Lanham, Maryland: University Press of America, 1977.

Ngugi wa Thiong'o with Ngugi wa Mirii. *I Will Marry When I Want.* London: Heinemann, African Writers Series, 1995.

_____. *The Devil on the Cross.* Nairobi: Heinemann, African Writers Series, 1987.

Njoku, John E. Eberegbulam. *The World of the African Woman.* Metuchen, New Jersey and London: Scarecrow Press, 1980.

Ntiri, Daphne Williams. *One Is Not a Woman, One Becomes: The African Woman in a Transitional Society, African Women Tell Their Story.* Troy, Michigan: Bedford Publishers, 1982.

Nwapa, Flora. *Efuru.* London: Heinemann, African Writers Series, 1966.

_____. *Idu.* London: Heinemann, African Writers Series, 1979.

_____. *One Is Enough.* Enugu, Nigeria: Tana Press, 1981.

Obbo, Christine. *African Women: Their Struggle for Economic Independence.* London: Zed Press, 1981.

Obiechina, E. *Culture, Tradition and Society in the West African Novel.* London: Cambridge University Press, 1975.

Oduyoye, Mercy Amba. *And Women, Where Do They Come In?* Lagos: Methodist Church Nigeria Literature Bureau, 1977.

_____. *Hearing and Knowing: Theological Reflections on Christianity in Africa.* Maryknoll, New York: Orbis Books, 1986.

_____, ed. *Orita: Ibadan Journal of Religious Studies* 10:2 (December 1976).

Oduyoye, Mercy Amba and Musimbi R. A. Kanyoro, eds., *The Will to Arise: Women, Tradition and the Church in Africa.* Maryknoll, New York: Orbis Books, 1992.

_____. *Tabitha Qumi.* Ibadan: Daystar Press, 1990.

Ogundipe, Chief (Mrs.) G. T. *The Ordination of Women, Methodist Church Nigeria.* Lagos: Methodist Church Nigeria Literature Bureau, 1977.

Ogundipe, Leslie Morala. *Re-Creating Ourselves: African Women and Critical Transformation.* Trenton, New Jersey: Africa World Press, 1994.

Ojo, J. S. Afolabi. *Yoruba Culture: A Geographic Analysis.* Ife: Ife University Press; London: London University Press, 1966.

Okot p'Bitek. *Acholi Proverbs.* Nairobi: Heinemann, 1985.

Okpewho, Isidore. *Myth in Africa.* Cambridge: Cambridge University Press, 1983.

Okure, Teresa. *The Johannine Approach to Mission*. Tübigen: ICB Mohr (Paul Siebeck), 1987.

_____. "A Theological View of Women's Role in Promoting Cultural/Human Development," *Ecclesiastical Review* 31 (December 1989).

Omoyajowo, Akin. *Cherubim and Seraphim: The History of an Independent Church*. New York: NOK Publishers, 1982.

_____. *The Cherubim and Seraphim in Relation to Church and State*. Ibadan: Claveriarum Press, 1975.

Oppong, Christine, ed. *Changing Family Studies*. Accra: University of Ghana, Institute of African Studies, 1972.

_____, ed. Colloquium on the Impact of Family Planning Programmes in Sub-Sahara Africa: Current Issues and Prospects. Lagos: 1980.

_____, ed. *Domestic Rights and Duties in Southern Ghana*. Legon Family Research Paper No. 1. Accra: University of Ghana, Institute of African Studies, 1974.

_____, ed. *Female and Male in West Africa*. London: George Allen and Unwin, 1983.

_____. *Marriage among Matrilineal Elite: A Family Study of Ghanaian Senior Civil Servants*. London: Cambridge University Press, 1974.

_____, ed. *Marriage, Fertility and Parenthood in West Africa*. Canberra: Australian National University, Department of Demography, 1978.

_____. *Middle Class African Marriage*. London: George Allen and Unwin, 1981.

Parvey, Constance. *The Community of Women and Men in the Church*. The Sheffield Report. Philadelphia: Fortress Press; Geneva: World Council of Churches, 1983.

_____. *Ordination of Women in Ecumenical Perspective*. Faith and Order Paper No. 106. Geneva: World Council of Churches, 1980.

Peel, John D. Y. *Aladura: A Religious Movement Among the Yoruba*. London: Oxford University Press for the International African Institute, 1968.

Rattray, Robert Sutherland. *Akan-Asante Folktales, Collected and Translated*. 1930; reprint, New York: AMS Press, 1983.

_____. *Ashanti*. Oxford, Clarendon Press, 1923; reprint Westport, Connecticut: Greenwood/African Universities Press, 1969.

_____. *Ashanti Proverbs*. Selected from Christaller. Oxford: Clarendon Press, 1916.

_____. *Ashanti Law and Constitution*. 1911; reprint New York: Negro University Press, 1969.

_____. *Hausa Folklore, Customs, Proverbs*. 1913; New York: Negro University Press, 1969.

_____. *The Leopard Priestess*. New York: Appleton, 1935.

_____. *Religion and Art in Ashanti*. Oxford: Clarendon Press, 1927; New

York: AMS Press, 1979.

_____. *Some Folk-Lore Stories and Songs in Chinyanja with English Translations and Notes*. New York: Negro Universities Press, 1969.

_____. *The Tribes of the Ashanti Hinterland*. Oxford: Clarendon Press, 1932.

Riis, Hans Nicholas. *Grammatical Outline and Vocabulary of the Oji Language with Special Reference to the Akwapim Dialect Together with a Collection of Proverbs of the Natives*. Basel: Basel Bahnmaier's Buchhandlung, 1854.

Robertson, Claire C. *Sharing the Same Bowl: A Socio-Economic History of Women and Class in Accra, Ghana*. Bloomington: Indiana University Press, 1984.

Russell, Letty M. *The Future of Partnership*. Philadelphia: Westminster Press, 1979.

_____. *Growth in Partnership*. Philadelphia: Westminster Press, 1981.

_____. *Household of Freedom*. Philadelphia: Westminster Press, 1987.

Sarbah, John Mensah. *Fanti Customary Laws*. London: Frank Cass & Co., 1968.

Schipper, Mineke. *Source of All Evil: African Proverbs and Sayings about Women*. Nairobi: Phoenix Press; London: Virgin Publishers, 1991.

Schlegel, Alice, ed. *Sexual Stratification, A Cross-Cultural View*. New York: Columbia University Press, 1977.

Schüssler Fiorenza, Elisabeth. *In Memory of Her: A Feminist Theological Reconstruction of Christian Origins*. New York: Crossroad Publishing Co., 1983.

Segun, Mabel Imohonede. *My Father's Daughter*. Lagos: African Universities Press, 1965.

Sichona, Francis J. *The Polygyny-Fertility Hypothesis Revisited: The Situation in Ghana*. Chapel Hill: University of North Carolina, Carolina Population Center, 1992.

Soyinka, Wole. *Ake: The Years of Childhood*. London: Rex Collings, 1981.

_____. *Myth, Literature, and the African World*. Cambridge: Cambridge University Press, 1976.

Steady, Filomena, ed. *The Black Woman Cross-Culturally*. Cambridge: Schenkam Publishing, 1981.

Sticher, Sharon, and Parpart, Jane. *Patriarchy and Class: African Women in Home and Workforce*. Boulder, Colorado: Westview Press, 1988.

Sundkler, Bengt. *Bantu Prophets*. London: Oxford University Press, 1961.

_____. *The Christian Ministry in Africa*. London: SCM Press, 1960.

Taylor, Archer. *The Proverb*. Hatboro, Pennsylvania: Folklore Associates; Copenhagen: Rosenkilde and Bagger, 1962.

Turner, Harold W. *African Independent Church: The Life and Faith of the Church of the Lord Aladura*. Oxford: Clarendon Press, 1967.

_____. *Bibliography of New Religious Movements,* Vol. 1: *Black Africa.* Boston: G. K. Hall & Co., 1977.

_____. *History of an African Independent Church: Church of the Lord Aladura.* Oxford: Clarendon Press, 1967.

Tutu, Desmond M. *Hope and Suffering.* Grand Rapids, Michigan: Eerdman's, 1985.

Ukpong, Justin S., ed. *Journal of Inculturation Theology* I:1 (1994) Port Harcourt, Nigeria: Catholic Institute of West Africa.

Vellenga, Dorothy Dee. "Who Is a Wife: Legal Expressions of Hetero-sexual Conflicts in Ghana," in Christine Oppong, ed., *Female and Male in West Africa.* London: George Allen and Unwin, 1983.

Walker, B. K., and W. S. Walker. *Nigerian Folktales as Told by Olawode Idowu and Omotayo Ayo.* 2nd ed. Hamden, Connecticut: Archon Books, 1980.

Ware, Helen, ed. *Women, Education, and Modernization of the Family in West Africa.* Canberra: The University Press, 1981.

Index

Abiodun, Captain (Captain Christiana Abiodun Akinsowon), 126, 130, 198

Adultery, 65

African Charismatic Churches. *See* African Instituted Churches

African Independent Churches. *See* African Instituted Churches

African Instituted Churches, 123-30, 198

"African Testament," 191

African Traditional Religion: blood taboos in, 116-20; community and, 114-15; divinities of, 110-15; rituals and, 195; values of, 12; women's leadership in, 126

Aidoo, Ama Ata, 9-10, 85, 102, 112

Akan-Asante Folktales (Rattray), 41, 42

Ake (Soyinka), 26-27

Aladura. *See* African Instituted Churches

Amoah, Elizabeth, 121, 122

Androcentrism, 183

Anthropology, Christian, 183

Augustine of Hippo, 5

Autonomy, women's, 106-108: abdication of, 195-96; marriage and, 151-53

Awe, Bolanle, 112

Banjo, Ore, 130

Barrenness, 69

"Better Life for Women," 83

Bible, the: as absolutized, 174-75; contextual reading of, 190; women and, 189-92

Blood, religious significance of, 115-20

Busia, Kofi Abrefa, 69-70

Change, the church and, 184-87

Cherubim and Seraphim church, 124, 126, 127, 130

Child-bearing, 49-52, 141-43

Children, 49-52

Choice, premundane, 23

Christian Catholic Apostolic Stone Church in Zion, 129

Christianity: effects on African women, 183; right-wing, 101

Church, the: African women and, 172-87, 189; definition of, 4; and sexism, 9

Church of the Lord, 129

Circumcision, female, 165

Community, African Traditional Religion and, 114-15

Complementarity, 177-78

Crowther, Samuel, 58-59

Daly, Mary, *Gyn/Ecology,* 86

Dependency relations, 63

Development, women's, 158-59

Dignity, human, 56-64

Divorce, 48, 68-70, 148-49

Dominance, male, 68

Dowyoro, Janet, 164

Economics, colonial, 104-105

Economy, the, women and, 99-101

Education, equal access to, 93

Egocentrism, 15

Egotism, 27

Family, women's role in, 90-93